T0213624

Lecture Notes of the Institute for Computer Sciences, Social Informatics and Telecommunications Engineering 202

More information about this series at http://www.springer.com/series/8197

Fulong Chen · Yonglong Luo (Eds.)

Industrial IoT Technologies and Applications

Second EAI International Conference, Industrial IoT 2017
Wuhu, China, March 25–26, 2017
Proceedings

 Springer

Editors
Fulong Chen
School of Mathematics and Computer
  Science
Anhui Normal University
Wuhu
China

Yonglong Luo
School of Mathematics and Computer
  Science
Anhui Normal University
Wuhu
China

ISSN 1867-8211 ISSN 1867-822X (electronic)
Lecture Notes of the Institute for Computer Sciences, Social Informatics
and Telecommunications Engineering
ISBN 978-3-319-60752-8 ISBN 978-3-319-60753-5 (eBook)
DOI 10.1007/978-3-319-60753-5

Library of Congress Control Number: 2017946058

Printed on acid-free paper

This Springer imprint is published by Springer Nature
The registered company is Springer International Publishing AG
The registered company address is: Gewerbestrasse 11, 6330 Cham, Switzerland

Preface

In recent years, the widespread deployment of wireless sensor networks, industrial cloud, industrial robot, embedded computing, and inexpensive sensors has facilitated industrial Internet of Things (IndustrialIoT) technologies and fostered some emerging applications (e.g., product lifecycle management). IndustrialIoT is the direct motivation and drive for industrial upgrading (e.g., implementing smart factory of Industrie 4.0).

With the support of all kinds of emerging technologies, IndustrialIoT is capable of continuously capturing information from various sensors and intelligent units, securely forwarding all the data to industrial cloud centers, and seamlessly adjusting some important parameters via a closed loop system. Also, IndustrialIoT can effectively detect failures and trigger maintenance processes, autonomously reacting to unexpected changes in production. However, we are still facing some challenges, for example, it is very difficult to capture, semantically analyze, and employ data in a coherent manner from heterogeneous, sensor-enabled devices (e.g., industrial equipment, assembly lines, and transport trucks) owing to the lack of measurement tools, collection protocols, standardized APIs, and security guidelines.

The 2017 International Conference on Industrial IoT Technologies and Applications was held during March 25–26, 2017, in Wuhu, China. The conference is organized by the EAI (European Alliance for Innovation). The aim of the conference is to stimulate interaction among researchers active in the areas of control, communications, industrial robot, industrial cloud, smart sensors and actuators, informatics, mobile computing, and security. All topics are in the context of the IndustrialIoT. The Program Committee received over 40 submissions and each paper was reviewed by at least three expert reviewers. We chose 25 papers after intensive discussions held among the Program Committee members. We appreciate the excellent reviews and lively discussions of the Program Committee members and external reviewers in the review process. This year we chose two prominent invited speakers: Prof. Walid Taha (Halmstad University), and Prof. Ji Zhang (University of Southern Queensland). The abstracts of their talks are included in these proceedings.

July 2017

Fulong Chen
Yonglong Luo

Organization

Steering Committee

Steering Committee Chair

Imrich Chlamtac   CREATE-NET and University of Trento, Italy

Steering Committee Members

Jiafu Wan   South China University of Technology, Guangzhou, China
Min Chen   Huazhong University of Science and Technology, China
Daqiang Zhang   Tongji University, China

Organizing Committee

General Chair

Fulong Chen   Anhui Normal University, Wuhu, China

General Co-chairs

Min Chen   Huazhong University of Science and Technology, China
Jiafu Wan   South China University of Technology, China
Yonglong Luo   Anhui Normal University, Wuhu, China

Technical Program Committee Co-chairs

Yan Zhang   University of Oslo, Norway
Yimu Ji   Nanjing University of Posts and Telecommunications, China
Chin-Feng Lai   National Cheng Kung University, Taiwan (China)
Jaime Lloret   Polytechnic University of Valencia, Spain
Tarik Taleb   Aalto University, Finland
Wei Wang   Hefei Polytechnic University, China
Yin Zhang   Huazhong University of Science and Technology, China

Workshop Chairs

Ji Zhang   University of Southern Queensland, Australia
Delu Zheng   South China University of Technology, China
Naijin Chen   Anhui Polytechnic University, China
Haiping Huang   Nanjing University of Posts and Telecommunications, China

Publicity and Social Media Chair

Houbing Song   West Virginia University, USA

Sponsorship and Exhibits Chair

Xiaoyao Zheng   Anhui Normal University, China

Publications Chair

Taochun Wang   Anhui Normal University, China

Local Chair

Chuanxin Zhao   Anhui Normal University, China

Web Chair

Ziyang Zhang   Anhui Normal University, China
Junru Zhu   Anhui Normal University, China

Conference Coordinator

Anna Horvathova   European Alliance for Innovation, Slovakia
Yimu Ji   Nanjing University of Posts and Telecommunications, China

Technical Program Committee

Yonglong Luo   Anhui Normal University, China
Min Chen   Huazhong University of Science and Technology, China
Jiafu Wan   South China University of Technology, China
Delu Zeng   South China University of Technology, China
Yin Zhang   Zhongnan University of Economics and Law, China
Haiping Huang   Nanjing University of Posts and Telecommunications, China
Yimu Ji   Nanjing University of Posts and Telecommunications, China
Ji Zhang   University of Southern Queensland, Australia
Yan Zhang   Simula Research Laboratory, Norway
Chin-Feng Lai   National Chung Cheng University, Taiwan (China)
Jaime Lloret   Polytechnic University of Valencia, Spain
Dongyao Jia   University of Leeds, UK
Houbing Song   West Virginia University, USA
Meikang Qiu   Pace University, USA
Yunsheng Wang   Kettering University, USA
Tarik Taleb   Aalto University, Finland
Wei Wang   Hefei Polytechnic University, China
Naijin Chen   Anhui Polytechnic University, China
Wenming Wang   Anqing Normal University, China
Wanggen Li   Anhui Normal University, China
Qun Fang   Anhui Normal University, China
Kaizhong Zuo   Anhui Normal University, China
Fulong Chen   Anhui Normal University, China
Chuanxin Zhao   Anhui Normal University, China

Taochun Wang   Anhui Normal University, China
Biao Jie   Anhui Normal University, China
Xiaoyao Zheng   Anhui Normal University, China

Abstract of Invited Papers

Rigorous Simulation

Walid Taha

School of Information Technology and Engineering, Halmstad University,
Halmstad, Sweden
walid.taha@hh.se

Abstract. The falling price of computational and communication components means that they will increasingly be embedded into physical products. Verifying the designs of the resulting "cyber-physical" products is challenging for several reasons. First, closed-form solutions for the behavior of physical systems rarely exist. Second, the most natural mathematical tool for modeling cyber-physical combinations, namely, hybrid (discrete/continuous) systems, exhibit pathologies that arise in neither purely continuous nor purely discrete systems. Third, the expressivity of existing continuous dynamics formalisms is generally lower than those used by domain experts.

To address these problems, we are developing a technology called "rigorous simulation". The back-end for rigorous simulation uses validated numerics algorithms, which compute guaranteed bounds for the precision of all solutions. We show that these algorithms can be extended to compute trajectories for some hybrid systems exhibiting Zeno behavior. Ongoing work suggests that chattering behavior can be similarly addressed. We make validated numerics more accessible to non-specialists through the use of a domain-specific language, based on hybrid ordinary differential equations, which we also extend to support partial derivatives and certain types of equational modeling. An implementation called "Acumen" has been built and used for several case studies. These include virtual testing of advanced driver assistance functions, bipedal robotics, and a range of model problems for teaching at both graduate and undergraduate levels.

The Industrial Internet of Things (IIoT) and Industrial Data Analytics

Ji Zhang

Faculty of Health, Engineering and Sciences, University of Southern Queensland, Toowoomba, QLD 4350, Australia
Ji.Zhang@usq.edu.au

Abstract. The Industrial Internet of Things (IIoT) is the next wave of innovation impacting the way the world connects and optimizes machines. It is also the driving force to generate a huge amount of big data which are valuable assets and can in turn push the advancement of IIOT. In this talk, I will review the current development of IIOT and the standards, pipeline and techniques for dealing with IIOT driven industrial data analytics. I will also present sound real-life case study of IIOT and industry data analytics and share some of our recent research work in these areas.

Contents

Bound Analysis for Anchor Selection in Cooperative Localization

Ping Zhang, Along Cao, and Tao Liu[✉]

School of Computer Science, Anhui Polytechnic University, Wuhu, China
{pingzhang,liutao}@ahpu.edu.cn, 154351635@qq.com

Abstract. Anchor selection refers to choosing a small portion of the nodes with known locations to ensure the unique localizability and/or improve the accuracy of cooperative localization. Focusing on the localization accuracy, conventional practice suggests that the anchors should be deployed on the perimeter of the network. This paper derives the perimeter anchor deployment strategy by performing a bound analysis for the Cramér-Rao lower bound (CRLB) which quantifies the localization accuracy. It is proved that the uniform perimeter anchor deployment strategy is the optimal to fix an isotropically discriminable relative configuration whose nodes are randomly deployed onto a two-dimensional plane. For the relative configuration specified by the internode distance measurements, we introduce an error metric to evaluate the anchor selection performance, together with an upper bound that is independent of anchor selection.

Keywords: Wireless sensor networks · Relative configuration · Kullback-Cleibler distance · Singular value decomposition · Internode distances

1 Introduction

Cooperative localization has attracted great interest recently because it meets the requirement of obtaining the node locations for the emerging wireless sensor networks and other large scale networks to perform various monitoring/surveillance tasks [1]. It uses the internode measurements, *e.g.*, connectivity, received signal strength (RSS), angel-of-arrival (AOA), angel-difference-of-arrival (ADOA), time-of-arrival (TOA), or time-difference-of-arrival (TDOA), to expand the localization area and/or improve the localization accuracy [2,3]. But the internode measurements provide only the relative location information [2,4]. To get the absolute locations, one should assign absolute locations to a small portion of the nodes, called anchors, *a priori*. Anchor selection, or named anchor deployment/placement, refers to determining which nodes should be specified as the anchors to ensure the coverage and/or improve the accuracy of cooperative localization.

© ICST Institute for Computer Sciences, Social Informatics and Telecommunications Engineering 2017
F. Chen and Y. Luo (Eds.): Industrial IoT 2017, LNICST 202, pp. 1–10, 2017.
DOI: 10.1007/978-3-319-60753-5_1

Ensuring the coverage of cooperative localization is usually known as the unique localizability problem. Given the observed data, *i.e.*, the internode measurements and the anchor locations, the network is said to be uniquely localizable if there is a unique set of node locations consistent with the given data. This problem is closely related to the graph rigidity [5]. That is, a network is unique localizable if and only if the corresponding graph (whose edges are composed of the ones related to the internode measurements and the ones between at least three, in two dimensional case, noncollinear anchors) is globally rigid. Testing the unique localizability of a network requires only polynomial time, but the realization problem is NP-hard [6]. To cope with this realization problem, a triangulation-based graph is constructed, where the realization time is polynomial with respect to the node number [6]. An extension of the triangulation-based graph is involving the wheel structure [7], and some special graphs can even be realized in linear time [8]. The minimum number of the anchors to guarantee the unique localizability was investigated in [9], and which nodes can be uniquely located under given anchor locations was explored in [10].

Besides the coverage, the localization accuracy is another object that can be improved by anchor selection. Focusing on the localization accuracy, most existing work suggested that the anchors should be placed on the perimeter of the network. By using the multi-hop distance approximation, the outmost corner anchor placement can be derived after transforming cooperative localization into conventional localization [11]. Simulations in [12] demonstrated that anchors deployed in the network center or covering a small area may cause large error. Instead of the outmost corner anchor placement, the near perimeter, but not the outmost, placement exhibited the best performance in the simulations. For some specific algorithms in cooperative localization [2,13], the experiments also support the perimeter anchor deployment strategy.

From another point of view, the internode measurements specify the network relative configuration [4], which depicts the "shape" of the network without considering the network's location and orientation [3]. This leads to a relative/transformation subspace decomposition, where the anchor selection seems mainly affect the error in the transformation subspace but not the error in the relative subspace [4,14]. Based on this discovery, a perimeter anchor deployment can be derived by minimizing the principal angle between anchor constraint subspace and the transformation subspace [15]. Besides, if we introduce the anchor location uncertainty but ignore the internode measurement noise, the uniform perimeter anchor deployment strategy can be proved to be the optimal when the nodes are randomly deployed on a two-dimensional plane [16].

This paper derives a uniform perimeter anchor deployment strategy by minimizing an approximation of the Cramér-Rao lower bound (CRLB) which quantifies the localization error. This approximation is obtained from a bound analysis for the CRLB, and is actually the CRLB under the assumption that the corresponding relative configuration is isotropically discriminable. Considering that the relative configuration specified by the noisy internode distance measurements is not isotropically discriminable in general, we introduce an error metric to evaluation the approximation performance, together with an upper bound that is independent of anchor selection.

The remainder of this paper is organized as follows. Section 2 derives the CRLB for the node locations under a statistical model for cooperative localization. For the derived CRLB, Sect. 3 introduces an approximation, based on which a uniform perimeter anchor deployment strategy can be derived when the nodes are randomly deployed on a two-dimensional plane. In Sect. 4, we conclude this paper.

2   Background

This section details the statistical model of the internode distance measurements and derives the CRLB for the unknown node locations under given anchor locations.

Let us consider a network composed of n nodes, whose relative configuration is specified by the internode distance measurements modeled as

$$y_{i,j} = d_{i,j} + \epsilon_{i,j}, \quad (i,j) \in \mathcal{E} \tag{1}$$

where $d_{i,j} = \|\mathbf{s}_i - \mathbf{s}_j\|$ denotes the Euclidean distance between the ith and the jth node, $\epsilon_{i,j}$, $(i,j) \in \mathcal{E}$, are independent and identical distributed Gaussian stochastic noises with zero mean and variance σ^2, and $\mathcal{E}$ denotes the index set of connected edges corresponding to the distance measurements. In this section, we assume the distance measurements are sufficient to guarantee the global rigidity of the network, and the distance measurements are symmetrical so that any index pair $(i,j) \in \mathcal{E}$ fulfills $i < j$.

The logarithm of the probability density function specified by (1) is

$$\log p(\mathbf{y}; \mathbf{s}) = -\frac{1}{2\sigma^2} \sum_{(i,j)\in\mathcal{E}} (y_{i,j} - d_{i,j})^2 + c \tag{2}$$

where the measurement vector $\mathbf{y} = [y_{i,j}]_{(i,j)\in\mathcal{E}}$, and the constant c is independent of $\mathbf{s}$. After taking the negative expectation of the second derivation of (2), we get the FIM of $\mathbf{s}$

$$\mathbf{J_s} = -\mathrm{E}\left[\frac{\partial^2 \log p(\mathbf{y}; \mathbf{s})}{\partial \mathbf{s}\partial \mathbf{s}^T}\right] = \sigma^{-2}\mathbf{F}^T\mathbf{F} \tag{3}$$

where the rows of $\mathbf{F}$ are the partial derivatives of $d_{i,j}$, $(i,j) \in \mathcal{E}$, with respect to the location vector $\mathbf{s}$, given by

$$\frac{\partial d_{i,j}}{\partial \mathbf{s}^T} = \left[\mathbf{0}_{1\times2(i-1)}, \boldsymbol{\tau}_{i,j}^T, \mathbf{0}_{1\times2(j-i-1)}, \boldsymbol{\tau}_{j,i}^T, \mathbf{0}_{1\times2(n-j)}\right] \tag{4}$$

where $\boldsymbol{\tau}_{i,j} = -\boldsymbol{\tau}_{j,i} = \frac{\mathbf{s}_i-\mathbf{s}_j}{\|\mathbf{s}_i-\mathbf{s}_j\|}$.

Internode distances specify only the relative configuration of the network, leaving the network location and orientation unknown. According to this fact, there exists a relative-transformation decomposition of the location subspace

$\mathbb{R}^{2n}$ [3,4]. The transformation subspace relates to the translation and rotation of the network, which is spanned by the columns of $\mathbf{V} = [\mathbf{1}_x, \mathbf{1}_y, \mathbf{v}]$ where $\mathbf{1}_x = [1, 0, \ldots, 1, 0]^T \in \mathbb{R}^{2n}$, $\mathbf{1}_y = [0, 1, \ldots, 0, 1]^T \in \mathbb{R}^{2n}$, and $\mathbf{v} = [s_{1,y}, -s_{1,x}, \ldots, s_{n,y}, -s_{n,x}]^T \in \mathbb{R}^{2n}$. The relative subspace relates to shape (including size) of the network, which is spanned by the columns of $\mathbf{U}$ which form an orthonormal basis of the null space of $\mathbf{V}^T$. Using a suitable $\mathbf{U}$, we can perform a compact singular value decomposition (SVD) of the FIM $\mathbf{J_s}$ in the relative subspace as

$$\mathbf{J_s} = \mathbf{U}\Lambda\mathbf{U}^T \tag{5}$$

where Λ is a diagonal matrix with diagonal elements $\lambda_1 \geq \lambda_2 \geq \cdots \geq \lambda_{2n-3} > 0$.

The unknown node locations can be uniquely estimated after setting at least three nodes as anchors. Here, we use $\mathcal{U}$ and $\mathcal{A}$ denote the index set of the unknown nodes and the anchor nodes, respectively, where $\mathcal{U} \bigcup \mathcal{A} = \{1, 2, \cdots, n\}$. After given m anchors, the CRLB of the unknown node locations can be represented as

$$\mathbf{C} = (\mathbf{H}^T \mathbf{J_s} \mathbf{H})^{-1} \tag{6}$$

where $\mathbf{H}$ is a $2n$-by-$2(n-m)$ matrix which is stacked in column by

$$\left[\mathbf{0}_{2\times 2(j-1)}, \mathbf{I}_2, \mathbf{0}_{2\times 2(n-j)} \right]^T, j \in \mathcal{U}$$

in column.

Throughout this paper, the optimal anchor set refers to the one minimizing the CRLB trace $\mathrm{tr}(\mathbf{C})$, which lower bounds the variance of any unbiased estimate and can be asymptotically achieved by maximum likelihood estimation (MLE).

3   Bound Analysis

It is somewhat difficult to derive the perimeter anchor deployment strategy from the analytic expression of (6). To cope with this problem, we introduce an approximation $b(\mathcal{A})$ of $\mathrm{tr}(\mathbf{C})$, where the difference between $\mathrm{tr}(\mathbf{C})$ and $b(\mathcal{A})$ is bounded as below.

Proposition 1. *The ratio between* $\mathrm{tr}(\mathbf{C})$ *and* $b(\mathcal{A})$ *is bounded as*

$$\lambda_1^{-1} \leq \frac{\mathrm{tr}\,(\mathbf{C})}{b(\mathcal{A})} \leq \lambda_{2n-3}^{-1}. \tag{7}$$

where λ_1 and λ_{2n-3} are the first and the $(2n-3)$th largest eigenvalues of the distance FIM $\mathbf{J_s}$, and

$$b(\mathcal{A}) = \mathrm{tr}\left(\left(\mathbf{H}^T \mathbf{U} \mathbf{U}^T \mathbf{H} \right)^{-1} \right)$$
$$\frac{n}{m} \left(\frac{(\bar{s}_{\mathcal{A},x} - \bar{s}_x)^2 + (\bar{s}_{\mathcal{A},y} - \bar{s}_y)^2 + \rho^2}{\rho_{\mathcal{A}}^2} + 2 \right) + 2(n-m) - 3 \tag{8}$$

where $\bar{s}_x = \frac{1}{n}\sum_{i=1}^n s_{i,x}$, $\bar{s}_y = \frac{1}{n}\sum_{i=1}^n s_{i,y}$, $\bar{s}_{\mathcal{A},x} = \frac{1}{m}\sum_{j\in\mathcal{A}} s_{j,x}$, $\bar{s}_{\mathcal{A},y} = \frac{1}{m}\sum_{j\in\mathcal{A}} s_{j,y}$, $\rho^2 = \frac{1}{n}\sum_{i=1}^n (s_{i,x} - \bar{s}_x)^2 + (s_{i,y} - \bar{s}_y)^2$, and $\rho_{\mathcal{A}}^2 = \frac{1}{m}\sum_{j\in\mathcal{A}} (s_{j,x} - \bar{s}_{\mathcal{A},x})^2 + (s_{j,y} - \bar{s}_{\mathcal{A},y})^2$.

The derivation of (7) and (8) can be found in Appendix A.

Minimizing $b(\mathcal{A})$ leads to the uniform perimeter anchor deployment strategy. In (8), $b(\mathcal{A})$ can be viewed as a function of $(\bar{s}_{\mathcal{A},x} - \bar{s}_x)^2 + (\bar{s}_{\mathcal{A},y} - \bar{s}_y)^2$ and $\rho_{\mathcal{A}}$ that are affected by the anchor selection. To minimize $b(\mathcal{A})$, $(\bar{s}_{\mathcal{A},x} - \bar{s}_x)^2 + (\bar{s}_{\mathcal{A},y} - \bar{s}_y)^2$ should be minimized, and $\rho_{\mathcal{A}}$ should be maximized. $(\bar{s}_{\mathcal{A},x} - \bar{s}_x)^2 + (\bar{s}_{\mathcal{A},y} - \bar{s}_y)^2$ evaluates the squared distance between the centroids of the anchors and the nodes. It can be reduced to zero if $\bar{s}_{\mathcal{A},x} = \bar{s}_x$ and $\bar{s}_{\mathcal{A},y} = \bar{s}_y$. $\rho_{\mathcal{A}}$ quantifies the diameter of the network composed of the anchors. To maximize it, the anchors should be deployed on the perimeter of the network. When the nodes are randomly deployed in a two-dimensional plane, deploying the anchors uniformly around the perimeter of the network meets the requirements above, so that it can be viewed as an optimal strategy to reduce $b(\mathcal{A})$.

What is the difference between minimizing $b(\mathcal{A})$ and minimizing $\mathrm{tr}(\mathbf{C})$? Here we provide four examples to demonstrate the difference between $b(\mathcal{A})$ and $\mathrm{tr}(\mathbf{C})$, seen in Fig. 1. These four examples differ in the node configuration, where the nodes are deployed regularly in a circular region in Fig. 1a, randomly in a circular region in Fig. 1b, regularly in a square region in Fig. 1c, and randomly in a square region in Fig. 1d. Figure 1e, f, g, and h display the CRLB trace $\mathrm{tr}(\mathbf{C})$, its lower bound $\lambda_1^{-1} b(\mathcal{A})$, and upper bound $\lambda_{2n-3}^{-1} b(\mathcal{A})$ as the functions of all anchor triplets selected from the nodes, sorted by the descending order of $b(\mathcal{A})$. From these figures, it can be found that there is a similar tendency in the variation of $\mathrm{tr}(\mathbf{C})$ and $b(\mathcal{A})$, so that minimizing $\mathrm{tr}(\mathbf{C})$ can be approximated by minimizing $b(\mathcal{A})$. However, there are local fluctuations of $\mathrm{tr}(\mathbf{C})$. Because of the fluctuations, the anchors selected by minimizing $b(\mathcal{A})$ may not be the ones minimizing $\mathrm{tr}(\mathbf{C})$, as seen in Fig. 1c and d. Therefore, the performance of the proposed approximation should be investigated.

3.1 Isotropic Discriminability

What is $b(\mathcal{A})$? By using relative-transformation decomposition, the location vector $\mathbf{s}$ can be reparameterized as

$$\mathbf{s} = \mathbf{U}\boldsymbol{\eta} + \mathbf{V}\boldsymbol{\zeta} \qquad (9)$$

where $\boldsymbol{\eta} \in \mathbb{R}^{2n-3}$ and $\boldsymbol{\zeta} \in \mathbb{R}^3$ refer to the coordinates in the relative and transformation subspace, respectively.

Under the assumption that the deformation of the relative configuration is isotropically discriminable, i.e., the FIM $\mathbf{J}_{\boldsymbol{\eta}} = \alpha \mathbf{I}_{2n-3}$, $\alpha > 0$, and no information on the global transformation is available, i.e., the FIM $\mathbf{J}_{\boldsymbol{\zeta}} = \mathbf{0}$, we have

$$\mathbf{J}_{\mathbf{s}} = \alpha \mathbf{U}\mathbf{U}^T. \qquad (10)$$

Throughout this paper, we ignore the factor α without loss of generality.

After setting m anchors, we get the CRLB of $\mathbf{s}$ from (6), whose trace is just $b(\mathcal{A})$. Comparing (5) and (10), we find that the approximation $b(\mathcal{A})$ is equivalent to an isotropic discriminability approximation of the deformation of the relative configuration, where the similarity can be evaluated by the eigenvalue ratio $\lambda_1 / \lambda_{2n-3}$.

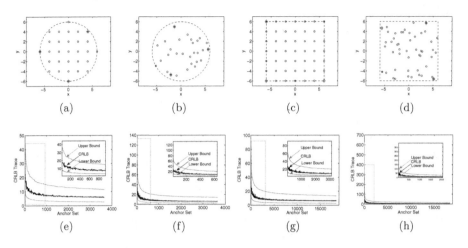

Fig. 1. Four examples: Fig (a), (b), (c), and (d) present the node configurations, where the anchor triplet selected by minimizing $b(\mathcal{A})$ (red empty diamonds: ◇) is compared with the one obtained by minimizing $\mathrm{tr}(\mathbf{C})$ (red solid circles: •). Figure (e), (f), (g), and (h) provide $\mathrm{tr}(\mathbf{C})$, its lower bound $\lambda_1^{-1}b(\mathcal{A})$, and upper bound $\lambda_{2n-3}^{-1}b(\mathcal{A})$ as the functions of all anchor triplets selected from the nodes, sorted by the descending order of $b(\mathcal{A})$. (Color figure online)

3.2   Performance Analysis

The performance of the approximation (8) can be quantified through the CRLB ratio $\frac{\mathrm{tr}(\mathbf{C}(\mathcal{A}_b))}{\mathrm{tr}(\mathbf{C}(\mathcal{A}_c))}$, where the numerator is the trace of the CRLB (6) corresponding to the anchor set $\mathcal{A}_b$ obtained by minimizing $b(\mathcal{A})$ and the denominator referring to the anchor set $\mathcal{A}_c$ obtained by minimizing the CRLB trace directly. This performance metric is bounded as below.

Proposition 2. *The CRLB ratio is bounded as*

$$1 \leq \frac{\mathrm{tr}(\mathbf{C}(\mathcal{A}_b))}{\mathrm{tr}(\mathbf{C}(\mathcal{A}_c))} \leq \frac{\lambda_1}{\lambda_{2n-3}}. \tag{11}$$

The proof is given in Appendix B.

The eigenvalue ratio λ_1/λ_{2n-3} is independent of the anchor selection. When λ_1/λ_{2n-3} approaches 1, the anchor set selected by minimizing $b(\mathcal{A})$ would be close to the optimal one. But in practice, although the CRLB ratios of the selected anchors are 1, 1, 1.0033, and 1.0287, the corresponding upper bounds λ_1/λ_{2n-3} are 4.3949, 5.4152, 4.9110, and 6.0145, respectively in Fig. 1a, b, c and d. Compared with the CRLB ratio, it seems that the upper bound λ_1/λ_{2n-3} tends to be conservative.

In fact, there is a negative result.

Proposition 3. *For fully connected networks, the eigenvalue ratio λ_1/λ_{2n-3} is bounded as*

$$\lambda_1/\lambda_{2n-3} \geq 2. \tag{12}$$

The proof can be found in Appendix C.

The equality in (12) holds under the condition that the nodes are uniformly deployed on a circle. As seen in Fig. 2, 49 nodes are uniformly deployed on a circle, with all pairwise distance measurements available. In this case, $\lambda_1/\lambda_{2n-3} = 2$, where $\lambda_1 = 49$ and $\lambda_{2n-3} = 24.5$. From Fig. 2b, it can be seen that the upper bound $\lambda_{2n-3}^{-1}b(\mathcal{A})$ is close to the CRLB trace $\text{tr}(\mathbf{C})$, thus the anchor set selected by minimizing $b(\mathcal{A})$ is the optimal in this trivial case.

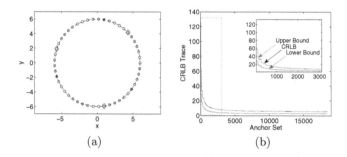

(a)   (b)

Fig. 2. Special case: Fig (a) presents the configuration of 49 nodes uniformly deployed on a ring, where the anchor triplet selected by minimizing $b(\mathcal{A})$ (red empty diamonds: $\diamond$) equals to (up to a symmetry) the one obtained by minimizing $\text{tr}(\mathbf{C})$ (red solid circles: $\bullet$). Figure (b) provides $\text{tr}(\mathbf{C})$, its lower bound $\lambda_1^{-1}b(\mathcal{A})$, and upper bound $\lambda_{2n-3}^{-1}b(\mathcal{A})$ as the functions of all anchor triplets selected from the nodes, sorted by the descending order of $b(\mathcal{A})$. (Color figure online)

4   Conclusion

In this paper, a uniform perimeter anchor deployment strategy is proved to be the optimal to fixing an isotropically discriminable relative configuration with randomly deployed nodes onto a two-dimensional plane. This strategy is used for anchor selection in cooperative location, where there exists deviation coming from the fact that the relative configuration specified by the internode distances is not isotropically discriminable in general. Theoretical analysis is performed to investigate the deviation, and more work is still needed to investigate the performance of the uniform perimeter anchor deployment strategy in future.

Acknowledgment. This research is partially supported by National Natural Science Foundation of China under Grant No. 61300170 and No. 61501005, Educational Commission of Anhui Province of China under Grant TSKJ2015B10, University Provincial Natural Science Foundation of Anhui Province under Grant No. KJ2016A057, and Research Starting Foundation of Anhui Polytechnic University under Grant No. 2015YQQ010.

A   Derivation of (7) and (8)

From (5), we have

$$\lambda_{2n-3}\mathbf{U}\mathbf{U}^T \le \mathbf{J_s} \le \lambda_1 \mathbf{U}\mathbf{U}^T \tag{13}$$

and thus

$$\lambda_{2n-3}\mathbf{H}^T\mathbf{U}\mathbf{U}^T\mathbf{H} \le \mathbf{H}^T\mathbf{J_s}\mathbf{H} \le \lambda_1\mathbf{H}^T\mathbf{U}\mathbf{U}^T\mathbf{H}. \tag{14}$$

Note that $\mathbf{C} = \left(\mathbf{H}^T\mathbf{J_s}\mathbf{H}\right)^{-1}$, we get

$$\lambda_1^{-1} \le \frac{\operatorname{tr}(\mathbf{C})}{b(\mathcal{A})} \le \lambda_{2n-3}^{-1} \tag{15}$$

after performing inversion and trace operation of (14).

To derive an analytical representation of $b(\mathcal{A})$, we use an column orthonormalized version of $\mathbf{V}$

$$\mathbf{V} = \left[\frac{1}{\sqrt{n}}\mathbf{1}_x,\ \frac{1}{\sqrt{n}}\mathbf{1}_y,\ \frac{\mathbf{v_s} - \frac{1}{n}\mathbf{1}_x^T\mathbf{v_s}\mathbf{1}_x - \frac{1}{n}\mathbf{1}_y^T\mathbf{v_s}\mathbf{1}_y}{\|\mathbf{v_s} - \frac{1}{n}\mathbf{1}_x^T\mathbf{v_s}\mathbf{1}_x - \frac{1}{n}\mathbf{1}_y^T\mathbf{v_s}\mathbf{1}_y\|}\right] \tag{16}$$

and thus $\mathbf{H}^T\mathbf{U}\mathbf{U}^T\mathbf{H} = \mathbf{I}_{2(n-m)} - \mathbf{H}^T\mathbf{V}\mathbf{V}^T\mathbf{H}$.

By applying the block matrix inversion formula and some matrix manipulations, we get

$$\operatorname{tr}\left(\left(\mathbf{I}_{2(n-m)} - \mathbf{H}^T\mathbf{V}\mathbf{V}^T\mathbf{H}\right)^{-1}\right) = \operatorname{tr}\left(\left(\mathbf{V}^T\left(\mathbf{I}_{2n} - \mathbf{H}\mathbf{H}^T\right)\mathbf{V}\right)^{-1}\right) + 2(n-m) - 3. \tag{17}$$

Note that

$$\mathbf{V}^T\left(\mathbf{I}_{2n} - \mathbf{H}\mathbf{H}^T\right)\mathbf{V} = \frac{m}{n}\begin{bmatrix} 1 & 0 & -\frac{\bar{s}_{\mathcal{A},y}-\bar{s}_y}{\rho} \\ 0 & 1 & \frac{\bar{s}_{\mathcal{A},x}-\bar{s}_x}{\rho} \\ -\frac{\bar{s}_{\mathcal{A},y}-\bar{s}_y}{\rho} & \frac{\bar{s}_{\mathcal{A},x}-\bar{s}_x}{\rho} & \frac{\tilde{\rho}_{\mathcal{A}}^2}{\rho^2} \end{bmatrix} \tag{18}$$

where $\bar{s}_x = \frac{1}{n}\sum_{i=1}^n s_{i,x}$, $\bar{s}_y = \frac{1}{n}\sum_{i=1}^n s_{i,y}$, $\bar{s}_{\mathcal{A},x} = \frac{1}{m}\sum_{j\in\mathcal{A}} s_{j,x}$, $\bar{s}_{\mathcal{A},y} = \frac{1}{m}\sum_{j\in\mathcal{A}} s_{j,y}$, $\rho^2 = \frac{1}{n}\sum_{i=1}^n (s_{i,x}-\bar{s}_x)^2 + (s_{i,y}-\bar{s}_y)^2$, and $\tilde{\rho}_{\mathcal{A}}^2 = \frac{1}{m}\sum_{j\in\mathcal{A}}(s_{j,x}-\bar{s}_x)^2 + (s_{j,y}-\bar{s}_y)^2$, we get

$$\left(\mathbf{V}^T\left(\mathbf{I}_{2n} - \mathbf{H}\mathbf{H}^T\right)\mathbf{V}\right)^{-1} = \frac{n}{m}\begin{bmatrix} 1 + \frac{(\bar{s}_{\mathcal{A},y}-\bar{s}_y)^2}{\rho_{\mathcal{A}}^2} & \frac{n(\bar{s}_{\mathcal{A},x}-\bar{s}_x)(\bar{s}_{\mathcal{A},y}-\bar{s}_y)}{-\rho_{\mathcal{A}}^2} & \frac{\rho(\bar{s}_{\mathcal{A},y}-\bar{s}_y)}{\rho_{\mathcal{A}}^2} \\ \frac{n(\bar{s}_{\mathcal{A},x}-\bar{s}_x)(\bar{s}_{\mathcal{A},y}-\bar{s}_y)}{-\rho_{\mathcal{A}}^2} & 1 + \frac{(\bar{s}_{\mathcal{A},x}-\bar{s}_x)^2}{\rho_{\mathcal{A}}^2} & \frac{\rho(\bar{s}_{\mathcal{A},x}-\bar{s}_x)}{-\rho_{\mathcal{A}}^2} \\ \frac{\rho(\bar{s}_{\mathcal{A},y}-\bar{s}_y)}{\rho_{\mathcal{A}}^2} & \frac{\rho(\bar{s}_{\mathcal{A},x}-\bar{s}_x)}{-\rho_{\mathcal{A}}^2} & \frac{\rho^2}{\rho_{\mathcal{A}}^2} \end{bmatrix} \tag{19}$$

where

$$\rho_{\mathcal{A}}^2 = \frac{1}{m}\sum_{j\in\mathcal{A}}(s_{j,x}-\bar{s}_{\mathcal{A},x})^2 + (s_{j,y}-\bar{s}_{\mathcal{A},y})^2. \tag{20}$$

Substituting (19) into (17), we get (8).

B   Proof of (11)

Let $\mathcal{A}_c$ and $\mathcal{A}_b$ denote the anchor set obtained by minimizing $\mathrm{tr}(\mathbf{C})$ and $b(\mathcal{A})$, respectively. After replacing $\mathbf{C}$ with $\mathbf{C}(\mathcal{A})$ to stress its dependence on the anchor selection, we get

$$\frac{\mathrm{tr}(\mathbf{C}(\mathcal{A}_b))}{\mathrm{tr}(\mathbf{C}(\mathcal{A}_c))} \geq 1 \tag{21}$$

$$\frac{b(\mathcal{A}_b)}{b(\mathcal{A}_c)} \leq 1. \tag{22}$$

From (7), we have

$$\mathrm{tr}(\mathbf{C}(\mathcal{A}_c)) \geq \lambda_1^{-1} b(\mathcal{A}_c) \tag{23}$$

$$\mathrm{tr}(\mathbf{C}(\mathcal{A}_b)) \leq \lambda_{2n-3}^{-1} b(\mathcal{A}_b) \tag{24}$$

and thus

$$\frac{\mathrm{tr}(\mathbf{C}(\mathcal{A}_b))}{\mathrm{tr}(\mathbf{C}(\mathcal{A}_c))} \leq \frac{\lambda_{2n-3}^{-1} b(\mathcal{A}_b)}{\lambda_1^{-1} b(\mathcal{A}_c)} \leq \frac{\lambda_1}{\lambda_{2n-3}} \tag{25}$$

where the right inequality is obtained by using (22).

From (21) and (25), we get

$$1 \leq \frac{\mathrm{tr}(\mathbf{C}(\mathcal{A}_b))}{\mathrm{tr}(\mathbf{C}(\mathcal{A}_c))} \leq \frac{\lambda_1}{\lambda_{2n-3}}. \tag{26}$$

C   Proof of (12)

Without loss of generality, we set $\sigma^2 = 1$. Then for a fully connected network, it can be verified that n is an eigenvalue of $\mathbf{J_s}$ with eigenvector proportional to $\mathbf{s} - \frac{1}{n}\mathbf{1}_x\mathbf{1}_x^T\mathbf{s} - \frac{1}{n}\mathbf{1}_y\mathbf{1}_y^T\mathbf{s}$. Note that the ith 2-by-2 diagonal block of $\mathbf{J_s}$ can be rewritten as $\sum_{j,j\neq i}\boldsymbol{\tau}_{i,j}\boldsymbol{\tau}_{i,j}^T$, and

$$\mathrm{tr}(\boldsymbol{\tau}_{i,j}\boldsymbol{\tau}_{i,j}^T) = \mathrm{tr}(\boldsymbol{\tau}_{i,j}^T\boldsymbol{\tau}_{i,j}) = 1, i \neq j \tag{27}$$

we have

$$\mathrm{tr}(\mathbf{J_s}) = \sum_{i=1}^{n} \mathrm{tr}(\sum_{j,j\neq i}\boldsymbol{\tau}_{i,j}\boldsymbol{\tau}_{i,j}^T) = n(n-1). \tag{28}$$

Since $\mathbf{J_s}$ is positive semidefinite with eigenvalues $\lambda_1 \geq \lambda_2 \geq \cdots \geq \lambda_{2n-3} \geq \lambda_{2n-2} = \lambda_{2n-1} = \lambda_{2n} = 0$, we get

$$\lambda_{2n-3} = \min_{i=2,3,\ldots,2n-3} \lambda_i \leq \frac{n(n-1)-n}{2n-4} = \frac{n}{2}. \tag{29}$$

Therefore, $\lambda_1/\lambda_{2n-3} \geq 2$ because $\lambda_1 \geq n$.

References

1. Patwari, N., Ash, J.N., Kyperountas, S., Hero III, A.O., Moses, R.L., Correal, N.S.: Locating the nodes: cooperative localization in wireless sensor networks. IEEE Signal Process. Mag. **22**(4), 54–69 (2005)
2. Patwari, N., Hero III, A.O., Perkins, M., Correal, N.S., O'Dea, R.J.: Relative location estimation in wireless sensor networks. IEEE Trans. Signal Process. **51**(8), 2137–2148 (2003)
3. Zhang, P., Wang, Q.: On using the relative configuration to explore cooperative localization. IEEE Trans. Signal Process. **62**(4), 968–980 (2014)
4. Ash, J.N., Moses, R.L.: On the relative and absolute positioning errors in self-localization systems. IEEE Trans. Signal Process. **56**(11), 5668–5679 (2008)
5. Jackson, B., Jordán, T.: Graph theoretic techniques in the analysis of uniquely localizable sensor networks. In: Mao, G., Fidan, B. (eds.) Localization Algorithms and Strategies for Wireless Sensor Networks, pp. 146–173. IGI Global (2009)
6. Eren, T., Goldenberg, O.K., Whiteley, W., Yang, Y.R., Morse, A.S., Anderson, B.D.O., Belhumeur, P.N.: Rigidity, computation, and randomization in network localization. In: Proceedings of IEEE Conference on Computer Communication, vol. 4, pp. 2673–2684 (2004)
7. Yang, Z., Liu, Y., Li, X.Y.: Beyond trilateration: on the localizability of wireless ad hoc networks. IEEE/ACM Trans. Netw. **18**(6), 1806–1814 (2010)
8. Aspnes, J., Eren, T., Goldenberg, D., Morse, A., Whiteley, W., Yang, Y., Anderson, B.D.O., Belhumeur, P.: A theory of network localization. IEEE Trans. Mobile Comput. **5**(12), 1663–1678 (2006)
9. Huang, M., Chen, S., Wang, Y.: Minimum cost localization problem in wireless sensor networks. Ad Hoc Netw. **9**(3), 387–399 (2011)
10. Yang, Z., Liu, Y.: Understanding node localizability of wireless ad hoc and sensor networks. IEEE Trans. Mobile Comput. **11**(8), 1249–1260 (2012)
11. Savvides, A., Garber, W., Adlakha, S., Moses, R., Srivastava, M.B.: On the error characteristics of multihop node localization in ad-hoc sensor networks. In: Zhao, F., Guibas, L. (eds.) IPSN 2003. LNCS, vol. 2634, pp. 317–332. Springer, Heidelberg (2003). doi:10.1007/3-540-36978-3_21
12. Li, X.L., Shi, H.C., Shang, Y.: Selective anchor placement algorithm for ad-hoc wireless sensor networks. In: Proceedings of IEEE International Confernce on Communications, pp. 2359–2363 (2008)
13. Chan, F., So, H.C., Ma, W.K.: A novel subspace approach for cooperative localization in wireless sensor networks using range measurements. IEEE Trans. Signal Process. **57**(1), 260–269 (2009)
14. Zhang, P., Lu, J., Wang, Q.: Performance bounds for relative configuration and global transformation in cooperative localization. ICT Express **2**(1), 14–18 (2016). special Issue on Positioning Techniques and Applications
15. Ash, J.N., Moses, R.L.: On optimal anchor node placement in sensor localization by optimization of subspace principal angles. In: Proceedings of IEEE International Conference on Acoustics of Speech, Signal Processing, pp. 2289–2292 (2008)
16. Zhang, P., Wang, Q.: Anchor selection with anchor location uncertainty in wireless sensor network localization. In: Proceedings of IEEE International Conference on Acoustics, Speech, Signal Processing, pp. 4172–4175 (2011)

Recharging Route Scheduling for Wireless Sensor Network Through Particle Swarm Optimization

Hengjing Zhang, Juan He, Runzhi Wang, Chuanxin Zhao[(⊠)],
Fulong Chen, and Yang Wang

School of Mathematics and Computer Science,
Anhui Normal University, Wuhu 241000, China
zhaocx@ahnu.edu.cn

Abstract. Wireless rechargeable sensor network can effective prolong the network lifetime through energy replenishment. However, how to schedule the energy replenishment still need to be carefully designed. In this paper, we proposed a novel route scheduling method for wireless sensor network to maximize network utility. Experiments results indicate that our method can more effective replenish energy than the compared method.

Keywords: Wireless rechargeable sensor network · Network utility · Particle swarm optimization · TSP

1 Introduction

With the rapid development of science technology, Internet of Things have caused more and more people's attention, such as wireless sensor networks (WSNs). WSNs mainly in the applications of surveillance and monitoring including environment sensing, nature disaster, target- tracking, structural health monitoring, etc. [1–3]. The traditional sensors [4–6] are mainly powered by batteries, but their limited battery capacity limits the large-scale deployment of wireless sensor networks. In other words, wireless sensor networks in the transmission process could not continue operations. Although there have been proposed energy saving method on the sensor in the past decade years, wireless sensor networks still left some problems and encountered bottleneck in the real deployments of WSNs and in wireless data communications.

To alleviate the limited capacity problem, researchers proposed to the renewable energy technology, which enables sensors to harvest ambient energy from their surroundings such as solar energy, wind energy, etc. [7–9]. However, the temporally–spatially nature of renewable energy makes it difficult to predict sensor capture rates. For example, it is shown that the difference of energy generating rates in sunny, cloudy and shadowy days can be up to three orders of magnitude in a solar collection system [10]. Therefore, the sensor can be charged so that the sensor has a stable energy. The recent breakthrough in the wireless power transfer technique based on strongly coupled magnetic resonances has drawn plenty of attentions [11]. Wireless power transmission

© ICST Institute for Computer Sciences, Social Informatics and Telecommunications Engineering 2017
F. Chen and Y. Luo (Eds.): Industrial IoT 2017, LNICST 202, pp. 11–23, 2017.
DOI: 10.1007/978-3-319-60753-5_2

technology is a promising technology to stable and high recharge rate wireless transmission power by Kurs et al. [12, 13].

Particle swarm optimization (PSO) is a population-based adaptive search optimization technique based on a simplified model of animal social behavior, first proposed by Kennedy and Eberhart in 1995. Such as fish school and bird populations. PSO was originally aimed at single-objective continuous optimization problem, it is a population-based optimization algorithm [14]. The basic principle of the PSO algorithm that each bird is abstracted as a particle, and the optimization results corresponding to the particle in space exploration position [14]. Therefore, the introduction of PSO algorithm can greatly improve the performance of WSN in the aspects of load balance, energy consumption and so on. PSO works with a population of particles. Particles move in the search space to find optimal solution. A particle adjusts its velocity before its movement according to some simple rules. Make use of the best position visited by each particle and the global best solution produced by the swarm to drive particles to a promising region.

In the paper, we propose multiple mobile wireless chargers to replenish sensors in a large scale WSN with wireless power transfer for a monitoring, making no sensor will run out of energy. We consider the flexibility of sensor energy charging mode, the sensor is charged by mobile Charger for on-demand routing and data routing and energy supplement. In order to avoid the termination of energy, we provide a method to transmission the energy from a mobile charger.

The rest of this paper is organized as follows. Section 2 reviews related work. Section 3 presents system model and notions. Section 4 proposes method. Section 5 evaluates the algorithm performance, and Sect. 6 concludes the paper.

2   Related Work

In order to prolong the service lifetime of the network, mobile chargers be used in wireless sensor networks. A few studies have been conducted to explore mobile chargers to replenish energy to sensors. Most existing studies considered sensor energy recharging and data collection routing jointly. For instance, Gu et al. [15] considered the problem of mobile strategy affects the survival time of direct network, which the author assumes the network is divided into several regions, and the cluster head is selected in the interior each area. The mobile node collects data directly from the cluster head. Its energy balance can be maintained by multi hop transmission. However, it will cause some data overflow and additional communication delay. Zheng et al. [16] designed a path selection probabilistic model and used the ACO algorithm to find the optimal path from the processing node to the destination node. But complexity of their proposed ACO algorithm is relatively high.

Guo et al. [17] proposed a framework for wireless energy supplements and mobile data collection based on the anchor point, considering that all kinds of capacity consumption and time vary with energy supplementation. In the energy balance, energy conservation and link capacity constraints, the problem of energy charge is considered to be the maximize utility. Zhao et al. [18] considered the combination of mobile data optimization and energy charging to achieve the energy complements range and latency data collection by using mobility. They have developed a charging and data collection problem as a way to adjust the data rate, flow routing, and link scheduling issues to achieve maximum network utility.

Similarly, Yang et al. [19] proposed a sleep multi-path routing protocol to save energy in directional diffusion by using desired path success and path dependency requirements to limit the number of active alternative paths. To improve the energy efficiency by reducing the length of the alternative paths, Ganesan et al. [20] proposed the braided multi-path protocol. In this protocol, rather than building completely disjoint paths, partially disjoint paths are constructed. In this protocol, instead of building a complete disjoint path, a partially disjoint path is constructed, which is a path-based failure that may fail on the edge while other edges are still available. Liu et al. [21] proposed topology control method for a multichannel multi-radio wireless network using directional antennas.

There are a few recent works using on-demand sensors to supplement the energy. Xu et al. [22] proposed a method to schedule K mobile chargers to add energy. The maximum charge time in the K charger is minimized for live sensors. Ren et al. [23] have recently investigated the deployment of a single mobile charger to charge under distance-constrained sensors. Approximate algorithm for the minimization of network utility [24] is proposed by Liang et al. By means of a charging sensor, under the energy constraints of each moving vehicle, moving vehicles are used to charge a set of charged sensors. For our work, we also take into accounted to minimize the total travel multiple mobile charger to maintain the permanent operation of the sensor network.

3 Problem Statement

How to schedule the charging vehicle to replenish the network directly affects the service life of the whole wireless sensor network. When there is only one charging vehicle in the entire network, it needs to traverse all sensor nodes in the network and add energy to them. Therefore, it is very important to choose the best path to traverse the network. We first assume that all sensors have reached the threshold of energy consumption, and they need for additional. And then we also assumed that the charging vehicle with infinite energy to support it to traverse all nodes and charge them, such as in Fig. 1. Through the above assumptions, the charging problem of wireless sensor network can be converted into Traveling Salesman Problem. Finally, the algorithm for dealing with this problem is proposed.

We can consider this problem as optimization problem. Let $S = \{s_1, s_2, \ldots, s_N\}$ be the set of sensors. We define a graph $G = (V, E)$ to represents the network, where V refers to the set of sensors and the base station (v0) and E denotes the paths between those sensors. There is an edge $(i, i + 1)$ between sensors i and sensor $i + 1$, $\forall i \in V$.

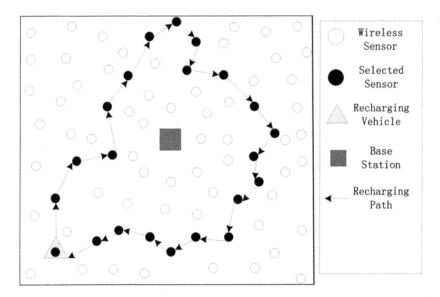

Fig. 1. Scheduling of recharging route for a wireless sensor network

Energy required by sensor node i is defined as e_i. $p_{i,i+1}$ is the energy consumed by a charging vehicle while move from sensor node i to sensor i + 1. Binary variable a_i equals 1 if sensor node i is recharged by charging vehicle; otherwise, it is 0. And binary variable $b_{i,i+1}$ equals 1 if the charging vehicle is move from sensor i to sensor i + 1; otherwise, it is 0. We define the total energy consumption of charging car during a charging tour as E_c. Table 1 lists the definitions of all notations.

Table 1. The parameters of network

Parameter	Value
Number of sensors N	20, 40, 60, 80, 100
The Upper limit of Iteration times	5000
Inertia weight w	0.5 f
Side length of sensing field L	200
Supply voltage	3 V
Charge threshold Ec	30
Consumption of Recharging Vehicles Em	0.56 J/m
Speed of Recharging Vehicles Vr	1 m/s
Magnification of $\sum 1/\mathbf{RE}$	500

We aim to find the maximum charging efficiency of the charging vehicle under the premise of ensuring the normal operation of sensor network, i.e., the ratio of the total energy demand of sensors to energy capacity of charging vehicle.

Maximize:

$$\sum_{i=0}^{N} a_i e_i / E_c \tag{1}$$

Subject to:

$$\sum_{i=0}^{N} b_{i,i+1} p_{i,i+1} > 0, \forall i \in s \tag{2}$$

$$\sum_{i=0}^{N} a_i e_i + \sum_{i=0}^{N} b_{i,i+1} p_{i,i+1} \leq E_c, \forall i \in s \tag{3}$$

$$a_{i,i+1} \in \{0,1\}, \forall i \in s \tag{4}$$

$$b_{i,i+1} \in \{0,1\}, \forall i \in s \tag{5}$$

In the above statement, constraint (2) shows that the charging vehicle moves at least once during a charging cycle. Constraint (3) ensures that the capacity of charging vehicle should not be depleted. Constraints (4) and (5) indicates that a_i and $b_{i,i+1}$ are all binary variables.

4 Proposed Method

4.1 Particle Swarm Optimization Algorithm

Particle swarm optimization has been used to solve resource assignment and network deployment [25, 26]. In the PSO, particle swarm search in an n dimensional space. In this space, each particle's position represents a solution to the problem. Particles search for new solutions by adjusting the position X. Every particle can remember their best solution, denoted as P_{id}. The best position of the particle swarm passed which is also the optimal solution to the current search, denoted as P_{gd}. Each particle has a velocity, denoted as V.

$$V_{id}' = \omega V_{id} + \eta_1 rand()(P_{id} - X_{id}) + \eta_2 rand()(P_{gd} - X_{id}) \tag{6}$$

The V_{id} means the velocity of the i particle at the d dimension. ω is the inertia weight. η_1, η_2 is the important parameters to adjusting P_{id} and P_{gd}. rand() is a random number generating function. In this way, we can get the next position of the particle.

$$X_{id}' = X_{id} + V_{id} \tag{7}$$

4.2 Charging Utility

We consider a modified PSO algorithm in this situation that there is only one recharging vehicles charging for the whole sensor cluster. For simplicity, we assume that all sensors have got the threshold of energy consumption so they all need additional energy. The recharging vehicle must pass all nodes to charge for all sensor nodes. In addition, it is assumed that the recharging vehicle has unlimited energy, it has enough energy to support itself to travel all nodes and charge all nodes. So the wireless charging sensor network can be converted into the TSP traveling salesman problem.

As the remaining energy of each sensor is different and the distance is also different. When recharging vehicle moves, it needs consume energy. Therefore, we define a charging utility criterion to measure the charging utility:

$$f(i) = \partial \frac{1}{RE_i} - e_m \times D_{i,j}, i,j = 0,1,2,\cdots,n, i \neq j \tag{8}$$

RE_i is the residual energy of sensor. e_m is the energy consumption when recharging vehicle drives one unit meters. $D_{i,j}$ is the pseudo Euclidean distance between sensor i and sensor j. ∂ is the constant coefficient.

When RE_i is small, the energy of sensor i is lower. As the result, the $\frac{1}{RE_i}$ is bigger, so the charging priority of the sensor i is higher and the charging utility is better. When $D_{i,j}$ is smaller, the energy the recharging vehicle consumes when it is moving is also less. In the contrary, the charging utility is better. Therefore, the standard can be well described for the charging utility.

We know the charging utility function of each sensor. According to this function, the fitness of each particle can be obtained:

$$fitness(k) = \sum (\partial \frac{1}{RE_i} - e_m \times D_{i,i+1}), i = 0,1,2,\cdots,n, k = 0,1,2,\cdots n \tag{9}$$

4.3 Improved PSO Algorithm

Because we have got the fitness, what we also need to know is the speed of particles. The speed determines the direction and distance they fly. Then the particles will follow the current optimal particle to search the best solution. We iterate this step to update the particle until we find the optimal solution or up to upper limit of the iteration. However, the basic PSO algorithm is used to solve the continuous problem. But we can't directly use formula (7) in the TSP problem. Therefore, we improved the PSO algorithm and introduced the exchange order to construct a special PSO algorithm. So we can use it to solve the traveling salesman problem. We introduce the following new speed formula.

$$V'_{id} = V_{id} \times \alpha(p_{id} - X_{id}) \times \beta(p_{gd} - X_{id}) \tag{10}$$

The α, β is the random number between 0 and 1. $\alpha(P_{id} - X_{id})$ means the basic exchange sequence $(P_{id} - X_{id})$ is retained at the probability α. $\beta(P_{gd} - X_{id})$ means the basic exchange sequence $(P_{gd} - X_{id})$ is retained at the probability β. So we can get this conclusion: when α is bigger, $(P_{id} - X_{id})$ is larger, the effect of P_{id} is bigger. Similarly, when β, $\left(P_{gd} - X_{id}\right)$ is larger, the effect of P_{gd} is bigger.

Next, we will describe the algorithm. First, we input the location and residual energy of each sensor nodes. We initial P_{id} and P_{gd} and randomly generated N particles. Each particle means a path to traverse all nodes. Next, according to the particle fitness function, we calculate the fitness of each particle. Then we start to iterate: we randomly change the path sequence and generate a new path and we calculate the fitness again. We compare it to the fitness of the best position of P_{id} the particle experiences. If better, we update P_{id}. Then, we also compare it to the fitness of the best position of P_{gd} the group experiences. If better, we update P_{gd}. If we can find the enough good position or up to the maximum number of iterations. We say we meet the ending conditions to end the cycle. Otherwise, continue to iterate. The flow chart of the algorithm is as Fig. 2:

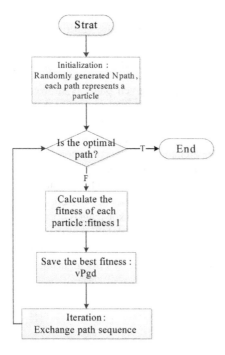

Fig. 2. The flowchart of method

5 Experiment and Simulation

In our simulation experiment, we laid N sensors at random in a square area whose side length L is 200. We laid a base station to receive sensor signal. Each sensor is equipped with CC2530 communication module and PIR to detect the target. The average current is 10 mA under 3 V voltage when the sensor is activated. It consumes 27 mA when they send or receive data package. The supply voltage range is between 2.0 V and 3.6 V, and we use 3 V in this experiment. Each sensor produces data package at constant speed, and each data package measures 20 bytes. During spare time the average current is 170 μA. We set the threshold value of the sensor is half of the whole power capacity. Recharging vehicle runs constantly at 1 m/s which consumes 0.56/m.

We realize the algorithm through Java and illustrate the result of the algorithm by diagram. We set these two auto-charging cars for two kinds of algorithms with same initial coordinates. Also, we set the initial coordinate of sensors randomly. We compare the results of CRSA and PSO: setting 5 sensor groups, and the sensor node numbers of these groups are 20, 40, 60, 80, 100, respectively.

5.1   Utility Evaluation

First of all, we evaluate the charging utility of the two algorithms. We compare the charging utility of the recharging vehicle under two algorithms. In the former condition, recharging vehicle charges the sensor through the charging path given by PSO. Meanwhile, recharging vehicle charges the sensor by the path given by CRSA in the second condition.

The comparison of charging utility within two algorithms that recharging vehicles charge all the sensors' nodes by the given paths is showed in Fig. 1 as below. The abscissa of the chart is the number of the sensors while the ordinate of the chart is the charging utility.

It illustrates by the Fig. 3 that when the scales of the sensors are 20, 40, 60, 80, 100, charging utilities of PSO are all larger than the corresponding ones of CRSA. In addition, with the scale of sensors enlarging the utility gap between these two algorithms becomes wider and wider. When the sensor's scale is small, the paths and given paths from PSO intelligent algorithm are less, when the sensor scale is 20, PSO algorithm only improves the charging utility by 37.2%. When the sensor scale is 40, the utility increases by 44.6%, while the scale is 60, it increases by 52.3%. Additionally, when the scale is 80 or 100, the utility is improved by 73.8% or 75.4% respectively. It demonstrates that the larger the scale is the better charging utility planned by PSO algorithm.

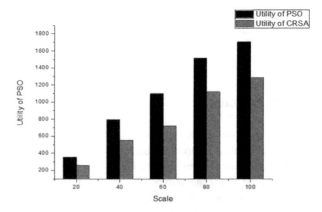

Fig. 3. The compared result of two algorithms for 5 networks

5.2 Convergence Analysis

Then, we will analyze the convergence of PSO. As followed, we compare these convergences in 5 different scales.

The Fig. 4 shows the convergence of PSO algorithm when sensor scale is 20. We can see from the graph that algorithm converges rapidly at 39th generation with a constant rate: 394.8.

As for the sensor group whose scale is 40, its algorithm convergence is shown by Fig. 5. The utility converges at 919th generation. Additionally, before the final convergence the utility convergent briefly for three times. At last, it finds a new best particle and converges. After the convergence, the utility maintains at 767.3.

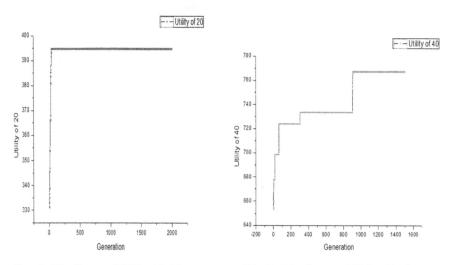

Fig. 4. The fitness of PSO with 20 sensors   **Fig. 5.** The fitness of PSO with 40 sensors

As for the sensor group whose scale is 60, its algorithm convergence is shown by Fig. 6. The utility converges at 1781th generation. After the final convergence, the utility maintains at 1032.1. Additionally, before the final convergence the utility convergent briefly for five times. At last, it finds a new best particle and converges.

As for the sensor group whose scale is 80, its algorithm convergence is shown by Fig. 7. The utility converges at 2472th generation. After the final convergence, the utility maintains at 1395.2. Additionally, before the final convergence the utility convergent briefly for nine times. At last, it finds a new best particle and converges.

As for the sensor group whose scale is 100, its algorithm convergence is shown by Fig. 8. The utility converges at 419th generation. After the final convergence, the utility maintains at 1664.1. Additionally, before the final convergence the utility convergent briefly for three times. At last, it finds a new best particle and converges.

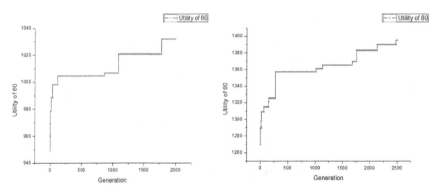

Fig. 6. The fitness of PSO with 60 sensors

Fig. 7. The fitness of PSO with 80 sensors

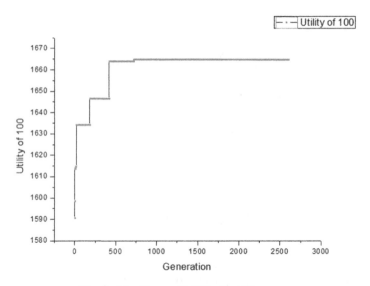

Fig. 8. The fitness of PSO with 100 sensors

5.3   Shortest Distance Assessment

We evaluate the shortest moving distance for sensors which is provided by recharging vehicles of two algorithms. We compare the shortest distances when sensor scale is 20, 40, 60, 80, 100 of two algorithms, respectively. Under the first circumstance, recharging vehicles plan the charging path and calculate the shortest distance by PSO algorithm. While under the second circumstance, recharging vehicles plan the charging path and calculate the shortest distance by CRSA algorithm.

It can be shown by Fig. 9 that with the sensor scale extending the distance for recharging vehicles need to move increases. However, it is not linear increase. When sensor scale increases from 60 to 80, the shortest moving distance for recharging vehicle increases apparently slower. When sensor scale is 20, the shortest distance planned by CRSA algorithm is 793 while it planned by PSO algorithm is 423. The shortest moving distance optimizes and improves by 87.5%. When sensor scale is 40, the shortest distance planned by CRSA algorithm is 1544 while it planned by PSO algorithm is 598. The shortest moving distance optimizes and improves by 158.3%. When sensor scale is 60, the shortest distance planned by CRSA algorithm is 2597 while it planned by PSO algorithm is 1145. The shortest moving distance optimizes and improves by 126.8%. When sensor scale is 80, the shortest distance planned by CRSA algorithm is 2971 while it planned by PSO algorithm is 1448. The shortest moving distance optimizes and improves by 105.2%. When sensor scale is 100, the shortest moving distance planned by CRSA algorithm is 4154 while it planned by PSO algorithm is 2546. The shortest moving distance optimizes and improves by 63.1%.

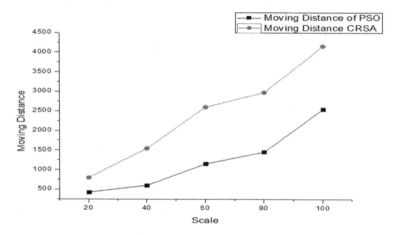

Fig. 9. The moving distance of 2 Algorithm

6 Conclusion

In this paper, we proposed a novel route scheduling method based on particle swarm optimization for wireless sensor network to maximize network utility. Experiments results indicate that our method can more effective replenish energy than compared method. Next, we will relax the assumption of energy to study the more real recharging scheduling for wireless network.

References

1. Yick, J., Mukherjee, B., Ghosal, D.: Wireless sensor network survey. Comput. Netw. **52**, 2292–2330 (2008)
2. Yick, J., Mukherjee, B., Ghosal, D.: Wireless sensor network survey. Comput. Netw. Int. J. Comput. Telecommun. Netw. **52**(12), 2292–2330 (2008)

3. Akyildiz, I.F., Su, W., Sankarasubramaniam, Y., Cayirci, E.: Wireless sensor networks: a survey. Comput. Netw. **38**(4), 393–422 (2002)
4. Zahmati, A.S., Abolhassani, B., Beheshti Shirazi, A., Bakhtiari, A.S: An energy efficient protocol with static clustering for wireless sensor networks, Int. J. Electron. Circuits Syst. **69** (2007)
5. Younis, O., Fahmy, S.: HEED: a hybrid, energy-efficient, distributed clustering approach for ad hoc sensor networks. IEEE Trans. Mob. Comput. **3**(4), 366–379 (2004)
6. Wei, D., Jin, Y., Vural, S.: An energy-efficient clustering solution for wireless sensor networks. IEEE Trans. Wireless Commun. **10**(11), 3973–3983 (2011)
7. Liang, W., Ren, X., Jia, X., Xu, X.: Monitoring quality maximization through fair rate allocation in harvesting sensor networks. IEEE Trans. Parallel Distrib. Syst. **24**(9), 1827–1840 (2013)
8. Kansal, A., Hsu, J., Zahedi, S., Srivastava, M.B.: Power management in energy harvesting sensor networks. ACM Trans. Embed. Comput. Syst. **6**(4), 32 (2007)
9. Ren, X., Liang, W., Xu, W.: Use of a mobile sink for maximizing data collection in energy harvesting sensor networks. In: Proceedings of 42nd international conference on parallel processing (ICPP), pp. 439–448. IEEE (2013)
10. Rahimi, M., Shah, H., Sukhatme, G., Heideman, J., Estrin, D.: Studying the feasibility of energy harvesting in a mobile sensor network. In: Proceedings of international conference on robotics and automation (ICRA), vol. 1, pp. 19–24. IEEE (2003)
11. Kurs, A., Karalis, A., Moffatt, R., Joannopoulos, J.D., Fisher, P., Soljacic, M.: Wireless power transfer via strongly coupled magnetic resonances. Science **317**, 83–86 (2007)
12. Lin, Z., Zhang, H., Wang, Y., Yao, F.: Energy-efficient routing protocol on mobile sink in wireless sensor network. Adv. Mater. Res. **787**, 1050–1055 (2013)
13. Gu, Y., Ji, Y., Li, J., Zhao, B.: ESWC: efficient scheduling for the mobile sink in wireless sensor networks with delay constraint. IEEE Trans. Parallel Distrib. Syst. **24**(7), 1310–1320 (2013)
14. Liang, Y., Yu, H.: PSO-based energy efficient gathering in sensor networks. In: Jia, X., Wu, J., He, Y. (eds.) MSN 2005. LNCS, vol. 3794, pp. 362–369. Springer, Heidelberg (2005). doi:10.1007/11599463_36
15. Zheng, W., Liu, S., Kou, L.: Dynamic mobile agent routing algorithm in sensor network. Control Decis. **25**(7), 1035–1039 (2010)
16. Guo, S., Wang, C., Yang, Y.: Mobile data gathering with wireless energy replenishment in rechargeable sensor networks. In: Proceedings of INFOCOM, pp. 1932–1940. IEEE (2013)
17. Zhao, M., Li, J., Yang, Y.: Joint mobile energy replenishment and data gathering in wireless rechargeable sensor networks. In: Proceedings of 23rd international tele-traffic congress (ITC), pp. 238–245. IEEE (2011)
18. Yang, O., Heinzelman, W.: Sleeping multipath routing: a trade-off between reliability and lifetime in wireless sensor networks. In: Proceedings of the 30th IEEE Conference on Global Telecommunications, GLOBECOM 2011, pp. 1–5 (2011)
19. Ganesan, D., Govindan, R., Shenker, S., Estrin, D.: Highly-resilient, energy-efficient multipath routing in wireless sensor networks. ACM SIGMOBILE Mob. Comput. Commun. Rev. **5**(4), 11–25 (2001)
20. Liu, Q., Jia, X., Zhou, Y.: Topology control for multi-channel multi-radio wireless mesh networks using directional antenas. Wirel. Network **17**, 41–51 (2010). doi:10.1007/s11276-010-0263-1
21. Xu, W., Liang, W., Lin, X.: Approximation algorithms for min-max cycle cover problems. IEEE Trans. Comput. (2013, to appear)
22. Ren, X., Liang, W., Xu, W.: Maximizing charging throughput in rechargeable sensor networks. In: Proceeding of ICCCN. IEEE (2014)

23. Liang, W., Xu, W., Ren, X., Jia, X., Lin, X.: Maintaining sensor networks perpetually via wireless recharging mobile vehicles. In: Proceeding of LCN. IEEE (2014)
24. Wang, C., Li, J., Ye, F., Yang, Y.: Multi-vehicle coordination for wireless energy replenishment in sensor networks. In: Proceeding of IPDPS. IEEE (2013)
25. Chuanxin, Z., Fulong, C., Ruchuan, W., Cheng, Z., Yonglong, L.: Multi-objective channel assignment and gateway deployment optimizer for wireless mesh network. J. Comput. Res. Dev. **52**(8), 1831–1841 (2015)
26. Zhao, C.-X., Wang, R.-C., Huang, H.-P., Sun, L.-J.: Cross-layer power allocation for multi-radio multi-channel Ad Hoc network. Syst. Eng. Electron. **33**(4), 894–899 (2011)

Tracking Movement Target by Using WebGIS on Video Surveillance System

Ji Bin[1(✉)], Xu Ting[1], Zhao Chuanxing[2], and Chu Yuezhong[1]

[1] School of Computer Science and Technology,
Anhui University of Technology, Ma'anshan 243032, China
I.1302793683@qq.com
[2] Department of Network Engineering,
Anhui Normal University, Wuhu 241000, China

Abstract. This paper addresses a novel video surveillance system based on camera monitoring network. The system is belong to the application layer of Internet of Things (IoT). In the system, all videos are mapped into the corresponding camera nodes on a WebGIS (Web geographic information system). A group of the related nodes can be attained automatically by the Nearest Neighbor search method. In the searched node, the target can be automatically found in the video by target detection algorithm based on clothing color, and tracked based on particle filter. When above searching works are finished in an interesting geographical area, a completed movement path of the target can be displayed on the map, meanwhile, an information summary table about the target's current location, current speed, current time and event's attribute can be created. It also automatically collects the target's relative video clips for improving the artificially monitoring work efficiency.

Keywords: WebGIS · Object tracking · Valuable video clips · Video surveillance system

1 Introduction

IoT applications has been being widely adopted [1, 2], which is becoming more intelligent. Its effects have been making incredible strides as a universal media solution for the many scenarios. In the near future, a large number of daily objects with computing and communication capabilities will be interconnected using standard Internet protocols [3, 4], and data collection and processing speed will be a challenge or a new perspective for us [5]. In the platform of IoT, intelligent video surveillance technology [6] has been quickly becoming a hot research and accessed wide attentions.

The video surveillance system can be regard as a perception layer of the cameras monitoring IoT. The coverage scope of the cameras monitoring IoT has been growing. With the increasing number of videos, the followed problem is that the efficiency of searching manually an interesting target is extremely low. Therefore, the searching task is encountering unmanageable troubles. However, with the development of the safe city's projects, the video surveillance system is playing increasingly an important role [7]. In the other hand, under the rapid development and extensive application of GIS [8, 9], the video surveillance system based on the GIS is becoming a more and more pressing need,

F. Chen and Y. Luo (Eds.): Industrial IoT 2017, LNICST 202, pp. 24–33, 2017.
DOI: 10.1007/978-3-319-60753-5_3

because videos can provide the objective motion and its location information in this field. Simon Denman [10] introduced a automatic surveillance in transportation hub which demonstrated target's performance on airport surveillance data. But this system can't show the movement path of the target within the geographic area. Bouwmans and his team [11] introduced the background detection technology from background modeling and pedestrian detection in terms of target recognition and tracking algorithms. Yilmaz, Wang [12] described the target tracking algorithm in detail from single camera and multi-cameras tracking. The works listed above are mainly limited to the single-source video, and the videos searching based on nodes network is still a difficulty. Therefore, an intelligent video surveillance system integrated WebGIS is quite promising.

This paper focuses on the design and implementation of the intelligent video Surveillance system from the perspective of human-computer interaction. It not only records the information of target's moving path on the map of WebGIS, but also automatically extracts the interested video clips included the suspect target. It improves the working efficiency for the monitoring staff.

2 Development Environment and Business Solution

2.1 Development Environment

This design uses the Linux operating system, which is a free and open source UNIX-like operating system. Firstly, Linux system can be more convenient because of using some lightweight and efficient open source software. Secondly, this design uses the computer vision technology with the OpenCV library to process the monitoring videos. Thirdly, this design uses Qt Creator for the preparation of human-computer interaction interface, which is a cross-platform C++ application framework and provides application developers to build art level graphical user interface. It is easy to extend and allow true component programming. It is a completed C++ program development framework and has a high degree of support for C++.

In summary, the design of the development environment:

Hardware platform:
CPU Intel Core i5-3210 M 2.50 GHz
Memory: 8 GB Kingston DDR3 SDRAM 1600 MHz
Graphics: Intel HD Graphics 4000 (2.13 GB)
Software platform:
Operating system: Fedora2.0
The program framework: Qt5.3.1
Integrated Development Environment: Qt Creator
Machine Vision Library: OpenCV2.4.7

2.2 Business Solution

This paper focuses on the intelligent video monitoring system based on the camera network map. The main research contents include the analysis about target state, cross-regional tracking, and the extraction of valuable videos. Based on the open source OpenCV machine vision library and WebGIS technology, this design realizes the functional requirements. The whole business's flow chart is as followed in Fig. 1;

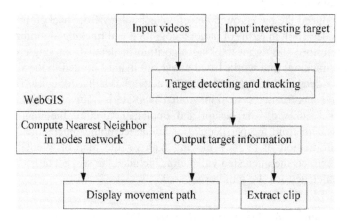

Fig. 1. Flow chart

The following topics should be explored in this paper.

1. Studying the recent moving target recognition algorithms and tracking algorithms and explore their advantages and disadvantages. We have studied the related algorithms and selected the algorithm which is suitable for the system, some of the algorithms should be modified to make them adapt to the demand of this system;
2. Studying the application of map information system services. We have called the Baidu map API using HTML language to write the appropriate codes and made the target move paths in the monitoring network;
3. Researching the continuous tracking algorithm in the multi-camera scenes. We have implemented the target cross-video analyzing and tracking in the monitoring network by the use of multi-threaded approach;
4. Studying the method of extracting valuable video clips. We have applied the corresponding cutting tools and download tools to extract the useful video clips from the video library, and achieve the function of 'preview,' 'save';

3   Using WebGIS

In recent years, GIS (Geographic Information System) has achieved increasingly wide application. WebGIS is the combination of Internet technology and GIS technology which is the GIS application in the network environment. From any node on the IoT, users can browse WebGIS map data and analyze spatial information. Web map service is becoming widely popular based on mature Web technology, computer technology and GIS technology. With the opening network technology, famous Online Map Service Providers almost welcome the third party softwares call their Map API in other applications.

This paper uses WebGIS (Baidu Map) API. In order to facilitate the user to search valid camera nodes in the map, we embed Baidu Map Webpage into the program. Through the Baidu Map API function we connect the map and video data library. When anyone clicks the camera button, the system can automatically load and play the video data from the video server. When the target is found in the related nodes, the icon color triggers a change from gray to yellow. When the automatically searching task has finished in the region, the movement path of the target can be played directly on the map. The path result is as shown in Fig. 2.

Fig. 2. The path on the Webcam Map

4   The Related Core Knowledge

4.1   Target Detection and Tracking in the Single Camera Scene

The process consists of two important steps: target detecting and target tracking.

In target detection algorithm, firstly we need obtain the feature of clothing-color by the operations of human interaction. After selecting body area of target, the color feature may be attained, and then, the similar color areas can be obtained by using a reverse projection method [13]. The clothing-color feature template is obtained after using region growing method [14] and contour of the lookup function [13]. This process of extracting the feature template is as shown in Figs. 3 and 4.

In target tracking algorithm, we use a particle filter tracking [15, 16] based on color histogram for target tracking. And its initial particle is the target which is identified by above target detection algorithm, and then according to the dynamic second order regression state transition equation to forecast the state of motion, the equation can be showed in formula (1):

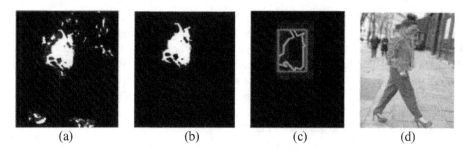

Fig. 3. The process of extracting the feature template about coat; (a) using reverse projection method; (b) using region growing method; (c) Extracting the outermost contour; (d) result of the contour

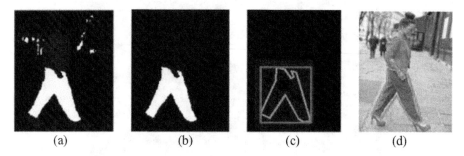

Fig. 4. The process of extracting the feature template about underwear; (a) using reverse projection method; (b) using region growing method; (c) Extracting the outermost contour; (d) result of the contour

$$\begin{cases} X = A_1 * (P_x - P_{x0}) + A_2 * (P_{xp} - P_{x0}) + B_0 * gsl\_ran\_gaussian(rng, TRANS\_X\_STD + P_{x0} \\ Y = A_1 * (P_y - P_{y0}) + A_2 * (P_{yp} - P_{y0}) + B_0 * gsl\_ran\_gaussian(rng, TRANS\_Y\_STD + P_{y0} \end{cases} \quad (1)$$

The coefficients set as follows: $A_1 = 2.0$, $A_2 = -1.0$, $B_0 = 1.0$, $TRANS\_X\_STD = 0.5$, where Px, Py are the coordinates of the center of current particle position, Px_0, Py_0 are the coordinates of the center of initial particle position, Pxp, Pyp are the coordinates of the center of previous particle position, $gsl\_ran\_gaussian()$ is gaussian distribution function to generate random numbers.

It can generates sampling points after above forecasting. Therefore, two histograms' color similarity of the predicting location and the initial position can be calculated by Bhattacharyya distance formula, which is as shown in formula (2) and (3):

$$\rho(\mathbf{p}, \mathbf{q}) = \sum_{i=1}^{N} \sqrt{p(i)q(i)} \quad (2)$$

$$d = \sqrt{1 - \rho(\mathbf{p}, \mathbf{q})} \quad (3)$$

In the above equations, the correlation coefficients are explained in Table 1;

Table 1. The correlation coefficients

q	The eigenvector of particle regions	$p(i)$, $q(i)$	The ith eigenvalue of eigenvectors **q**, **p**
p	The eigenvector of the target template	N	The number of features
d	Bhattacharyya distance	$\rho(\mathbf{p}, \mathbf{q})$	Similarity coefficient

(a)

(b)

(b)

(d)

(e)

(f)

Fig. 5. The effects of single-camera scene in the target tracking; (a) 50th frame; (b) 100th frame; (c) 150th frame; (d) 200th frame; (e) 250th frame; (f) 300th frame

This Bhattacharyya distance is as weight. It can automatically adjust particle weight and modify the original boundary location according to the weight, which can falls on the target, i.e. target tracking is finished. Until the target disappears in a single camera scene, the whole tracking effects is as followed in Fig. 5.

4.2   The Search Method About Neighborhood Areas

All videos data need be mapped the corresponding nodes of monitoring IoT. In an interested geographical scope which is selected manually, each node where the target passes by should be found by using the nodes search algorithm. The flow chart of the algorithm is shown in Fig. 6. Firstly, a start node should be found after the man-machine interaction, then the video in the node can be detected whether there is a video segment with having the target. Secondly, this node is regard as a core node, the neighbor nodes round this core one will search the object in next one. If one of the nodes finds the target, the node continues to track the moving target until the target leaves this monitoring scene, meanwhile the rest nodes terminate searching. And this node will be regard a new core node for going on subsequent searching. The above operation is repeated, until the target leaves the monitoring region, meanwhile, the moment means the target detecting and the target tracking work over.

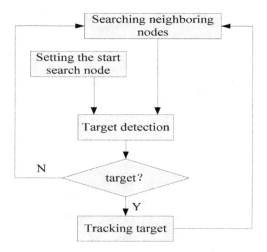

Fig. 6. The Search algorithm about neighborhood areas

The neighbor nodes round the core one are searched by the multi-threaded pro-cessing program inherited from the Qt with the base class QThread. Once one of threads finds the target, the others threads will be aborted.

The following code is a definition of this class:

```
class Tracer : public QThread
{
public:
    explicit Tracer(QObject *parent = 0);
    Tracer(QString filename, const CvScalar &color, int md = NORMAL, int bTime =
0);
    ~Tracer();
    void run();
    IplImage* getResultFrame() const;
    void stop();
    int getBeginTime() const;
    int getEndTime() const;
    int getCurrentTime() const;
    int getEndFoundTime() const;
    int getBeginFoundTime() const;
    float getSpeed() const;
    bool isFound() const;
    bool isInArea() const;
    QString getVedioName() const;
    QString getEvent();
•••//Since the content is omitted;
};
```

Qt performs thread operation in the thread class by rewriting the run () function. Here, the run () function implements a tracking algorithm, which has been described above in detail.

4.3   Results of Human-Computer Interaction Operation

Based on the above analyses;

(1) Achieving a movement target information record about a series of target's state characteristics in the monitoring video, including its current location, current speed, current time and event's attribute (to determine whether it's abnormal), as shown in Fig. 7;

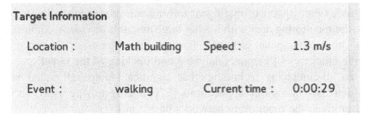

Fig. 7. Information record

(2) Forming a target information summary table after finishing the searching process of the target in the interesting monitoring network area, which includes the node's position name, the time of target's appearance, the time of target's disappearance and time span, as shown in Fig. 8, monitoring staff can preview and download these videos.

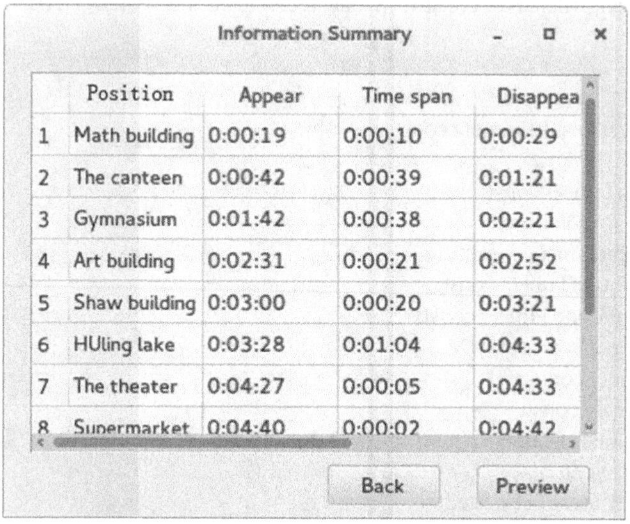

	Position	Appear	Time span	Disappea
1	Math building	0:00:19	0:00:10	0:00:29
2	The canteen	0:00:42	0:00:39	0:01:21
3	Gymnasium	0:01:42	0:00:38	0:02:21
4	Art building	0:02:31	0:00:21	0:02:52
5	Shaw building	0:03:00	0:00:20	0:03:21
6	HUling lake	0:03:28	0:01:04	0:04:33
7	The theater	0:04:27	0:00:05	0:04:33
8	Supermarket	0:04:40	0:00:02	0:04:42

Information Summary

Back   Preview

Fig. 8. Information summary

5 Summary

This design combines the video data on the camera nodes of monitoring IoT and WebGIS. In the specified geographical areas, it can search an interesting target. The system can extract of the corresponding nodes where the target passed by and show its moving path. By manually giving the target area, the system can intelligently detect and track the target, and summary the state information about the target, and provide the functions about preview and download target's video clips according to information summary table for police works.

This video surveillance system runs on the application layer of monitoring IoT. It combines the knowledge of specific industry and the scientific achievements. The application needs the support of intelligent information processing technology, which can analyze the monitoring area with having large amounts of videos. Simultaneously, it provides human-computer services through an interactive interface, greatly improving the efficiency of manual analyzing and tracking of the target.

IoT as an all-embracing technology has significant potential, social value and application demands in various applications [17]. Intelligentizing video surveillance system will promote the monitoring networks based on IoT.

Acknowledgments. This work was supported by the grant of the Academic Natural Science Research Project of AnHui, No. KJ2017A069 & KJ2016A085.

References

1. Giusto, D., Iera, A., Morabito, G., Atzori, L.: The Internet of Things. Springer, New York (2010). ISBN 978-1-4419-1673-0
2. Mazhelis, O., Tyrvainen, P.: A framework for evaluating Internet-of-Things platforms: application provider viewpoint. In: IEEE World Forum Internet of Things (WF-IoT), pp. 147–152 (2014)
3. Ray, P.P.: A survey on Internet of Things architectures. J. King Saud Univ. Comput. Inf. Sci. **3**(6), 290–302 (2016)
4. Atzori, L., Iera, A., Morabito, G.: The Internet of Things: a survey. Comput. Networks **10** (28), 2787–2805 (2010)
5. Miorandi, D., Sicari, S., De Pellegrinia, F., Chlamtac, I.: Internet of things: vision, applications and research challenges. Ad Hoc Netw. **10**(7), 1497–1516 (2012)
6. Wang, X.: Intelligent multi-camera video surveillance: a review. Pattern Recogn. Letters **34** (1), 3–19 (2012)
7. Sun, T., Xia, Y., Gan, Y.: Discussion on integration of urban video surveillance system. Procedia Eng. **15**, 3255–3259 (2011)
8. Li, X., Hua, Y.: The integration and application of GIS and DVS. Sci. Surv. Mapping **33**(2), 200–203 (2008)
9. Zhang, L., Yuan, H.: The design and development of electric map in video surveillance system. Comput. Eng. Appl. **19**, 107–111 (2004)
10. Denman, S., Kleinschmidt, T., Ryan, D., Barnes, P., Sridharan, S., Fookes, C.: Automatic surveillance in transportation hubs: no longer just about catching the bad guy. Expert Syst. Appl. **42**, 9449–9467 (2015)
11. Bouwmans, T., Vachon, B.: Background modeling using mixture of gaussians for foreground detection: a survey. Recent Patents Comput. Sci. **1**(3), 219–237 (2008)
12. Yilmaz, A., Javed, O., Shah, M.: Object tracking: a survey. ACM Comput. Surv. **38**(4), 1–29 (2006)
13. Xingyun, M.: OpenCV3 Programming Entry. Publishing House of Electronics Industry, Beijing (2015)
14. Hojjatoleslami, S.A., Kittler, J.: Region growing: a new approach. IEEE Trans. Image Process. **7**(7), 1079–1083 (1998)
15. Li, Y., Lu, Z., Gao, Q.: Particle filter and mean shift tracking method based on multi-feature fusion. J. Electron. Inf. Technol. **32**(2), 411–415 (2010)
16. Zhiyu, Z.: Popular Particle Filtering Algorithm and its Application in Video Target Tracking, p. 1. National defense Industry Press, Beijing (2015)
17. Zhao, C., Chen, F., Wang, R., Zhao, C., Luo, Y.: Multi-objective channel assignment and gateway deployment optimizer for wireless mesh network. J. Comput. Res. Dev. **52**(8), 1831–1841 (2015)

Mobile Attitude Transmission and Aircraft Control Strategies Based on WIFI

Chenlong Li, Tao Liu[✉], Yi-wen Dou, and Jun Qiang

School of Computer and Information,
Anhui Ploytechnic University, Wuhu, Anhui, China
{Lclcug, liutao, yiwend, chiang_j}@ahpu.edu.cn

Abstract. Four rotor aircraft controlled by remote controller has obvious disadvantages which including high cumulative error, and poor portability and low dynamic response and those decrease the user's sense of substitution and result in poor touch experiences. This paper proposes a set of control strategies and applies them in flight control and mobile phone terminal. Firstly, STM32 is used to solute the attitude of aircraft by DMP based on MPU6050 and communicates with the Smartphone by wireless WIFI communication module based on ESP8266. Secondly, the attitude solution of Smartphone is calculated by JAVA development kit and the adjusted Euler angle will be sent to flight control terminal so as to follow the phone attitude. Simulation and the actual test results show that our proposed strategies have good stability and portability.

Keywords: STM32 · ESP8266 · MPU6050 · Quaternion · Attitude algorithm

1 Introduction

It is not portable to use remote control of carrier attitude in the conventional method. The smartphone device is used as a remote control device, which has good touching experience, high portability and practicability, and supports magnetic, gravity and gyroscope sensors. It can control the micro-four-wing aircraft through mobile phone attitude. In order to achieve attitude transmission, flight control board need to configure the WIFI module.

Attitude calculation is one of the most important technologies in the field of flight control, which is widely used in aeronautics and astronautics, industrial robots and other popular fields. It is the key technology of inertial navigation system [1]. In order to accurately calculate the attitude information of the carrier, it is necessary to fuse the data of various sensors to achieve the purpose of complementary advantage. In this paper, the board of flight control integrates the MPU6050 to solve the carrier attitude. Using smart phones integrated magnetic sensor, gravity sensor, the remote control solves the carrier attitude through the Android API, and transfer Euler angles to the flight control side through the WIFI, In order to achieve the purpose of mobile phone control carrier attitude.

© ICST Institute for Computer Sciences, Social Informatics and Telecommunications Engineering 2017
F. Chen and Y. Luo (Eds.): Industrial IoT 2017, LNICST 202, pp. 34–42, 2017.
DOI: 10.1007/978-3-319-60753-5_4

2   System Framework and Hardware Design

2.1   System Framework

The hardware of the system includes mobile phone as remote control and flight control board. STM32 microcontroller connects the gyroscope(MPU6050) through the IIC interface to complete the attitude sensor data collection. The original data is processed by the main control processor to generate quaternions, which is converted into Euler angle [2, 3]. The STM32 is connected to the ESP8266 via the LVTTL serial interface. Set it to COM-AP mode to accept smart phone attitude data. The raw data (acceleration, gyro) as well as the attitude sensor data can be sent through the UART serial communication to the host computer for analysis (Fig. 1).

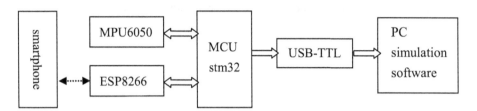

Fig. 1.   System architecture

2.2   Hardware Design of Flight Control Board

The STM32F407 communicates with the attitude sensor MPU-6050 by GPIOB interface of the PB8/PB9. Communication using iic protocol. PC0 of STM32F407 connects MPU6050 interrupt request, AD0 connects low level. Thus, the access address of the MPU 6050 is 0x68. The pins TXD, RXD, and RST of the ESP8266 module are connected to PB11, PB10, and PF6 of the MPU. The hardware connection is shown in Fig. 2.

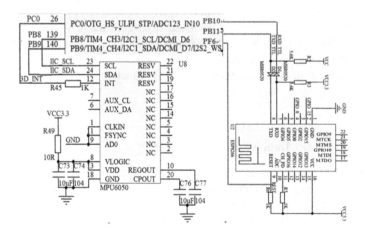

Fig. 2.   The hardware connection diagram of flight control board

3 System Software Design

3.1 Smartphone Attitude Estimation

When using orientation and movement sensors in Android, two coordinate systems are defined: the global coordinate system, and a device coordinate system. Both coordinate systems are illustrated in Fig. 3. Euler angle(azimuth/yaw, pitch, roll angle) is formed between the device coordinate system and the global coordinate system, when the Smartphone attitude change [4]. The Android platform provides two sensors that let you determine the position of a device: the geomagnetic field sensor and the orientation sensor. the orientation sensor is a synthetic sensor that calculates rotation angle of the global coordinate system with respect to the device coordinate system using the accelerometer, the magnetometer, and possibly the gyroscope if available. [5] We can use these sensors to calculate the Euler angle, the specific steps are as follows:

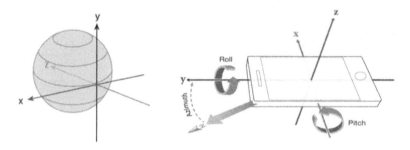

Fig. 3. Coordinate system

Step 1: Create a sensor manager and a sensor listener and instantiate it.
Step 2: Regester and monitor the geomagnetic sensor and the gravity sensor. When the sensor data change, callback the SensorEventListener, and obtain the real-time change data through the SensorEvent.
Step 3: A rotation matrix can be obtained from getRotationMatrix() or getRotationMatrixFromVector(), using the geomagnetism sensor and gravity sensor to generate the attitude rotation matrix. ns). [5]
Step 4: The rotation matrix can then be passed to function getOrientation() to get the orientation (azimuth, pitch, and Roll).

3.2 Design of WIFI Data Transmission Strategy

Establishing TCP communication in wireless local area network. The flight control terminal server is established in a wait state, waiting for the mobile phone client connection. When a client request is received, the server generates a message to the client. In the client, smart phone use the constructor to create the connection to server through the IP address and port.

Wireless WIFI module ESP8266, used to receive smart phone gesture and control data. In order to ensure the reliability of data transmission, you need to customize a set of transmission protocols to prevent interference by other signals. As shown in Table 1:

Table 1. Transfer protocol

Function	Header	Type code	data		End of message
Flight control signal	MH	00-10	XXXXXX		ME
phone attitude	MH	11	XXXX XXXX XXXX		ME

The "MH" in the transport protocol represents the protocol header. "ME" represents the protocol tail, and is used to determine the start and end of a data transmission. There are two types of code: "00" that remote control command data, "01" that control the attitude data. The valid data of the attitude data are 12 bits, which are 4 Roll angle data, 4 Pitch angle data and 5 Yaw angle data.

3.3   The Software Design of STM32 Flight Control Board

STM32 as the control part of the whole system, the algorithm through Keil MDK5 Integrated development tools to achieve. The main idea of the flight control program is to initialize the MCU (serial port, interrupt, timer, IIC, etc.), wireless module, MPU6050 initialization after power on. Flight control system interrupted every 0.5 ms,

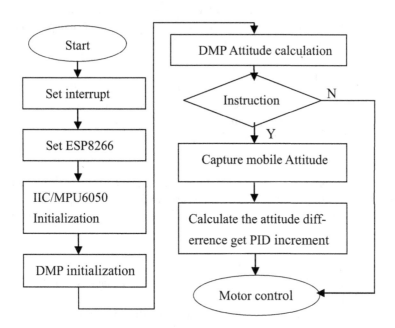

Fig. 4. Control flow chart

each interrupt will check once the wireless module data reception, to ensure that the flight control information is real-time. The raw data of the system acceleration, angular velocity of the IMU is read once every two milliseconds to complete the quaternion attitude calculation. In order to simulate the flight controller and mobile terminal, STM32 relies on timer interrupt to perform sampling, and send the data to PC via RS232 serial port. Real-time display MPU6050 and the phone's sensor status curve, and display 3D pose. Figure 4 shows the overall control flow.

(1) *Attitude solving algorithm based on DMP*

MPU6050 is used to realize the attitude calculation of the carrier, which not only simplifies the code design, but also reduces the burden of the MCU. The MCU does not need the attitude solving process, so it has more time to process other events and improve the system real-time. The main processes include MPU6050 initialization and DMP attitude calculation.

MPU6050 comes with a digital motion processor (DMP), and InvenSense provides a MPU6050 embedded motion-driven library. We can convert our raw data directly into quaternion, and Finally, Euler angles are calculated, yaw, roll and pitch are obtained. After DMP processing, MCU can directly read out the number of quaternion and the corrected gyro data, acceleration data from the FIFO cache of MPU6050. It is very important to convert quaternion to the Euler angle in the process of Attitude calculation. In 3D graphics, the commonly used method to solve the problem of coordinate system rotation direction cosine method and Quaternion method [6]: method of direction cosine calculation to obtain three angle data of attitude. Assume that the rotation angles around the x, y, and z axes are θ, ϕ, ψ, the rotation matrix such as formula (1), therefore, Transformation of reference coordinate system to the carrier coordinate system can be achieved by the product of these three independent transformations, $R_Z\psi R_Y\theta R_X\phi = A$ [7], as shown in the formula (2)

$$R_X\phi = \begin{bmatrix} 1 & 0 & 0 \\ 0 & \cos\phi & \sin\phi \\ 0 & -\sin\phi & \cos\phi \end{bmatrix} \quad R_Y\theta = \begin{bmatrix} \cos\theta & 0 & -\sin\theta \\ 0 & 1 & 0 \\ \sin\theta & 0 & \cos\theta \end{bmatrix}$$

$$R_Z\psi = \begin{bmatrix} \cos\psi & \sin\psi & 0 \\ -\sin\psi & \cos\psi & 0 \\ 0 & 0 & 1 \end{bmatrix} \tag{1}$$

$$A = \begin{bmatrix} \cos\psi\cos\theta & \sin\psi\cos\theta & -\sin\theta \\ \cos\psi\sin\theta\sin\phi - \sin\psi\cos\phi & \sin\psi\sin\theta\sin\phi + \cos\psi\cos\phi & \cos\theta\sin\phi \\ \cos\psi\sin\theta\cos\phi + \sin\psi\sin\phi & \sin\psi\sin\theta\cos\gamma - \cos\psi\sin\phi & \cos\theta\cos\phi \end{bmatrix} \tag{2}$$

The calculation of attitude matrix with direction cosine method, no Equation degradation problem, but needs to solve 9 differential equations, so the real-time performance is bad and the calculation is large. Quaternion method needs to obtain rotation axis and rotation angle. Compared with the direction cosine attitude matrix differential equation, the computational cost is obviously reduced [8].

The representation of the quaternion is given in Eq. (3). The reference coordinate system rotates a corner θ. The direction of the rotation axis is determined by the imaginary part of the number of four elements. The value (cos α, cos β, cos γ) indicates the direction cosine value between the axis of rotation axis N and the reference coordinate system.

$$q = \lambda + p_1 i + p_2 j + p_3 \tag{3}$$

$\lambda = \cos\frac{\theta}{2}$, $p_1 = \sin\frac{\theta}{2}\cos\alpha$, $p_2 = \sin\frac{\theta}{2}\cos\beta$, $p_3 = \sin\frac{\theta}{2}\cos\gamma$. The quaternion can be transformed into attitude matrix A by using the trigonometric formula

$$A = \begin{bmatrix} p_0^2 + p_1^2 - p_2^2 - p_3^2 & 2(p_1 p_2 + p_0 p_3) & 2(p_1 p_3 - p_0 p_2) \\ 2(p_1 p_2 - p_0 p_3) & P_0^2 + p_2^2 - p_1^2 - p_3^2 & 2(p_2 p_3 + p_0 p_1) \\ 2(p_1 p_3 + P_0 p_2) & 2(p_2 p_3 - P_0 p_1) & p_0^2 + p_3^2 - p_1^2 - p_2^2 \end{bmatrix} \tag{4}$$

$$\phi = \arctan\left(\frac{A(2,3)}{A(3,3)}\right); \psi = \arctan\left(\frac{A(1,2)}{A(1,1)}\right); \theta = \arcsin(A(1,3)) \tag{5}$$

According to the formula (2), the formula (4) gets the Euler angle formula of the quaternion formula is as follows: [9]:

$$\phi = \arctan((2 \times p2 \times p3 + 2 \times p0 \times p1)/(p_0^2 - p_1^2 - p_2^2 + p_3^2)) \tag{6}$$

$$\psi = \text{atan2}(2 \times (p1 \times p2 + p0 \times p3)/(p_0^2 + p_1^2 - p_2^2 - p_3^2)) \tag{7}$$

$$\theta = \text{asin}(-2 \times p1 \times p3 + 2 \times p0 \times p2) \tag{8}$$

Thus, a calculation formula for roll ϕ, yaw ψ, and pitch θ is obtained. Pitch accuracy: 0.° range: −90.0 DEG +90.0 DEG <—>; roll angle and heading angle accuracy: 0.1° range: −180.0 DEG +180.0 DEG <—>, through Dmp_get_data (float *pitch, float *roll, float *yaw) attitude.

(1) *ESP8266 settings and software design*

ESP8266 module connects the WIFI device phone as a wireless WIFI hotspot. We need to configure the ESP8266 for the COM-AP mode. According to the different application scenarios the mode includes 3 sub models: TCP server, TCP client, UDP. Work mode can be configured with AT instructions. [10, 12] Serial Wireless AP WIFI mode, TCP server configuration, as shown in Table 1.

The bottom driver of STM32 mainly includes the sending and receiving of AT instruction, the module state detection, the acquisition of IP/MAC and the establishment of TCP connection, as well as the data transmission and reception of the mobile phone and module (Table 2).

Table 2. Esp8266 work mode configuration

Send instructions	Effect
AT + CWMODE = 2	Set the module WIFI mode to AP mode
AT + CWSAP = "ESP8266", "12345678", 1, 4	Set the AP parameters of the module: SSID is ESP8266, password is 12345678, channel number is 1, and the encryption mode is WPA_WPA2_PSK
AT + CIPMUX = 1	Turn on multiple connections
AT + CIPSERVER = 1,8086	Turn on SERVER mode, set the port to 8086
AT + CIPSEND = 0,25	Sending 25 byte packets to ID0

4   Related Testing

4.1   WIFI Related Testing

WIFI communication test mainly include the communication between the PC and the aircraft and the communication between the mobile phone APP and the aircraft. Test method: In the test, first connect the aircraft as WIFI hotspots, and then enter a set account password. Connection is successful, after successful connection, PC or APP is required to open the TCP client, connected to the aircraft's TCP server. The server IP address is 192.168.4.1, port 8086. We can send remote frame data to aircraft after the connection is established. The mobile phone attitude data use the serial debugging assistant to simulate, mobile phone use the existing network assistant APP. Simulation of the Euler angle of smart phone is as shown in Fig. 7. The red curve represents roll; yaw is the gray curve; the blue curve is pitch.

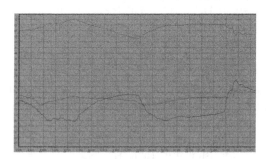

Fig. 7. Simulation of the Euler angle of smart phone (Color figure online)

4.2   Flight Attitude Testing

In order to observe the changes of MPU6050 data in real time and evaluate the performance of the algorithm, this paper uses the serial communication to send the sensor data and the Euler angle data generated by the algorithm to the host computer. The usart1_niming_report function is used to package data, calculate the checksum, and then reported to the PC software; mpu6050_send_data function for the original data to the accelerometer and gyroscope, waveform display for sensor data. The usart1_report_imu function is used to display the frame, flight control, real-time 3D display MPU6050 attitude sensor data, etc.

Figure 8 shows the original data of MPU6050 (three axis acceleration, three axis gyroscope). The waveforms show that the data are unstable and there is noise. Figure 9 shows the filtered Euler angle (pitch, roll, yaw) after a continuous sampling of the data waveform. Test results show that the DMP attitude solution can effectively suppress the noise and obtain the stable and smooth data.

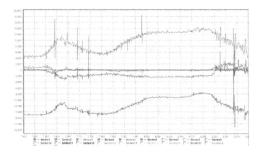

Fig. 8. waveform of the original data of gyroscope

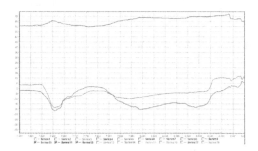

Fig. 9. attitude waveform of gyroscope

5 Conclusions

In this paper, the attitude solution of mobile phone based on the JAVA development kit is realized, and the smartphone's Euler angle is transmitted to the flight control side. Flight control board uses DMP of MPU-6050 gyroscope to achieve the carrier attitude calculation. Experimental results show that the proposed approach not only has low noise but also has high dynamic response. The system can meet the requirements of the aircraft attitude control system. However, the MPU-6050 itself does not have a fusion magnetometer, so the carrier in the yaw angle has accumulated error, the system can further expand the three-axis magnetometer to compensate for the shortcomings.

Acknowledgements. This work was supported by the National Natural Science Foundation of China (No. 61300170), the University Provincial Natural Science Foundation of Anhui Province (No. KJ2016A057), the Natural Science Foundation of Anhui Province (16080MF147), the Major Projects of Nature Science Research in Universities of Anhui (No. KJ2015ZD06).

References

1. Zhang, R.H., Jia, H.G., Chen, T., et al.: Analysis of Attitude of Strapdown Inertial Navigation System Based on Quaternion Method. Editorial Office Optics Precis. Eng. **16**(10), 1963–1970 (2008)
2. Zhang, Y.: Proficient in the STM32F4 (library function version), pp. 13–14. Beihang University press (2015)
3. Huang, W.K., Wu, F.J.: The development of actual combat guide robot volume, pp. 95–97. Machinery Industry Press (2014)
4. Wang, Z.P., Tang, X.H., Wang, Y.F.: Research on attitude recognition technology of aircraft based on MEMS accelerometer. Piezoelectric Acoust. Opt. **29**(2), 224 (2007)
5. Milette, G., Stroud, A.: Professional Android Sensor Programming, pp. 87–97. Tsinghua University Press (2013)
6. Guo, L.L., Zhao, H.: The spatial coordinate conversion algorithm of the accelerometer data of the mobile phone in the mobile phone is applied. Comp. Appl. **36**(02), 301–306 (2016)
7. Wang, X.P., Zhang, T.G.: Strapdown inertial navigation technology, 2nd edn. National Defence Industry Press (2007)
8. Sun, D., Tian, Z., Han, L.: Simulation on quaternion calculate attitude angle of the strapdown inertial navigation system. J. Projectiles Rockets Missiles Guidance **29**(1), 51–54 (2009)
9. Zhao, J.J., Chen, B., Yang, L.B.: Geodetic coordinate transformation algorithm based on four element number and its implementation. Comput. Eng. Appl. **49**(4), 202–205 (2013)
10. Molloy D.: Wireless Communication and Control. Exploring Raspberry Pi, pp. 535–575 (2016)
11. Liu, X.H., Li, J.B.: Four rotor attitude control system based on STM32. Comput. Meas. Control **22**(3), 762 (2014)
12. Rudinskiy, M.: ECE 4999 Independent Project: Wi-Fi Communication Using ESP8266 & PIC32 Mikhail Rudinskiy Completed for Dr. Bruce Land

Optimization Bottleneck Analysis in GPU-Based Aiming at SAR Imaging

Wang Shi-Yu[✉], Zhang Sheng-Bing, An Jian-Feng,
Huang Xiao-Ping, and Wang Dang-Hui

School of Computer Science,
Northwestern Polytechnical University, Xi'an 710129, China
onion0709@mail.nwpu.edu.cn

Abstract. Application Defect induced by GPU Aiming at SAR Imaging are studied. It is the first time the issue of application defect induced by GPU is addressed in SAR field. In GPU-based SAR imaging system, application defect induced by resources competition can significantly decrease the granularity of parallelism. To solve this problem, the GPU-based SAR imaging system with CUDA is firstly modeled. Secondly, conditions of parallel granularity loss rate by using CUDA are obtained based on time output feedback scheme. Thirdly, more importantly, find the difficulties and bottlenecks in the optimization of SAR imaging operation is proposed according to the measured conditions of parallel granularity loss rate. Finally, optimization bottleneck analysis through FFT function and linear matrix interpolation scheme, and numerical simulations are made to demonstrate the effectiveness of the proposed scheme.

Keywords: GPU · SAR imaging · Parallel computing · Optimization bottleneck analysis

1 Introduction

SAR (Synthetic Aperture Radar) remote sensing data, with its unique advantages is gradually used in the field of earth observation. The amount of data contained in a SAR image is usually very large. Considering that the traditional serial processing method has a certain lag, in practical application, operation rate is one of the key factors of SAR image processing.

The current SAR imaging processing algorithms mainly include RDA algorithm, CS (Scaling Chirp) algorithm, and the ωKA algorithm. The three algorithm flowcharts are shown in Fig. 1.

At present, most of the SAR imaging systems based on the CPU of the personal computer, workstation or large computing server, are carried out on such hardware in the system. Besides, in order to make the CPU-based imaging system be fully applied and further accelerate the speed of SAR echo data processing, the design of the software architecture also needs a lot of human input.

CUDA (Compute Unified Device Architecture) providing a parallel programming model and software environment will fully mobilize the powerful parallel computing

© ICST Institute for Computer Sciences, Social Informatics and Telecommunications Engineering 2017
F. Chen and Y. Luo (Eds.): Industrial IoT 2017, LNICST 202, pp. 43–52, 2017.
DOI: 10.1007/978-3-319-60753-5_5

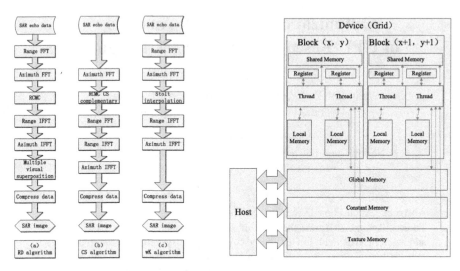

Fig. 1. Three kinds of SAR algorithm flow   **Fig. 2.** CUDA storage model

power of GPU, so that GPU can play its inherent advantages in solving complex computational problems. Hierarchical management is shown in Fig. 2.

With its rapid development, GPU is widely used to solve the problem of the calculation of massive remote sensing data processing [3]. However, using GPUs for scientific computing has been mostly dominated by those with needs for a large number of tightly-coupled floating-point operations such as the n-body problem [4].

At present, the research on the acceleration of SAR imaging is mainly reflected in the improvement of the SAR algorithm [6] and the efficient application of the CUDA architecture [7–9]. In this paper, the CUDA architecture is used to accelerate the SAR imaging, identify the bottlenecks in the process of acceleration, and point out the focus of the work for future SAR imaging.

The paper is structured as follows: The second part analyzes the specific algorithm of SAR imaging and the details of the formula. And the parallelism of the SAR imaging arithmetic unit is analyzed and designed in the third part, while the fourth part presents the experimental data and the parallel bottleneck analysis. The conclusion is given in the fifth part.

2   The Analysis of SAR Imaging Arithmetic Operator

From the previous description, SAR imaging steps can be summed up, although the imaging algorithms have different characteristics and advantages, but each SAR imaging algorithm basically contains FFT (IFFT), phase multiplication and interpolation of these three kinds of computing components. Most of the computing cost also comes from the three arithmetic units (Calculation Sample: 1024×1024 SAR image data matrix).

2.1 FFT (IFFT) Arithmetic Operator

N finite length sequence of X (n) DFT and IDFT operation process is as follows (Table 1):

$$X(k) = DFT[x(n)] = \frac{1}{N}\sum_{n=0}^{N-1} x(n)W_N^{nk} \quad k = 0,\ldots,N-1 \tag{1}$$

$$x(n) = IDFT[X(k)] = \frac{1}{N}\sum_{n=0}^{N-1} X(k)W_N^{-nk} \quad n = 0,\ldots,N-1 \tag{2}$$

$$W_N^{nk} = \exp(-2nk\pi i/N) \tag{3}$$

Table 1. DFT calculating amount

Amount of computation	N-point DFT	Complex multiplication	Complex addition
DFT[x(n)]	N-point X (k)	N^2	N (N – 1)

2.2 The Interpolation of Arithmetic Operator

SAR image processing achieves the sample position mainly by the interpolation. In accuracy and computation requirements, 8 point sinc interpolation is generally used. What's more, Sinc interpolation method concerns the use of the original function y in the value of the other points, weights sinc function, and gets the value of Y (x) at X. The interpolation operation procedure is as follows:

$$y(x) = \sum_{i=-\infty}^{\infty} y(i)\sin c(x-i) \tag{4}$$

$$\sin c(x) = \frac{\sin(\pi x)}{\pi x} \tag{5}$$

Therefore, it is necessary for sinc interpolation truncation, the P sinc interpolation, and interpolation formula for range curvature correction (Table 2):

$$s'(m,n) = s(m,n+\Delta n) = \sum_{i=-p/2}^{p/2-1} s(m,n+n'+i)\sin c(franc-i). \tag{6}$$

Table 2. Interpolation calculating amount

Amount of computation	N-point Y (X)	Sine calculation	Complex multiplication
Y (x)	8-pointX (k)	8 N	8 N

2.3   Phase Multiplication Arithmetic Operator

In the process of the CS imaging algorithm, the three phase multiplication algorithm is included. The signal in the form of Doppler domain is as follows:

$$S_1 = (f_t, \tau, r)$$

$$= CG(-\frac{r\lambda f_1}{2v^2})m(-\frac{2R_f(f_t, r)}{c})\exp\{-j\pi K_m(f_t, r) \cdot$$

$$[\tau - \frac{2R_f(f_t, r)}{c}]^2\} \cdot \exp\{-j\frac{4\pi r}{\lambda}\gamma(f_t)\}$$

(7)

The first phase is multiplied in the azimuth FFT, the completion of the CS is realized by the RCMC operation:

$$S_2(f_\tau, \tau, r) = S_1(f_\tau, \tau, r) \cdot H_1(f_\tau, \tau, r).$$

(8)

In Formula (8):

$$H_1(f_t, \tau, r) = \exp\{-j\pi K_m(f_t, r_{ref}) \cdot C_s(\tau - \tau_{ref})^2\}.$$

(9)

$$\tau_{ref} = \frac{2}{c}r_{ref}[1 + C_s(f_t)]$$

(10)

τ_{ref} is generally used as the center of the imaging and mapping band as well as a fixed reference distance.

The second phase is multiplied by the distance to FFT, as well as the completion of RCMC, SRC and distance compression:

$$S_3(f_t, f_\tau) = S_2(f_t, f_\tau) \cdot H_2(f_t, f_\tau).$$

(11)

In Formula (11):.

$$H_2(f_t, f_\tau) = \exp\{-j\pi\frac{f_\tau^2}{K_m(f_t, r_{ref})[1 + C_s(f_t)]}\}\exp\{j\frac{4\pi}{c}r_{ref}C_s(f_t)f_\tau\}.$$

(12)

Third phase multiplication in the distance to IFFT after the completion of the azimuth compression and phase correction:

$$S_4(f_t, \tau) = S_3(f_t, \tau) \cdot H_3(f_t, \tau).$$

(13)

In Formula (13) (Table 3):

$$H_3(f_t, \tau) = \exp\{j\frac{2\pi}{\lambda}c\tau \cdot \gamma(f_t) + j\Delta\}.$$

(14)

Table 3. Phase multiplication calculating amount

Amount of computation	N-point Y (X)	Complex multiplication
Y (x)	N-point X (k)	N

$$\Delta = \pi K_m \frac{C_s(\tau - \tau_{ref})^2}{1 + C_s} \tag{15}$$

3 Parallel Architecture for Computing Components

Multiple FFT parallel computing, data exist before and after dependence [12, 13]. Therefore, in the calculation process, FFT calculation process in each block there is a pipeline to wait for the calculation process [14]. As shown in Fig. 3.

Interpolation and phase multiplication calculation no data dependencies. Therefore, Parallel computation of multi channel block, multiple threads can be calculated in parallel. As shown in Fig. 4.

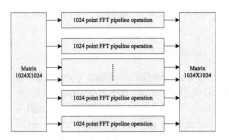
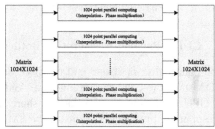

Fig. 3. FFT multi path parallel computing architecture

Fig. 4. Interpolation, Phase multiplication parallel computing architecture

4 Experimental Results and Analysis

4.1 Experimental Computing Platform

(1) Hardware Platform:

>   CPU Model: Intel(R) Core(TM) i5-3230M;
>   CPU Dominant Frequency: 2.6 GHz;
>   System Memory: 8.00 GB;
>   GPU Model: NVIDIA GeForce 840M;
>   GPU Dominant Frequency: 1.12 GHz;
>   The Number of SM: 3;
>   The Number of SP: 3128;
>   Memory Interface: 64-bit;

Memory Bandwidth: 14.4 GB/s;
Memory Dominant Frequency: 900 MHz;

(2) Software Platform

Operating System: Microsoft Windows 8.1;
Test Platform: Visual Studio 2013;
CUDA v7.5;
Calculation Sample: 1024 × 1024 SAR image data matrix

4.2 Computational Optimization Ratio

See (Table 4).

Table 4. GPU/CPU speedup ratio

Arithmetic unit	CUDA mode	Sine calculation	CPU mode
FFT	7.7 ms	2.665 s	346.1
Interpolation	7.9 ms	1.8 s	227.8
Phase multiplication	15 ms	0.055 s	3.67

4.3 CUDA Parallel Acceleration Bottleneck Analysis

If the data matrix is at one end of GPU, data first entered the memory global, when CUDA starts the CPU computing core. And then, the data is written to memory share, and GPU operations on the data in share memory. The data migration generated a corresponding time, but GPU inside the SM did not appear to wait for the phenomenon of hunger, and the full load of work is always kept. Therefore, the data migration in the chip fails to affect the calculation of the acceleration optimization. However, there are only three SMs in the GPU.

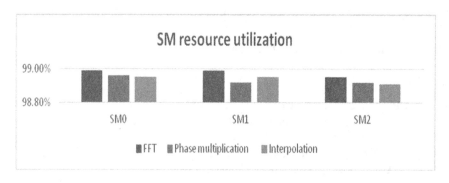

Fig. 5. SM resource utilization

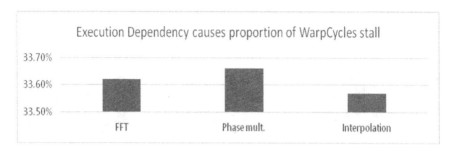

Fig. 6. Execution dependency causes proportion of WarpCycles stall

The internal SM of GPU is in full load working state, which is shown in Fig. 5. The utilization rate of SM has reached 100%, and there is no waiting for data. Therefore, the data migration in the chip does not affect the optimization efficiency of the operation (Fig. 6).

Throughout the clock cycle, more than 80% of the clock cycle is executed in kernel, so there is no reason for warps to block the next instruction, which is shown in Fig. 7.

Fig. 7. No eligible of warp issue efficiency

Both the SAR imaging algorithm and parallel computing have been developed towards a mature phase, and plenty of research results have been obtained in these fields [23, 24]. CUDA program contains three kinds of executive unit, namely thread, block and grid. In CUDA programming, a grid is divided into a number of blocks, and then, a block is divided into multiple threads. The division is based on the task characteristics and the hardware characteristics of GPU itself. The division of tasks will also affect the final implementation of the results (Figs. 8 and 9).

In GPU hardware resources, SP (streaming processor) is the most basic processing unit of GPU, and all the operations will be implemented on the SP. Besides, GPU in parallel computing will be ultimately reflected in a number of SP parallel computing. Any SP with some allocation of resources, including storage, memory and register, consists of a SM (streaming multiprocessor). The current GPU contains a limited

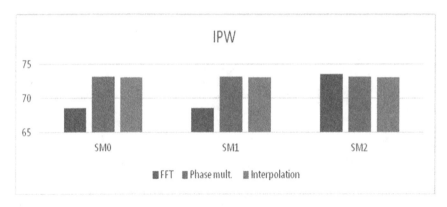

Fig. 8. Instructions per warp

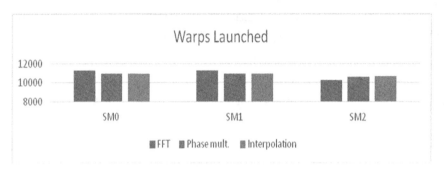

Fig. 9. Warps launched

number of SM and SP. When taking GPU as an example in this experiment, the GPU contains three SMs, each of which contains 128 SPs.

In the process of executing the CUDA program, a SM performs a block task, and at the same time, a SP performs a thread task. However, in the execution program of GPU, the warp is considered as the unit, and a warp is a thread group that contains 32 threads.

In the parallel processing SAR image data matrix and the operation process of three kinds of computing components, the task is divided into 1024 blocks, and the operation of each point is assigned to 1024 threads. When taking the FFT operation of the SAR image matrix as an example, each line of data is assigned to a block which consists of 1024 threads, and each thread performs the FFT operation of the corresponding point in the row data.

The compute-resource allocation process of the parallel algorithm in GPU is analyzed, and at the same time, there will be 1024 blocks, and among them, each block contains 1024 threads to be executed. As above, the parallel algorithm requires 1024 SM processing corresponding to the 1024 blocks, Each SM requires 1024 SPs corresponding to each of the 1024 threads in the block. Only to meet the needs of these hardware resources, the algorithm can be truly parallel computing. However, from the GPU resource list, SM and SP resources in GPU are relatively limited, and the experiment with the GPU contains 3 SMs, and each SM contains 128 SPs. Therefore, in the implementation of the CUDA program, only three blocks can be executed in parallel at one time. The CUDA program contains 1024 blocks, such as the 3 SMs to be seen as a computing unit, and besides, every 3 block is considered as a unit. If you need to complete 1024 blocks, the 3 SMs sequence needs to be conducted for 342 times. 1024 blocks are actually calculated in a serial manner 342 times. Each block contains 1024 threads, while each SM in the SP executes a thread, but each SM contains 128 SPs. Similarly, with the 128 SPs as a computing unit and 128 threads as a pending computing unit, the 1024 threads need to be calculated in a serial mode eight times. Therefore, due to the limitation of GPU's own hardware resources, the parallel optimization efficiency of the SAR image matrix processing program is of great limitation.

SFU, as a special function of SM can achieve six kinds of transcendental functions, including common sine, cosine, logarithm, exponential, reciprocal and square root. However, when each thread needs to use SFU, each of the four threads requires a serial use of SFU. it seriously affects the parallel optimization efficiency between threads. For example, in the process of interpolation, as shown in Table 5, the sine and the reciprocal operation are involved. In this case, each of the four interpolations of the thread must be done after the serial operation of the sine and the countdown to complete the entire interpolation algorithm. What's more, this process turns the parallel operation between threads into the serial operation between threads, and the advantage of CUDA parallel computing is lost.

Table 5. Interpolation operation time in different degree of parallelism

Degree of parallelism	1-thread	2-threads	4-threads	8-threads	1024-threads
Operation time	6.6 ms	6.7 ms	6.6 ms	6.6 ms	7.7 ms

5 Conclusion

In GPU-based SAR imaging system, application defect induced by resources competition can significantly decrease the whole system performance. To solve this problem, the SAR imaging system is firstly modeled on CPU and GPU in view of the idea that CPU rate can be replaced by GPU, and the speedup ratio of system with GPU-based is also given. Then, the principle of GPU-based that the parallel granularity loss rate is analyzed, and the deceleration ratio of SAR imaging with CUDA is also given. Finally, the bottleneck of GPU-based SAR imaging system is analyzed, and the bound on SAR imaging speedup ratio that GPU-based without increasing power consumption is proposed. The effectiveness of the proposed inference is demonstrated by numerical simulations. It is shown that GPU-based SAR imaging system with resource bottleneck operation rate can not be further improved.

Note that only three key operating cells in multiple SAR imaging algorithms in the paper, however, similar analysis can be made of other operating cell in SAR imaging algorithm. The scheme proposed in this paper achieve heuristic result has some values of guidance in acceleration research of SAR Imaging.

How to increase the calculating speed in real-time SAR imaging is an open problem. In addition, application on GPU-based has little room for improving performance more. For future work, we plan to deeper investigation of arithmetic unit oriented to application of SAR imaging.

References

1. Larsen, E.S., Mc Allister, D.: Fast matrix multiplies using graphics hardware. In: 2001 ACM/IEEE Conference on Supercomputing (CDROM). ACM Press (2001)
2. General-Purpose Computation Using Graphics Hardware. http://www.gpgpu.org/
3. YANG, C., Wu, Q., Hu, H., Shi, Z., Chen, J., Tang, T.: Fast weighting method for plasma PIC simulation on GPU-accelerated heterogeneous systems. J. Cent. South Univ. **20**, 1527–1535 (2013)
4. NVIDIA CUDA: Compute Unified Device Architecture http://developer.nvidia.com/object/cuda.html
5. Li, Z., Wang, J., Liu, Q.H.: Frequency-domain backprojection algorithm for synthetic aperture radar imaging. IEEE Geosci. Remote Sens. Lett. **12**(4), 905–909 (2015)
6. Sheng, H., Wang, K., Liu, X., Li, J.: A fast raw data simulator for the strip map SAR based on CUDA via GPU. In: IGARSS, pp. 915–918 (2013)
7. Dąbrowski, R., Chodarcewicz, Ł., Kulczyński, T., Niedźwiedź, P., Przedniczek, A., Śmietanka, W.: Accelerating USG image reconstruction with SAR implementation on CUDA. In: Kim, T., Cho, H., Gervasi, O., Yau, S.S. (eds.) FGIT 2012. CCIS, vol. 351, pp. 316–329. Springer, Heidelberg (2012). doi:10.1007/978-3-642-35600-1_47
8. Denham, M., Areta, J., Tinetti, F.G.: Synthetic aperture radar signal processing in parallel using GPGPU. J. Supercomput. **72**(2), 1–17 (2015)
9. Long, H.: Research and implementation of synthetic aperture radar parallel imaging algorithm. Master thesis, University of Electronic Science and Technology (2001)
10. Benson, T.M., Campbell, D.P., Cook, D.A.: Gigapixel spotlight synthetic aperture radar backprojection using clusters of GPUs and CUDA. In: 2012 IEEE Radar Conference (RADAR), pp. 0853–0858. IEEE (2012)
11. Kong, F., Zhao, J., Yue, B.: Research on parallel processing of SAR imaging algorithm. In: Proceedings of the 2nd Asian-Pacific Conference on Synthetic Aperture Radar, pp.784–787 (2009)
12. Swarztrauber, P.N.: FFT algorithms for vector computers. Parallel Comput. **1**, 45–63 (1984)
13. Cooley, J., Tukey, J.: An algorithm for the machine calculation of complex Fourier series. Math. Comput. **19**(90), 297–301 (1965)
14. Ogata, Y., Endo, T., Maruyama, N., Matsuoka, S.: An efficient, model-based CPU-GPU heterogeneous FFT library. In: Proceedings of the 17th International Heterogeneity in Computing Workshop (in conjunction with IPDPS 2008) (2008)
15. Solimene, R., Catapano, I., Gennarelli, G., Cuccaro, A.: SAR imaging algorithms and some unconventional applications: a unified mathematical overview. IEEE Signal Process. Mag. **31**(4), 90–98 (2014)
16. Capozzoli, A., Curcio, C., Liseno, A.: Fast GPU-based interpolation for SAR back projection. Progress Electromagn. Res. **133**, 259–283 (2013)

Research Based on Data Processing Technology of Industrial Internet of Things

Shu-Ting Deng[✉] and Cong Xie

College of Information Engineering, Guangxi University of Foreign Languages,
Nanning, 530222, China
385884384@qq.com

Abstract. With the increasingly wide application of Internet of Things technology in the industrial field, Industrial Internet of Things provides a viable and convenient service for the development of intelligent industry, meanwhile more and more countries pay attention to the development of Industrial Internet of Things. The data of Industrial Internet of Things have features such as massive polymorphism, dynamic heterogeneity, relevance, real-time etc.

These features become resistance in the process of data to create value. This paper explores the issues and challenges of data of Industrial Internet of Things, and studies data processing technology deeply. It provide some help to improve data management of Industrial Internet of Things.

Keywords: Industrial Internet of Things · Data · Data processing technology

1 Introduction

With the development of computer technology, industrial economy and communication technology, especially the development of Internet of Things technology which is widely used in the field of industry, these will change the modern industrial production process, management mode and management concept. Industrial Internet of Things will bring another information revolution to modern industry. In recent years, the rapid growth of new industry requires more and more intelligence of industry. Industrial Internet of Things provides a feasible and convenient service for the development of intelligent industry. At present, the massive data mining and massive using indicates that the era of big data has come. More and more countries pay attention to the development of Industrial Internet of Things. The data of industrial Internet of Things have features such as massive polymorphism, dynamic heterogeneity, relevance, real-time etc. These features become resistance in the process of data to create value. Big data will become the main way and key elements of industrial productivity and competitiveness, thus data processing technology is one of the key technologies of industrial Internet.

© ICST Institute for Computer Sciences, Social Informatics and Telecommunications Engineering 2017
F. Chen and Y. Luo (Eds.): Industrial IoT 2017, LNICST 202, pp. 53–60, 2017.
DOI: 10.1007/978-3-319-60753-5_6

2   Related Concepts: Industrial Internet of Things

Internet Of Things shorted as IOF is the object and object connected to the Internet. At present, industrial IOF has not yet clear and accepted definition. It mainly refers to the intelligent terminal, mobile computing model, ubiquitous mobile network communication applied to all aspects of industrial production. It coordinates data analysis and action, promotes industrial efficiency, and improves manufacturing efficiency so as to realize intelligent industry. It is an industrial system that connects the digital world with the physical world through sensors and actuators. Industrial IOF needs to meet the following three requirements: the first is time accurate synchronization requirements; second is the accuracy of communication; third is the high adaptability of industrial environment.

3   Characteristics of Data in Industrial Internet of Things System

The architecture of Industrial Internet of Things is divided into data acquisition layer, data transmission layer, data integration layer and data application service layer. It plays an important role in the intelligent industry in the whole work system. Data processing will be one of the most important technologies for Industrial Internet of Things, so understanding the characteristics of massive data for Internet of Things, is the key to deal with big data of industrial Internet of Things. The data of industrial Internet of Things have features such as massive polymorphism, dynamic heterogeneity, relevance, real-time etc.

3.1   Massive Polymorphism

The system of industrial Internet of Things, usually contains multiple wireless sensor networks which contains very many sensor nodes, and the amount of data collected by sensor nodes is massive. Sensor nodes in the sensor network can be judged by the pressure, vibration, sound, etc., so the data obtained are various. Different data have different formats, units, precision, etc., thus the data of industrial Internet of Things is dynamic.

3.2   Dynamic Heterogeneity

There are some differences in the physical material and system design in the sensor system of industrial Internet of Things, which causes the data that produced in the industrial production process to be different in quantity, progress and so on. Data measured by different sensors may also vary at different times. Dynamic heterogeneity is an important feature of industrial Internet of Things data. This feature leads to industrial Internet of Things in data storage mode is difficult to unify.

3.3   Relevance

The data of industrial Internet of Things is not independent, and it have a certain connection. The data acquired by industrial Internet of Things in the production process and data attributes belong to a whole not a single one can be omitted. There are many correlations between data in space, time and other dimensions, therefore, in industrial production, data transmission, storage, use, such as the process must pay attention to the integrity and accuracy of data attributes.

3.4   Real-Time

The data real-time requirement is prominent in the application process of industrial Internet of Things whose system requires high real-time information for the sensor nodes of the data acquisition. Data real-time performance ensure that important data get more transmission time in the transmission process, thus data enables information to be aggregated faster to nodes, faster integration, and faster analysis and conclusions, so the system can make all kinds of decisions faster according to these conclusions.

Wireless sensor needs to complete the task of sensing, transmission, coordination and other tasks in the industrial Internet of Things system. In the whole process, it will produce massive data, the more data collected, the more junk information will be. We study the data processing technology of industrial Internet of Things according to different industrial production demand.

4   The Data Processing Technology of Industrial Internet of Things

The data of industrial Internet of Things have features such as massive polymorphism, dynamic heterogeneity, relevance, real-time etc. These features make data processing need to solve the following the problem of key technologies.

4.1   The Data Storage Demand of Industrial Internet of Things

The data adopted by the industrial Internet of Things is real-time and massive. Data from sensor nodes, variety of intelligent terminal equipment and generated by variety of physical objects in the production process must be transferred to control center. data is collected, analyzed, and calculated by using data mining and analysis tools, and it is supported and serviced ultimately. The storage of industrial Internet of Things data needs the support of database, data warehouse, network storage and cloud storage technology. The research on storage, retrieval and query of mass data in industrial Internet of Things is beneficial to data acquisition and application. There is a big difference between wireless sensor database management system and traditional database system in the industrial Internet of Things system. Major expression is the in following few aspects.

First, in the industrial Internet of Things system, wireless sensor nodes have only limited capacity and computing power, and its function is limited by battery capacity and network routing. Traditional database system can query and process database independently, not affected by computer network distributed process communication.

Second, in the industrial Internet of Things system, data sensed by ireless sensor node can not be sent back to the central processing node, and it must use certain control mechanism and method to analyze the data, and then transmit the data, thereby reducing the amount of data transmission.

Third, in the industrial Internet of Things system, it must be "data centric". If some wireless sensor nodes fail due to power exhaustion, other nodes should be rebuilt in accordance with the requirements of ad hoc networks, and data transmission, data fusion will also change, so database management systems must adapt to these changes while the traditional database system does not appear this situation.

4.2   The Data Storage Technology of Industrial Internet of Things

4.2.1   Storage Mechanism

Data storage mechanism of industrial Internet of Things adopts two forms: storage mechanism and traction mechanism. Each data node provides data to the global view for providing a global view. Through global view, we can quickly locate the required nodes and reduce query time. Individual network node commonly need use of non relational technology for data storage. To Two kinds of data of temporal flow and spatial flow of industrial Internet of things, we can file data by creating traction algorithms automatically and find the best solution by using traction technology.

4.2.2   Data Management System Architecture and Model of Industrial Internet of Things

At present, most of the industrial IOT database management systems adopt semi distributed structure according to the data characteristics of wireless sensor nodes. There are two main data models in Wireless Sensor Networks: one is to perceive the data as a distributed database; another is to consider each wireless sensor network as a distributed database system. Semi distributed structure is generated under the combination of traditional database technology and network technology, and its physical space is dispersive. Data are distributed in various nodes of wireless sensor networks, but it has unity in logic and data is independent. Semi distributed database management adopts control mode and global control centralized, decentralized or decentralized.

4.2.3   Data Query

Data query of industrial Internet of Things relates to different types of data objects and data size and scope is very extensive. The data system of industrial IOT is composed of several independent network nodes which has a different storage mode. Because the amount of data is increasing, and the heterogeneity and interoperability exist in real-time data, data query must maintain the integrity of the data.

Data query language requires structured data query, and it can be extended to XML and can inquire web pages, documents, etc. Stored data can be stored in time series that helps to improve query performance and response.

4.3 The Data Fusion Technology of Industrial Internet of Things

Wireless sensor network is an important part of the perception of industrial Internet of Things. Because of its constraints of energy, storage capacity and transmission energy, it consumes the most energy in the data transmission process, therefore, the data must be analyzed, integrated and then transmitted by a certain control mechanism and method in the transmission process. Thereby, the transmission of data quantity is reduced. Data fusion process (As shown in Fig. 1).

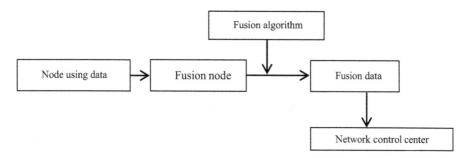

Fig. 1. Data fusion process

Data fusion technology involves a wide range of methods. According to different rules, there are many classification standards. There are three kinds of data fusion technologies in industrial wireless sensor networks: classification according to the data content before and after fusion, or classification according to the relational of data semantics before and after data fusion, or classification according to the level of fusion operations. This paper studies the technology of data fusion in industrial Internet of Things according to the different level of fusion operation.

4.3.1 Data Level Fusion

Data level fusion named as "pixel fusion" is the primary data fusion. Data acquired by sensor is data oriented fusion that usually depends on the type of sensor and that is a combination of pixel classification. Its working principle is that immediately expand data fusion in its initial state after sensor nodes collecting data, and then classifying and discriminating the collected data for reducing redundant information. Data level data fusion diagram shown in Fig. 2. Data fusion can maintain data integrity, and the obtained data is more detailed and accurate than the obtained data from other methods, however, the channel bandwidth and energy consumption in the data transmission are very high.

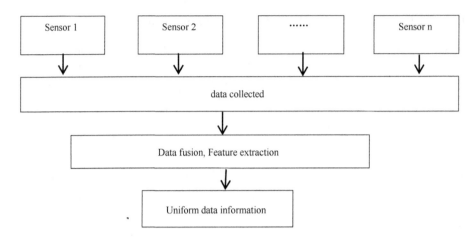

Fig. 2. Data fusion diagram

4.3.2   Feature-Level Fusion

The feature-level fusion of data is the fusion of monitoring object features, through feature extraction, the data is represented as a series of features reflecting things. Its working principle is that sensor nodes of industrial Internet of Things collect data information of an object. According to the specific situation, the characteristic data get by sensor node is extracted, and forming characteristics, providing data information description according to certain circumstances. Feature-level data fusion diagram shown in Fig. 3. Through the feature-level fusion technology, the data collected by the sensor node only needs to transmit the extracted part, that can greatly reduce the amount of information transmission and shorten the transmission time. Feature-level data fusion applications require certain regularity, and we need to clear the distribution of nodes of industrial Internet of Things for purposeful division, but each node is randomly distributed that causes the feature-level data fusion applications to be limited accordingly.

4.3.3   Decision-Level Fusion

The decision-level fusion is application oriented fusion whose working principle is similar with feature-level data fusion according to application requirements. The sensor node takes the characteristic data to an object in the concrete situation and refines the information to form a vector of features. Decision-level fusion operations include data feature parameters, and identifying and classifying characteristic parameters, and dividing the provided data information. That allows you to obtain decision information that satisfies application requirements through logic.

In the industrial Internet of Things, decision-level fusion data affects the final decision, that has a high degree of flexibility, good fault tolerance, etc., but decision-level fusion is based on specific criteria and programs. Data fusion needs to continue to study from practical issues, and it makes the fusion results more in line with the actual requirements.

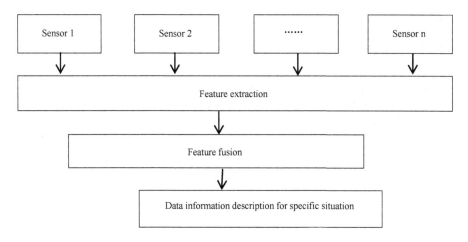

Fig. 3. Data fusion diagram

5   Conclusion

In recent years, the rapid development of new industry requires more and more intelligence of industry. Industrial Internet of Things provides a viable and convenient service for the development of intelligent industry. There is a large amount of data in industrial Internet of Things that will cause waste of resources in the system transmission process. The data of Industrial Internet of Things have features such as massive polymorphism, dynamic heterogeneity, relevance, real-time etc. These features become resistance in the process of data to create value. This paper explores the issues and challenges of data of Industrial Internet of Things, and studies data processing technology deeply. It provide some help to improve data management of Industrial Internet of Things.

References

1. Mo, Q.: Research on data fusion algorithm based on Internet of Things. LiaoNing University (2014)
2. Yu, T.: Research on perception terminal and data management of Internet of Things. WuHan University (2015)
3. Wen, Z., Zhang, Q.: Analysis and research of database technology based on massive data processing of Internet of Things. Intell. Process. Appl. (2014)
4. Feng, H.: Research on mass data fusion technology in Internet of Things workshop. Nanjing University of Aeronautics & Astronautics (2015)
5. Ling, X., Wei, C.: Research on data fusion technology of Internet of Things based on artificial bee colony algorithm. In: Combined Machine Tool and Automatic Machining Technology (2013)
6. Wen, Z., Zhang, Q.: Analysis and research of database technology based on massive data processing of Internet of Things. Intell. Process. Appl. **6** (2014)
7. Li, X.: Research and application of heterogeneous data integration technology in Internet of Things. Beijing University of Posts and Telecommunications (2012)

8. Chen, H.: The application of the integration of networking and big data. Nanjing University of Posts and Telecommunications (2015)
9. Li, B.: The design and application of the Internet of Things data center. Wuhan University of Technology (2013)
10. Li, S., Luo, G.: Overview of industrial networking technology and application. Telecommun. Netw. Technol. **3** (2014)
11. Zhong, D.: Analysis of mass data processing based on Internet of Things. Commun. Des. Appl. **8** (2015)
12. Shen, S., Zhenyang: Internet of Things architecture and its standardization. J. Nanjing Univ. Posts Telecommun. **2** (2015)
13. Liu, Y.: Data processing technology of Internet of Things. Inf. Comput. **7** (2012)

An Optimized Clustering Method with Improved Cluster Center for Social Network Based on Gravitational Search Algorithm

Liping Sun, Tao Tao, Fulong Chen, and Yonglong Luo[(✉)]

Engineering Technology Research Center of Network and Information Security,
Anhui Normal University, Wuhu 241000, China
ylluo@ustc.edu.cn

Abstract. Data clustering is a kind of data analysis techniques for grouping the set of data objects into clusters. To make use of the advantages of distance measure and nearest neighbor method, we present a hybrid data clustering algorithm based on GSA and DPC (GSA-DPC) algorithm. The optional clustering center set is selected by DPC algorithm. In turn, we optimize the clustering center set to achieve the best clustering distribution under the fame of GSA. Its performance is compared with four related clustering algorithms. The simulation results demonstrate the effectiveness of the presented algorithm.

Keywords: Data clustering · Gravitational Search Algorithm · Density peaks clustering · Social network

1 Introduction

Data clustering aims to divide objects into groups according to some measure of their similarities, so that objects in the same cluster are more similar to each other while other objects in different clusters [1]. With the aid of clustering method, the hidden patterns and trends within data can be revealed [2]. Clustering analysis has been widely applied for scientific and engineering applications [3,4].

At present, the typical clustering methods mainly include partitioned, hierarchical, density and etc. Similarity measure method can have an important impact on clustering algorithms. Distance measure and nearest neighbor method are two widely used measurement methods. K-means algorithm [5] is a classic of distance-based clustering algorithm, which is well known for its efficiency and easily to achieve clustering results with spherical clusters. Density peaks clustering (DPC) algorithm [6] could recognize arbitrary shape clusters on the basis of the nearest neighbor method.

Gravitational Search Algorithm (GSA) [7] is a heuristic optimization method for solving continuous optimization problems. To make use of the advantage of two kinds of distance measurement method, DPC algorithm is applied for the best cluster centers candidates, and the distance-based measure of cluster quality is defined for the fitness function of GSA.

© ICST Institute for Computer Sciences, Social Informatics and Telecommunications Engineering 2017
F. Chen and Y. Luo (Eds.): Industrial IoT 2017, LNICST 202, pp. 61–71, 2017.
DOI: 10.1007/978-3-319-60753-5_7

2   Analysis of DPC Algorithm

DPC algorithm provides a new method for data clustering. The algorithm is based on the assumption that cluster centers are characterized by neighbors with relatively lower local density and by a relatively large distance from points with higher densities. Let $O = \{o_1, o_2, ..., o_N\}$ be a dataset of N vectors in $\mathbb{R}^l$. Let d_{ij} denotes the distance between the data point o_i and o_j. For N data points, distance matrix $D = \{d_t | d_t$ is the distance between two data points, $t = 1, 2, ...N^2\}$. Let p(p is set for 2% in [6]) is the percentage of the number of data point set $O.d_c \in D$ is a cutoff distance, where $c = \lfloor N^2 * p + 0.5 \rfloor$.

For each data point i, its local density ρ_i and its distance δ_i from points of higher density are defined by Eqs. (1) and (2), respectively.

$$\rho_i = \sum_j \chi(d_{ij} - d_c). \tag{1}$$

$$\delta_i = \min_{j:\rho_j > \rho_i} (d_{ij}). \tag{2}$$

where $\chi = 1$ if $d_{ij} < d_c$ and $\chi = 0$ otherwise.

For the data point with highest density, its δ_i is defined by Eq. (3).

$$\delta_i = \max_j (d_{ij}). \tag{3}$$

Rodriguez and Laio [6] also present another local density computation as Eq. (4).

$$\rho_i = \sum_j exp^{(-d_{ij}^2/d_c^2)}. \tag{4}$$

Table 1. DPC on Zoo dataset with different values of p.

p	d_c	Indicators				
		ACC	NMI	REC	F_M	E_V
2%	0	0.3762	0.3482	0.2744	0.3523	0.6477
4%–8%	1.00	0.6337	0.7219	0.6848	0.5998	0.4002
9%	1.03	0.6337	0.7227	0.6855	0.6011	0.3989
10%	1.41	0.6040	0.6968	0.6518	0.5784	0.4216

d_c is the only given parameter in [6], which is used in Eqs. (1) and (4). Experimental results indicate that d_c is zero for the experiment on zoo data set, which will cause the error that division by zero. As shown in Table 1, clustering evaluation indices demonstrate that the quality of the clustering results for zoo is low when $d_c = 0$. It also demonstrates that the value of d_c has significant influence on the performance of the DPC algorithm. This shortage of DPC algorithm means the choice of d_c may lead to wrong choice of cluster centers. And once the clustering centers are identified, the remaining data points would be allocated to a wrong cluster.

3   Analysis of GSA Algorithm

GSA is a kind of heuristic optimization method which is inspired by the law of gravity and mass interactions. We apply GSA to solve clustering problems in this paper for optimizing the selection of clustering centers to achieve the best clustering distribution. Let the i-th agent be a $K * l$-dimensional vector which is represented as $X_i = \{\underbrace{x_{11}^i x_{12}^i ... x_{1l}^i}_{C_1} \cdots \underbrace{x_{j1}^i x_{j2}^i ... x_{jl}^i}_{C_j} \cdots \underbrace{x_{k1}^i x_{k2}^i ... x_{kl}^i}_{C_K}\}$, where C_i corresponds to the center of ith-cluster. The mass value of the X_i is calculated as follows.

$$m_i(t) = \frac{fit_i(t) - worst(t)}{best(t) - worst(t)}. \tag{5}$$

$$M_i(t) = \frac{m_i(t)}{\sum_{j=1}^N m_j(t)}. \tag{6}$$

Where $M_i(t)$ and $fit_i(t)$ represent the mass value and the fitness value of the agent X_i at time t, respectively. $worst(t)$ and $best(t)$ are defined as follows for a minimization problem as follows.

$$best(t) = \min_{j \in \{1, \cdots, N\}} fit_j(t). \tag{7}$$

$$worst(t) = \max_{j \in \{1, \cdots, N\}} fit_j(t). \tag{8}$$

The acceleration of the agent X_i by the law of motion is calculated as follows.

$$a_i^d(t) = G(t) \sum_{j \in Kbest, j \neq i}^N rand_j \frac{M_j(t)}{R_{ij}(t) + \varepsilon}(x_j^d(t) - x_i^d(t)). \tag{9}$$

$$v_i^d(t+1) = rand_i \times v_i^d(t) + a_i^d(t). \tag{10}$$

$$x_i^d(t+1) = x_i^d(t) + v_i^d(t+1). \tag{11}$$

Where $Kbest$ is the set of first K agents with the best fitness value and biggest mass value, which is initialized to the value K_0 at the beginning of the GSA. ε is a decimal very close to zero but not zero used to avoid the error that division by zero whenever the similarity between agent x_i and agent x_j is equal to zero. The agent's next velocity $v_i^d(t+1)$ and position $x_i^d(t+1)$ are all based on the current value, respectively. The $rand$ is a uniformly distributed random number in the interval $[0, 1]$.

4   GSA-DPC Clustering Algorithm

Given a data set O, the goal of a clustering algorithm is to obtain a partition $I = \{I_1, I_2, \cdots, I_K\}$ which satisfies $I_i \neq \emptyset$, for $\forall i; \bigcup_{i=1}^{K} I_i = O, I_i \cap I_j = \emptyset$, for $\forall i \neq j$. The widely used in cluster analysis for measuring the quality of finding clusters is the total mean-square quantization error (MSE) [8]. In this paper, the fitness of a clustering on data point set O with cluster C, which is defined as follows.

$$fit(O, C) = \sum_{j=1}^{K} \sum_{o_i \in C_j} \|o_i - C_j\|^2. \tag{12}$$

Where $\|o_i - C_j\|$ denotes the similarity between the point v_i and clustering center C_j.

Recall is a typical criterion to evaluate the performance of clustering algorithm, which is defined as follows.

$$Recall = \frac{\#true\ positive decisions}{\#true\ positive\ decisions\ + \#false\ negative\ decisions}. \tag{13}$$

We elaborate cluster center selection based on DPC algorithm as follows.

Algorithm 1. Cluster center selection based on DPC algorithm

Input: the set of data points $O = \{o_1, o_2, \cdots, o_N\}$, parameter p, number of clusters K.
Output: the cluster center candidate set $C = \{C_1, C_2, \cdots, C_K\}$.
1. Calculate distance matrix D by the similarity measure
2. Sort D by ascending
3. Let d_c be the $\lfloor N^2 \times p + 0.5 \rfloor$ -th element in D
4. While $d_c = 0$
5. $p \leftarrow 2 * p$
6.   Let d_c be the $\lfloor N^2 \times p + 0.5 \rfloor$-th element in D
7. Endwhile
8. Calculate $\{\rho_i\}_{i=1}^{N}$ according to Eq. (1) or (4)
9. Calculate $\{\delta_i\}_{i=1}^{N}$ according to Eqs. (2) and (3)
10. Calculate $\{\gamma_i = \rho_i \times \delta_i\}_{i=1}^{N}$
11. Sort $\{\gamma_i\}_{i=1}^{N}$ by descending
12. Choose the first K elements of $\{\gamma_i\}_{i=1}^{N}$ as $\{\gamma_i\}_{i=1}^{K}$
13. Choose K data points of O corresponding to the index of each element in $\{\gamma_i\}_{i=1}^{K}$ as cluster center candidate set C

The proposed GSA-DPC algorithm works as follows.

Algorithm 2. GSA-DPC algorithm

Input: the label vector of cluster center:$C \in \mathbb{R}_{i,K*l}$
Output: the cluster assignment I
1. Initialize an initial population : $X = \{X_1, X_2, \cdots, X_s\}$:
2. $X_1 \leftarrow C$
3.   For $i = 2$ to s do
4. $X_i = [x^1_{11}x^1_{12} \cdots x^1_{1l} \cdots x^1_{j1}x^1_{j2} \cdots x^1_{K1}x^1_{K2} \cdots x^1_{Kl}] \times rd$, where rd is a uniformly
       distributed random number in the interval $(0, 1]$
5.   Endfor
6. do
7.   Calculate similarity metric between o_i and C_j, for each
     $o_i \in O \wedge C_j \in X_t, i = 1, 2, \cdots, N, j = 1, 2, \cdots, K, t = 1, 2, \cdots, s$
8.   Allocate each data point to the closest cluster center with $IDX_t(t = 1, 2, \cdots, s)$
9.   Evaluate the fitness for each $X_t(t = 1, 2, \cdots, s)$ according to Eq. (12)
10. Choose the best cluster assignment I by evaluate the recall indicator using Eq.
(13)
11. Calculate the agent's mass value using the Eqs. (5)-(8)
12. Calculate the agent's acceleration using the Eq. (9)
13. Calculate the agent's velocity using the Eq. (10)
14. Update the searching space X through move the agents using Eq. (11)
15. Until the stop criteria is reached

---

5   Experimental Results

In this section, the performances of GSA-DPC algorithm are tested through different types of the experiments. We compared our algorithm with density peaks clustering (DPC) algorithm [6], gravitational search algorithm for clustering (GSA-C) [7], Kmeans algorithm [5], and GSA-Kmeans (GSA-KM) algorithm [9] in Accuracy (ACC), Normalized Mutual Information (NMI), Recall (REC), F-measure (F_M), Expect Value (E_V). All the algorithms have been executed upon datasets for 20 times.

5.1   Experimental Results on UCI and Synthetic Datasets

As shown in Table 2, 12 data sets from the UCI machine learning repository (http://archive.ics.uci.edu/ml/) are tested in this paper. We also compared our algorithm with the other four algorithms by four 2-D synthetic datasets. The most famous similarity metric between data points of UCI and synthetic datasets is measured by Euclidean distance (as shown Eq. (14)).

$$d(o_i, o_j) = \sqrt{\sum_{t=1}^{l}(o_i^t - o_j^t)^2}. \tag{14}$$

The comparison of the algorithms in this paper is shown in Table 3. GSA-DPC algorithm outperforms others in both low-dimensional and high- dimensional data sets. To be specific, the clustering results on zoo data set indicate

Table 2. The details of UCI datasets.

DataSets	#Object	#Features	#Clusters
Iris	150	4	3
Wine	178	13	3
Glass	214	9	6
Heart	303	13	2
Liver	345	6	2
Pima	768	8	2
Vote	435	16	2
Breast	277	9	2
Wpbc	198	33	2
Zoo	101	16	7
Sonar	208	60	2
Vehicle	846	18	4

that our method has overcome the low performance caused by the value of d_c. In other words, we optimize the clustering center set to achieve the best clustering distribution.

The aggregation data set is composed of 788 data points and has instances from each of 7 classes. The compound data set contains 399 data instances and divided into 6 classes. The jain data set has 373 samples forming 2 classes. The flame data set is composed of 240 data instances and 2 classes are represented. Figure 1 presents the clustering results of our algorithm with comparison to the other methods. As shown, GSA- DPC gets perfect results on different synthetic datasets. As shown in Table 4, the experimental results illustrate our algorithm is effective in finding clusters of arbitrary shape, density and distribution.

5.2 Experimental Results on Social Networks

The comparison experiments have been carried on four typical social networks, including dolphin social networks (Dolphins), books about US politicians (Polbooks), Zachary's karate club (Karate), and American college football (football) (As shown in Table 5). Due to the characteristics of social network, the similarity metric between data points is measured by correlation coefficients (as shown Eq. (15)).

$$R(o_i, o_j) = \frac{Cov(o_i, o_j)}{\sqrt{Cov(o_i, o_i)Cov(o_j, o_j)}}. \tag{15}$$

Table 3. The results of comparison experiments on UCI datasets.

Algorithm	Iris					Wine				
	ACC	NMI	REC	F_M	E_V	ACC	NMI	REC	F_M	E_V
GSA-DPC	0.940	0.826	0.887	0.890	0.110	0.962	0.866	0.933	0.925	0.075
DPC	0.553	0.653	0.555	0.670	0.330	0.787	0.555	0.648	0.673	0.327
GSA-C	0.887	0.742	0.798	0.811	0.189	0.956	0.854	0.923	0.914	0.086
Kmeans	0.826	0.708	0.751	0.779	0.221	0.927	0.810	0.882	0.881	0.119
GSA-KM	0.888	0.743	0.800	0.812	0.188	0.954	0.848	0.919	0.910	0.090
Algorithm	Glass					Heart				
	ACC	NMI	REC	F_M	E_V	ACC	NMI	REC	F_M	E_V
GSA-DPC	0.492	0.283	0.407	0.404	0.596	0.791	0.265	0.663	0.676	0.324
DPC	0.509	0.299	0.341	0.432	0.568	0.696	0.137	0.563	0.622	0.378
GSA-C	0.435	0.302	0.386	0.375	0.625	0.691	0.122	0.570	0.596	0.404
Kmeans	0.433	0.324	0.384	0.392	0.608	0.669	0.103	0.558	0.583	0.417
GSA-KM	0.434	0.327	0.383	0.393	0.607	0.708	0.140	0.581	0.609	0.391
Algorithm	Liver					Pima				
	ACC	NMI	REC	F_M	E_V	ACC	NMI	REC	F_M	E_V
GSA-DPC	0.572	0.002	0.512	0.638	0.362	0.701	0.073	0.588	0.667	0.333
DPC	0.513	0.000	0.510	0.520	0.480	0.618	0.002	0.550	0.629	0.371
GSA-C	0.556	0.000	0.511	0.605	0.395	0.668	0.052	0.590	0.597	0.403
Kmeans	0.546	0.000	0.510	0.591	0.409	0.667	0.050	0.589	0.601	0.399
GSA-KM	0.557	0.000	0.511	0.605	0.395	0.668	0.052	0.590	0.597	0.403
Algorithm	Vote					Breast				
	ACC	NMI	REC	F_M	E_V	ACC	NMI	REC	F_M	E_V
GSA-DPC	0.878	0.490	0.809	0.791	0.209	0.706	0.078	0.647	0.657	0.343
DPC	0.876	0.506	0.807	0.787	0.213	0.516	0.000	0.582	0.540	0.460
GSA-C	0.851	0.444	0.778	0.765	0.235	0.617	0.045	0.622	0.596	0.404
Kmeans	0.852	0.438	0.778	0.770	0.230	0.641	0.051	0.626	0.615	0.385
GSA-KM	0.867	0.469	0.793	0.774	0.226	0.604	0.041	0.619	0.589	0.411
Algorithm	Wpbc					Zoo				
	ACC	NMI	REC	F_M	E_V	ACC	NMI	REC	F_M	E_V
GSA-DPC	0.730	0.011	0.644	0731	0.269	0.835	0.813	0.822	0.880	0.120
DPC	0.672	0.033	0.618	0.695	0.305	0.376	0.348	0.274	0.352	0.648
GSA-C	0.627	0.026	0.660	0.595	0.405	0.776	0.794	0.814	0.812	0.188
Kmeans	0.596	0.026	0.652	0.576	0.424	0.694	0.762	0.775	0.722	0.278
GSA-KM	0.601	0.027	0.654	0.577	0.423	0.701	0.790	0.829	0.733	0.267
Algorithm	Sonar					Vehicle				
	ACC	NMI	REC	F_M	E_V	ACC	NMI	REC	F_M	E_V
GSA-DPC	0.567	0.015	0.507	0.508	0.492	0.395	0.137	0.313	0.328	0.672
DPC	0.510	0.000	0.498	0.524	0.476	0.363	0.142	0.285	0.358	0.642
GSA-C	0.498	0.012	0.499	0.577	0.423	0.363	0.130	0.295	0.368	0.632
Kmeans	0.545	0.006	0.502	0.523	0.477	0.362	0.111	0.307	0.316	0.684
GSA-KM	0.549	0.008	0.503	0.518	0.482	0.363	0.112	0.308	0.316	0.684

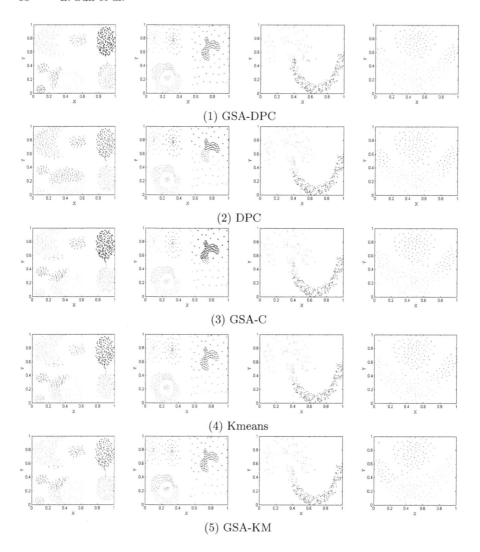

Fig. 1. Cluster assignment of artificial datasets.

We demonstrate the feasibility of our algorithm by experiments and simulations on social network data sets. Table 6 illustrates the performances of all the methods in this paper. DPC method does not need to iterate in the algorithm. Regardless of DPC algorithm, our algorithm is the most stable within the remaining four algorithms.

Table 4. The results of artificial datasets.

Algorithm	Aggregation					Compound				
	ACC	NMI	REC	F_M	E_V	ACC	NMI	REC	F_M	E_V
GSA-DPC	0.855	0.847	0.916	0.803	0.197	0.671	0.717	0.757	0.654	0.346
DPC	0.787	0.894	0.906	0.802	0.198	0.667	0.736	0.742	0.643	0.357
GSA-C	0.787	0.842	0.903	0.766	0.234	0.584	0.701	0.730	0.632	0.368
Kmeans	0.784	0.825	0.877	0.759	0.241	0.593	0.693	0.713	0.629	0.371
GSA-KM	0.818	0.839	0.906	0.772	0.228	0.643	0.716	0.746	0.651	0.349
Algorithm	Jain					Flame				
	ACC	NMI	REC	F_M	E_V	ACC	NMI	REC	F_M	E_V
GSADPC	0.918	0.588	0903	0.874	0.126	0.867	0.462	0.801	0.778	0.222
DPC	0.895	0.577	0.898	0.837	0.163	0.788	0.413	0.696	0.678	0.322
GSA-C	0.882	0.527	0.882	0.818	0.182	0.845	0.423	0.773	0.746	0.254
Kmeans	0.882	0.527	0.882	0.818	0.182	0.849	0.441	0.779	0.751	0.249
GSA-KM	0.882	0.527	0.882	0.818	0.182	0.840	0.407	0.767	0.740	0.260

Table 5. The details of SNS datasets [10–13].

DataSets	#Nodes	#Links	Source
Football	115	613	American college football (football)
Karate	34	78	Zachary's karate club (Karate)
Polbooks	105	441	books about US politicians (Polbooks)
Dolphins	62	159	dolphin social networks (Dolphins)

Table 6. The result of SNS datasets.

Algorithm		Football					Karate				
		ACC	NMI	REC	F_M	E_V	ACC	NMI	REC	F_M	E_V
GSA-DPC	Max	0.826	0.872	0.791	0.810	0.190	0.912	0.574	0.826	0.831	0.470
	Min	0.826	0.872	0.791	0.810	0.190	0.618	0.040	0.500	0.530	0.169
	ST.D	0.000	0.000	0.000	0.000	0.000	0.081	0.146	0.088	0.085	0.085
DPC	Max	0.817	0.862	0.744	0.783	0.217	0.500	0.046	0.485	0.639	0.361
	Min	0.817	0.862	0.744	0.783	0.217	0.500	0.046	0.485	0.639	0.361
	ST.D	0.000	0.000	0.000	0.000	0.000	0.000	0.000	0.000	0.000	0.000
GSA-C	Max	0.896	0.906	0.853	0.869	0.365	0.882	0.492	0.780	0.783	0.470
	Min	0.704	0.740	0.577	0.635	0.131	0.618	0.040	0.500	0.530	0.217
	ST.D	0.058	0.044	0.080	0.071	0.071	0.079	0.137	0.087	0.077	0.077
Kmeans	Max	0.870	0.887	0.787	0.817	0.392	0.941	0.677	0.883	0.883	0.345
	Min	0.635	0.759	0.510	0.608	0.183	0.529	0.000	0.487	0.655	0.117
	ST.D	0.080	0.042	0.097	0.077	0.077	0.088	0.159	0.091	0.063	0.063
GSA-KM	Max	0.800	0.872	0.758	0.766	0.596	0.853	0.401	0.735	0.734	0.266
	Min	0.574	0.598	0.397	0.404	0.234	0.853	0.401	0.735	0.734	0.266
	ST.D	0.095	0.117	0.138	0.158	0.158	0.000	0.000	0.000	0.000	0.000
Algorithm		Polbooks					Dolphins				
		ACC	NMI	REC	F_M	E_V	ACC	NMI	REC	F_M	E_V
GSA-DPC	Max	0.676	0.340	0.596	0.590	0.535	0.774	0.247	0.702	0.662	0.480
	Min	0.486	0.098	0.429	0.465	0.410	0.548	0.006	0.553	0.520	0.338
	ST.D	0.059	0.071	0.050	0.034	0.034	0.065	0.084	0.043	0.041	0.041
DPC	Max	0.705	0.541	0.725	0.723	0.277	0.677	0.284	0.604	0.593	0.407
	Min	0.705	0.541	0.725	0.723	0.277	0.677	0.284	0.604	0.593	0.407
	ST.D	0.000	0.000	0.000	0.000	0.000	0.000	0.000	0.000	0.000	0.000
GSA-C	Max	0.686	0.332	0.586	0.597	0.548	0.742	0.185	0.668	0.630	0.482
	Min	0.448	0.077	0.428	0.452	0.403	0.371	0.000	0.546	0.518	0.370
	ST.D	0.064	0.074	0.056	0.041	0.041	0.099	0.058	0.037	0.034	0.034
Kmeans	Max	0.781	0.454	0.751	0.711	0.385	0.887	0.510	0.845	0.809	0.444
	Min	0.648	0.339	0.664	0.615	0.289	0.387	0.108	0.561	0.556	0.191
	ST.D	0.041	0.032	0.024	0.024	0.024	0.149	0.150	0.106	0.098	0.098
GSA-KM	Max	0.781	0.470	0.760	0.702	0.405	0.871	0.475	0.824	0.785	0.484
	Min	0.638	0.318	0.650	0.595	0.298	0.371	0.000	0.548	0.516	0.215
	ST.D	0.061	0.052	0.039	0.041	0.041	0.176	0.190	0.113	0.108	0.108

6   Experimental Results

In this work, a hybrid clustering method based on gravitational search algorithm
(GSA) and density peaks clustering (DPC) algorithm is presented. It tries to
exploit the merits of two algorithms simultaneously. The performance of the
proposed algorithm is compared with four related approaches. The comparison
results show the effectiveness of the proposed method.

Acknowledgment. This work is supported by the National Natural Science Foundation of China (No. 61602009, No.61672039, No. 61572036), Anhui Provincial Natural Science Foundation (No. 1608085MF145), Research Program of Anhui Province Education Department (No. KJ2015A067).

References

1. Jain, A.K.: Data clustering: a review. ACM Comput. Surv. **31**(3), 264–323 (1999)
2. Bonab, M.B., Hashim, S.Z.M., Bazin, N.E.N., Alsaedi, A.K.Z.: An effective hybrid of bees algorithm and differential evolution algorithm in data clustering. Math. Probl. Eng. **2015**(2), 1–17 (2015)
3. Jain, A.K., Dubes, R.C.: Algorithms for clustering data. Technometrics **32**(32), 227–229 (2015)
4. Ashouri, M., Yousefi, H., Basiri, J., Hemmatyar, A.M.A., Movaghar, A.: PDC: prediction-based data-aware clustering in wireless sensor networks. J. Parallel Distrib. Comput. **81–82**, 24–35 (2015)
5. Macqueen, J.: Some methods for classification and analysis of multivariate observations In: Proceeding of Berkeley Symposium on Mathematical Statistics and Probability (1967)
6. Rodriguez, A., Laio, A.: Clustering by fast search and find of density peaks. Science **344**(6191), 1492–1496 (2015)
7. Rashedi, E., Nezamabadi-Pour, H., Saryazdi, S.: GSA: a gravitational search algorithm. Intell. Inf. Manage. **04**(6), 390–395 (2012)
8. Güngör, Z., Ünler, A.: K-harmonic means data clustering with simulated annealing heuristic. Appl. Math. Comput. **184**(2), 199–209 (2007)
9. Hatamlou, A., Abdullah, S., Nezamabadi-Pour, H.: A combined approach for clustering based on k-means and gravitational search algorithms. Swarm Evol. Comput. **6**, 47–52 (2012)
10. Lusseau, D., Schneider, K., Boisseau, O.J., Haase, P., Slooten, E., Dawson, S.M.: The bottlenose dolphin community of Doubtful Sound features a large proportion of long-lasting associations. Behav. Ecol. Sociobiol. **54**(4), 396–405 (2003)
11. Zachary, W.W.: An information flow model for conflict and fission in small groups. J. Anthropol. Res. **33**(4), 473 (1977)
12. Girvan, M., Newman, M.E.J.: Community structure in social and biological networks. Proc. Natl. Acad. Sci. U.S.A. **99**(12), 7821–7826 (2002)
13. Newman, M.E.: Finding community structure in networks using the eigenvectors of matrices. Phys. Rev. E Stat. Nonlinear Soft Matter Phys. **74**(3 Pt 2), 92–100 (2006)

Elastic Resource Provisioning System Based on OpenStack Cloud Platform

Zheng Zhang$^{(\boxtimes)}$, Hao Xu, Ke Chen, and Pingping Shan

College of Software, Nanyang Institute of Technology, Nanyang 473000, Henan, China
sawest@163.com

Abstract. As open source private cloud platform, OpenStack provides basic resource service which has features of stability reliability and security. Function components of OpenStack platform were deployed and installed. Integrated basic resource pool was built. Based on open API of platform, applying JAVA native interface, elastic resource provisioning system was implemented which adops software architecture of B/S. The system has functions of establishment distribution and real-time adjustment of dynamic resource. In order to manage elastic resource of plateform expediently the system provides personalization module and favorable user interface.

Keywords: Elastic resource · Cloud platform · OpenStack · B/S · JNI

1 Introduction to OpenStack

OpenStack is open-source software which provides a basic platform for deployment cloud facilitates the deployment and management of virtual machine and serves as a public/private cloud for virtual computing and storage. OpenStack mainly include Nova virtual computing service, Swift storage service, Glance virtual image registration distribution service [1–4].

1.1 System Structure of OpenStack

OpenStack cloud platform mainly includes seven components with different functions:

Nova computing component is the core of OpenStack platform and responsible for computing part and implementing corresponding strategies. Other components are scheduled through Nova component. Same as Amazon EC2 and RackspaceCloud-Servers, Nova component provides functions, including example operation, network management, user control and access to the cloud by other items.

Swift object storage component is a distributed object storage component with similar functions to Hadoop. In addition, Swift is used to store the image files to create virtual machine.

Cinder block storage component adds enduring storage service for virtual machine. Block storage component provides an infrastructure management data volume and interacts with OpenStack computing service as well as offers data volume for examples.

© ICST Institute for Computer Sciences, Social Informatics and Telecommunications Engineering 2017
F. Chen and Y. Luo (Eds.): Industrial IoT 2017, LNICST 202, pp. 72–82, 2017.
DOI: 10.1007/978-3-319-60753-5_8

Quantum network component provides networking service, which means to create IP address of virtual machine and manage the network system structure through API.

Keystone authentication component is responsible for access management and service catalogue. Amongst, access management takes charge of authorization and access establishment of users and involves concepts, including users, tenants and roles. Besides, service catalogue can only be provided for users after each service of OpenStack is registered in Keystone. Endpoint is the access point of the corresponding service.

Horizon component provides visualized GUI image interface and makes the users to operate various resources of OpenStack platform [5–8].

1.2   Command Line Management Tool of OpenStack

OpenStack cloud platform has two different methods to manage the cloud resources. The first one is to realize the management over cloud resources by Horizon, a GUI image interface based on Web while the second one is to manage the resources by portals of OpenStack command line.

(1) Check the OpenStack cloud platform service
      nova-manage service list
(2) Create examples of virtual machine
      nova boot [name of virtual machine] --flavor [type of virtual machine] --image [ID of virtual machine image] --security-groups default-nic --net-id = [ID of the network which the virtual machine belongs to]
(3) Stop, suspend and delete the virtual machine
      nova stop [vm-name]
      nova suspend [vm-name]
      nova delete [vm-name]

2   System Design

Elastic resource allocation system is based on OpenStack cloud platform and realizes JAVA localized encapsulation of open API interface as well as allocates various resources in resource pool dynamically, which mainly include image management module, virtual machine management module, network management module and tenant information module, etc. in order to provide an excellent user interface.

2.1   System Software Structure

Elastic resource allocation system is divided into three layers. The bottom layer establishes elastic resource pool through OpenStack cloud platform and provides infrastructure service. The middle layer realizes the encapsulation of local components by using the open API programming interface of OpenStack and provides functional support for the upper layer. In addition, the upper layer realizes the management system of B/S structure based on J2EE technical design as well as manages and allocates various resources in resource pool. Figure 1 shows the system software structure.

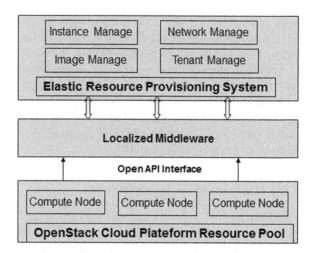

Fig. 1. Elastic resource allocation system software structure

2.2 Scheduling of OpenStack Cloud Platform Resource Pool

OpenStack cloud platform is established on the basis of server cluster. Then, the hardware resources at the bottom layer are abstracted as logic resources and are responsible for managing and scheduling virtual logic resources. The resource pool in the cluster includes the sum of resources of all the computing joints in the cluster. The logic resource pool develops API programming interface for the upper layer and provides transfer of infrastructure.

Resource scheduling refers to allocate the M heterogeneous and available resources to N mutually-independent application tasks in order to minimize the total task completion time and make full use of the resources. Resource allocation serves as a key component of cloud computing and its efficiency directly influences the working performance of cloud computing environment. The central controller of OpenStack, Nova is responsible for managing the resource computing of the whole cloud. Instead of providing any virtual capabilities, Nova makes the interactions between Libvirt API and host of virtual machine possible and provides external processing interface through Web service API. OpenStack makes use of the management program to provide the corresponding abstract relations between the application programs and the hardware. Therefore, a pool is equipped behind the server, network or storage device of each virtual machine, which makes the request response and resource allocation more flexible and effective [9].

Based on OpenStack open-source cloud platform framework, the functions of platform resource monitoring and dynamic resource scheduling are expanded into the computing module, Nova in order to include the monitoring and scheduling functions into this platform. Thus, corresponding function deployment can be accomplished when the platform is being deployed. In addition, service-oriented concept is adopted to manage the virtualized resources and realizes the optimal match between the physical resources at the bottom layer and the services at the upper layer by combining the resource scheduling & allocation with service type and working load. Figure 2 shows the design framework.

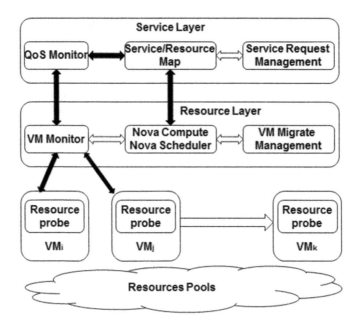

Fig. 2. Strategic framework of virtual resource scheduling

The scheduling algorithm locates all the virtual machines whose load is higher than the upper threshold in the virtual machine cluster and adopts the optimal adaptive algorithm to find the physical machine whose physical resource load is the highest but does not exceed the upper threshold for physical load after the scheduling process; then, the virtual machine is transferred to this physical machine and both the resource vector magnitude and the load of physical machine are updated.

2.3   Cluster Management Middleware

Multi-cluster management middleware is mainly responsible for shielding the multi-computing cluster distribution of the bottom cluster layer. The platform management layer transfers the middleware to accomplish resource integration and provides related information about each sub-cluster or sub-platform managed by the platform when operations, including virtual machine creation, storage management and information collection, need to be carried out in order to realize the goal of scheduling all the resources distributed across the whole platform during resource transfer.

Multi-cluster management middleware is a dynamic linkage module encapsulated through JNI technique by developing API interface provided by OpenStack cloud platform. On the basis of infrastructure platform, multi-cluster management, resource collection, storage service and virtual machine service are realized. In addition, management middleware can not only transfer OpenStack platform resources but simplify and encapsulate the transfer process in order to provide realization of functional module for the application system at the upper layer and increase the flexibility and scalability of elastic resource allocation system. The realization process includes following steps:

(1) Receive the transfer request of functional module in elastic resource allocation system.
(2) According to the request type, write the corresponding processing script, which contains the resource scheduling command identified by OpenStack cloud platform, into the memory and implement it.
(3) Cloud platform cluster makes corresponding disposals according to the command and returns the results back to the middleware.
(4) Middleware converts the format of feedback data from cloud platform to send the data in a format which complies with system transmission protocol to the system module.

Table 1 shows the main contents encapsulated by JAVA localized middleware:

Table 1. Middleware interface encapsulation table

Name of encapsulation interface	Name of functions transferred by upper module	Middleware realizing function
Example of inquiring virtual machine	private native String novaListJNI()	JNIEXPORT jstring JNICALL novaListJNI (JNIEnv *, jobject)
Inquiry image	private native String novaImageListJNI ()	JNIEXPORT jstring novaImageListJNI (JNIEnv *, jobject)
Example of initiating virtual machine	private native String novaBootJNI (String flavorId, String imageId, String name)	JNIEXPORT jstring JNICALL novaBootJNI (JNIEnv *, jobject, jstring, jstring, jstring)
Example of stopping virtual machine	private native void novaSuspendJNI (String instanceId);	JNIEXPORT void JNICALL novaSuspendJNI (JNIEnv *, jobject, jstring)
Example of deleting virtual machine	private native void novaDeleteJNI (String instanceId);	JNIEXPORT novaDeleteJNI (JNIEnv *, jobject, jstring);

Middleware is responsible for encapsulating the scheduling commands and converting the format of data transmitted. The existence of middleware can greatly reduce the coupling among the layers in software structure and provide convenience for system function expansion in the future.

2.4   Elastic Resource Allocation System

Elastic resource allocation system realizes the management over various resources in cloud platform in modules and is mainly divided into five major modules: image management module, virtual machine management module, network management module, user information management module and auxiliary function module. Amongst, the image module achieves the functions of creating images by image files, viewing existing images and creating images by virtual machine snapshot; virtual machine module achieves the functions of creating, initiating, stopping and deleting virtual machine; user information module achieves the functions of importation, revision and view of user information; network module achieves the functions of generating floating IP and its binding with virtual machine; auxiliary function module achieves the functions of server performance inspection and real-time synchronization of system background data., etc.

The system background is realized by JAVA programming language and achieves control over major computing joints in cloud platform by class function, RmtShellExecutor through remote access.

2.4.1   Virtual Machine Management Module

Aiming at virtual machine resources, this module can realize the functions of virtual machine creation by images, management and control of virtual machine as well as view of virtual machine information.

(1) Creation of virtual machine. Select the type of image, set the configuration parameters (memory size, CPU and hard disk) of the virtual machine and generate virtual machines in batches.
(2) Management and control of virtual machine. Initiate, suspend, stop or delete designated virtual machine resources according to ID, name and type of virtual machine.
(3) View of virtual machine information. View the information about existing virtual machines in cloud platform, which mainly includes ID, name, status, network of virtual machines and operations supported by virtual machines.

2.4.2   Image Management Module

Images are master files used to derive virtual machines in cloud platform and create image files according to the standard image creation procedure for OpenStack cloud platform:

glance   add   name="win7"   is_public=true   container_format=ovf disk_format=raw < win7.img

Image management module can upload, create, view images and make images by virtual machine snapshot. Amongst, the snapshot function can use the storage of current state of virtual machine to copy virtual machines with the same contents. Figure 3 shows the snapshot function in image management module:

Location:[Create Image From VM]
VM ID:
Image Name:
Create
Cancel

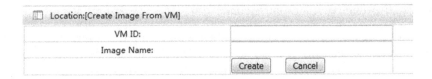

Fig. 3. Image management module snapshot function figure

2.4.3 Network Management Module

Each virtual machine operating in elastic resource allocation system corresponds to two IPs, one fixed inner network IP and one floating IP. The floating IP needs to be bond with virtual machine. Therefore, the network management module is responsible for batch creation and binding of floating IP.

2.4.4 User Information Management Module

User information management module is responsible for batch creation, deletion, revision and inquiry of user information in cloud platform. To facilitate the administrators to add batch user information, the administrators can fill in user information according to given format and put the information into an Excel sheet and then upload the sheet. The basic information about the virtual machine bond to the user can be inquired about in user information module.

2.4.5 Auxiliary Management Module

Auxiliary management module is responsible for viewing the operation state of server background resources, including the utilization rate of CPU, occupation rate of memory and utilization rate of exchange partition, etc. The auxiliary system administrators judge the operation condition of server in order to create virtual machine rationally and allocate corresponding hardware resources. Figure 4 shows the operation effect of auxiliary module.

top - 21:39:19 up 12 days, 19:25, 2 users, load average: 0.00, 0.01, 0.05
Tasks: 465 total, 1 running, 163 sleeping, 0 stopped, 301 zombie
Cpu(s): 2.7%us, 0.5%sy, 0.0%ni, 96.6%id, 0.0%wa, 0.0%hi, 0.2%si, 0.0%st
Mem: 49454660k total, 42469808k used, 6984852k free, 200288k buffers
Swap: 50320380k total, 0k used, 50320380k free, 39245240k cached

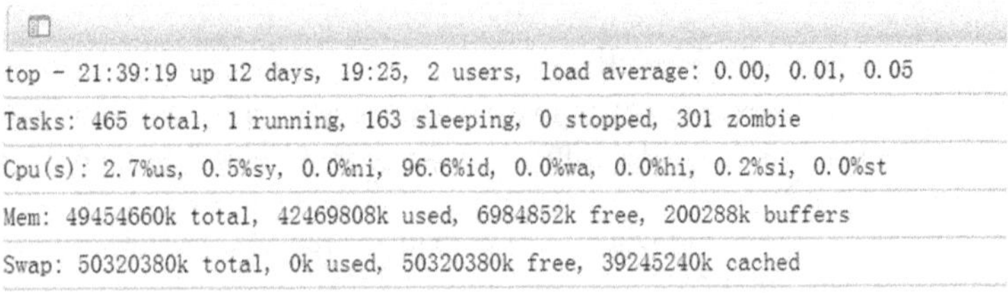

Fig. 4. Operation effect of auxiliary module

3 Key Technologies for System Realization

3.1 OpenStack API Authentication and Request Workflow

Authentication is required when the system accesses the OpenStack services. Firstly, authentication request should be sent to obtain the authentication token. Therefore, valid certificate must be provided in order to request the authentication token. When the system sends OpenStack API request, the token information is put into the X-Auth-Token head of HTTP request message. The token has a valid term and will become invalid after the term [10, 11]. OpenStack API authentication and request workflow process is as follows (Table 2):

(1) Access the authentication service access point of cloud platform, request for the authentication token. A valid certificate is included in the request sent, which contains following request parameter sheet:
    When the request is successfully sent, the server will return back an authentication token.
(2) Place the token into the head of X-Auth-Token of HTTP request message to send API request. Keep using this token to send API request until the operation is finished or the server returns to 401 Unauthorized [12, 13].
(3) When 401 Unauthorized error occurs, please request for a new token.

Table 2. Request parameter of certificate table

Parameter	Type	Description
username (required)	xsd:string	Username. If you cannot provide username and password, token must be provided
password (required)	xsd:string	Password of this user
tenantName (elective)	xsd:string	Name of tenant. Both tenant ID and name are elective but cannot be used at the same time. If these two properties are designated, the service will return 400 error request
tenantId (elective)	capi:UUID	ID of tenant. Both tenant ID and name are elective but cannot be used at the same time. If these two properties are designated, the service will return 400 error request. If you do not know tenantId, you can send a "" as a request for tenantID and gain this ID from the returned message
token (elective)	capi:UUID	Token. If you cannot provide token, user name and password must be provided

3.2 Localized Interface Realization Technology

Localized interface is shortened as JNI (Java Native Interface) to provide API for realize communications between JAVA language and other languages. In this system, the virtual machine scheduling command in OpenStack cloud platform is encapsulated into executable scripts and then stored into memory. The background of elastic resource allocation system is realized by JAVA language, which adopts JNI technology to execute the scripts in local servers and obtain relevant data to return back to system background. Take the virtual machine initiation function for example [14], the realization steps are as follows:

(1) Statically load the dynamic linkage library of localized interface encapsulation in system background function module. The code is as follows:

```
static
{
System.loadLibrary("novaList");
}
```

(2) Declare localized realization method, transfer the localized realization. The code is as follows:
    private native String novaBootJNI (String flavorId, String imageId, String name);
(3) Accomplish localized realization in C language. The method is declared as follows:
    JNIEXPORT jstring JNICALL Java_com_execute_ssh_ExecuteSSH_nova-BootJNI (JNIEnv * env, jobject jo, jstring flavorId, jstring imageId, jstring name)

4   System Performance Test

During performance test, electromagnetic calculation algorithm, FDTD algorithm is operated on each virtual machine in elastic resource allocation system for performance test. This algorithm possesses the features of medium communication amount and large calculation amount and can carry out multi-core parallel calculation in a single machine or among multiple machines through network connection, thus achieving the test on calculation capability and network environmental calculation capability.

4.1   Calculation Performance Test for Single Virtual Machine

This test is carried out on the physical machine and the virtual machine created by elastic resource allocation system respectively. Table 3 shows the testing hardware configuration environment.

Table 3. Single-point test environment

Resource type	Resource name	Description	Quantity
Physical resource	DELL workstation	Octa-core CPU, 16 GB memory	1
Platform resource	Platform virtual machine	Octa-core VCPU, 16 GB memory	1

FDTD algorithm is used in these two environments for four calculations respectively. Table 4 shows the calculation results.

Table 4. Single-point test result

Resource type	First test results	Second test result	Third test result	Fourth test result	Average time
Physical resources	3997 s	4003 s	3978 s	3877 s	3963.75 s
Platform resource	4015 s	4211 s	4008 s	3997 s	4057.75 s

The average of the results of four calculations is obtained and thus the calculation time under platform virtual machine environment is about 1.02 times the calculation time of physical machine. The tests show that the operation performance in virtual machine environment is close to the performance of physical machine. Through platform automatic task operation and resource monitoring, the users can obtain the flexibility in operation and environment management with low performance loss.

4.2   Calculation Performance Test for Multiple Virtual Machine

This test adopts four sets of machines for calculation of FDTD cases. The testing environment for each set is the same as the environment in single machine test. Likewise, four calculations are carried out in these two environments respectively. Table 5 shows the calculation time results:

Table 5. Multi-point test result

Resource type	First test results	Second test result	Third test result	Fourth test result	Average time
Physical resource	4181 s	4103 s	4456 s	4480 s	4305 s
Platform resource	4691 s	4589 s	4983 s	5016 s	4819.75 s

Similarly, the average of the results of four calculations is obtained and thus the calculation time for virtual resources provided by the platform is about 1.12 times the calculation time of physical machine. The original calculation time is 89.3% of the calculation time under platform environment. Therefore, it can be seen that the performance loss of virtual machine environment provided by the platform is only about 10%. In addition, it can be seen that after the network delay is introduced, the calculation time of both the physical machine and the virtual machine environment increase. Although the time increases, this distributed calculation environment provides stronger calculation environment, which actually solves a more complex problem and obtains higher calculation precision. In the meanwhile, the calculation environment provided by the platform greatly simplifies the deployment and management of distributed calculation environment and facilitates the users.

5   Conclusion

Elastic resource allocation system realizes the scheduling and management of virtual resources based on OpenStack platform. Its main functions include virtual machine management and control, network resource management, user information management and image module management. The system provides humanized image interface and allocates the virtual resources flexibly and efficiently for the users.

References

1. Fei, X., Jing, Y., Liming, L.: Design and implementation of computer lab self-service platform based on openstack. Comput. Modern. **7**, 52 (2013)
2. Mingli, W., Tianhong, R., Yebai, L.: Application and research of resource management technology based on openstack private cloud platform. Ind. Technol. Innov. **2**(3), 334–341 (2015)
3. Shaoka, Z., Liyao, L., Xiao, L., Cong, X., Jiahai, Y.: Architecture and scheduling scheme design of tsinghua cloud platform based on openstack. J. Comput. Appl. **33**(12), 3335–3338, 3349 (2013)
4. Jinpeng, H., Qin, L., Chunming, H.: Research and design on hypervisor based virtual computing environment. J. Softw. **18**(8), 2016–2026 (2007)
5. Xianfeng, S., Junchuan, J., Xiaojun, Z.: Private cloud APCS platform design based on virtualization technology. Comput. Eng. **38**(8), 200–212 (2011)
6. Zhao, W.M., Wang, Z.L., Luo, Y.W.: Dynamic memory balancing for virtual machines. ACM SIGOPS Oper. Syst. Rev. **43**(3), 37–47 (2009)
7. Zhang, J., Gu, Z., Zheng, C.: Survey of research progress on cloud computing. Appl. Res. Comput. **27**(2), 429–433 (2010)
8. Wensheng, Z.: Application research of software virtualization in computer lab. China Electr. Power Educ. **8**, 113–114 (2012)
9. Mell, P., Grance, T.: The NIST definition of cloud computing (draft). NIST **800**(145), 7 (2011)
10. Zhuhua, W.: Analysis of Core Technologies of Cloud Computing. Posts & Telecom Press, Beijing (2011)
11. Qiang, X., Zhenjiang, W., Computing, C.: Application Development Practices. China Machine Press, Beijing (2012)
12. OpenStack. OpenStack Documentation [EB/OL]
13. http://docs.openstack.org. Accessed 16 Sep 2012
14. Peng, L.: Cloud Computing, 2nd edn. Publishing House of Electronics Industry, Beijing (2011)
15. Hua, Z.: Application of cloud computing technology in construction of university green computer labs. Value Eng. **11**, 180–181 (2012)

Edge Affine Invariant Moment for Texture Image Feature Extraction

Yiwen Dou[(⊠)], Jun Wang, Jun Qiang, and Ganyi Tang

College of Information and Computing Sciences, Anhui Polytechnic University,
Wuhu 241000, Anhui, People's Republic of China
yiwend@sina.com

Abstract. Texture image feature extraction is one of hot topics of texture image recognition in recent years. As to this, a novel technique for texture image feature extraction based on edge affine invariant moment is presented in this paper. Firstly, each texture image is checked by a short step affine transformation Sobel algorithm initially. Then, the corresponding texture image feature named edge affine invariant moment will be calculated and added to feature vector set. Subsequently, cluster analysis will be loaded upon the set by K-means algorithm and the categorized texture image can be obtained. Three simulation experiments closed to real environment over the two well-known Brodatz and KTH-TIPS texture databases are performed in order to test the efficiency of our proposed algorithm.

Keywords: EAIM (edge affine invariant moment) · Feature extraction · K-means · SSAT (short step affine transformation Sobel)

1 Introduction

Image texture analysis is a hot issue in many fields such as computer vision [1], image retrieval [2], image processing [3] and machine vision [4] etc. Its ambiguous definitions lead to non-unified framework structure for image texture analysis till now. In spite of different research contents about texture image segmentation [5], classification [6], synthesis [7], retrieval [8] and restoration [9] etc., its essential work is to extract texture features [10]. At present, the main goal of texture feature extraction is good robustness and high computational efficiency.

The typical method of texture feature extraction includes two major categories. One is based on point feature and another based on gray feature. The feature vector of SIFT or SURF is extracted from the texture feature based on the feature extraction. Because SIFT is not a global feature descriptor, Yong Xu et al. [11] proposed a multi-fractal spectrum method which can extract the global feature descriptor of texture images. This SIFT-like descriptor had been applied to both static and dynamic textures and resulted in good extraction performance. Jayaraman et al. [12] used SURF to obtain the iris texture features, and these features will be used to classify initial iris color feature data. The method ultimately improves the accuracy of iris recognition. Those feature extractions based on point feature can obtain too much point features and

© ICST Institute for Computer Sciences, Social Informatics and Telecommunications Engineering 2017
F. Chen and Y. Luo (Eds.): Industrial IoT 2017, LNICST 202, pp. 83–90, 2017.
DOI: 10.1007/978-3-319-60753-5_9

are easily disturbed by many kinds of noise. Obviously, they fail to meet the practical application requirements of texture feature extraction.

Siqueira et al. [13] used Gaussian multi-scale expression and image pyramid to extend the gray level co-occurrence matrix so as to obtain multi-scale texture feature. They applied their algorithm to five benchmark texture data sets and got a good recognition effects. However, in the calculation of the gray level co-occurrence matrix, it is necessary to calculate the probability of the co-occurrence of the pixels in the distances and directions and it also needs to calculate more texture features. So the drawbacks of texture feature extraction based on gray feature become more and more prominent.

In recent years, the research based on line features, especially on the edge feature is more state-of-the-art. Compared with point and surface features, line features can not only reduce noise interference factors but also improve calculation efficiency.

In this paper, we propose a feature extraction method based on edge affine invariant moments (EAIM) for texture image feature extraction. The edge image is obtained by short step affine transformation Sobel algorithm (SSAT [14]) and then its edge affine invariant moment will be calculated to build feature vectors. Finally, the K-means algorithm [15] is used to classify texture images in feature vectors space.

The rest of this paper is organized as follows. In Sect. 2, we briefly introduce some related work about texture image feature extraction methods and SSAT. The detailed derivation process of the proposed EAIM is described in Sect. 3. In Sect. 4, experiment results are analyzed and discussed. Finally, conclusions and further research are addressed in last section.

2   Related Work

2.1   Short Step Affine Transformation Sobel

Usually in complex environment, images will be enormously affected by light changing. At that time, we cannot get good edge information because of low illumination. In [14],

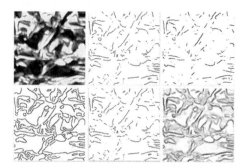

Fig. 1. Edge images obtained by different edge extraction methods (The first row shows the original image, Prewitt and Roberts segmentation effects, respectively. The second row shows canny, sobel and SSAT segmentation effect, respectively.)

the authors proposed SSAT method which is used affine invariance to extract image edge directly. In order to reduce the influence of light interference, we will use this edge extraction algorithm to promote the real-time ability of our scheme.

As can be seen from Fig. 1, Canny operator preserves the best details of the edge image and the distinction between the target and the background is also shown better than the others. SSAT algorithm outperform the Prewitt, Roberts and Sobel operator because its mechanism.

2.2   Sift and Surf

SIFT descriptors [16] are obtained by using difference of Gaussian (DoG) and gradient histogram based on 128-dimensional vector. The application of this feature description to object classification is the classic strategy of pattern recognition. SURF local feature description [17] is built on the SIFT algorithm. SURF's box filter obtains multi-scale pyramid images by convoluting the original image and performs fast Hessian matrix approximation in the integral image. These strategies make SURF obtaining faster feature points calculation.

However, as to complicated and overloaded texture image, more feature points mean the algorithm will spend more time to calculate and it results in wasting the recognition efficiency. So SIFT and SURF are all less used to extract the texture features in real.

From Fig. 2, we can see that texture feature extraction using feature points can not carry out accurate texture image description which will greatly affect the effect of classification recognition.

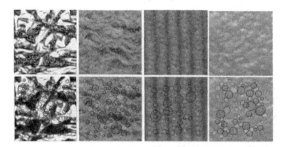

Fig. 2. SIFT and SURF feature extraction of texture images (The first and the second row are SIFT and SURF feature extraction respectively.)

2.3   Gray Level Co-occurrence Matrices

GLMC [18] is used as a statistical method to describe the image texture information method. First, the matrix is constructed according to the direction and distance between those image pixels, and then the meaningful statistical features are extracted from the matrix to describe the texture. Because the texture is the adjacent pixel or the adjacent region on the grayscale geometric position of the relationship between the character-izations or the statistics in the same position of the relationship between a pair of gray-scale pixel correlation, you can use some conditional probability of this pair of pixels to describe its texture characteristics. However, because of the huge computa-tional complexity, it is not the first choice in real-time systems.

The process of extracting texture features is introduced briefly. In the following we will give a series of mathematical description and a set of edge affine invariant moments.

3   Edge Affine Invariant Moment

3.1   Edge Moment

The basic definition of the $(p + q)$th continuous edge moments [19] in 2D is given below:

$$e_{pq} = \int_L x^p y^q ds \qquad (1)$$

where L is the edge curve of closet region Ω, $p, q = 0, 1, 2, \cdots$, $ds = \sqrt{(dx)^2 + (dy)^2}$.

3.2   Edge Affine Invariant Moment

In practical applications, we define the edge center moment as follows:

$$\mu_{pq} = \int_L (x - \bar{x})^p (y - \bar{y})^q ds \qquad (2)$$

Due to the discretization of CCD equipment, the edge center moment should be considered as written by discrete form. Naturally, the smaller the physical distance along the axis x and the axis y in the imaging plane of the CCD device, the closer the value of the discrete-form edge moment approximates the continuous form. Here we give a set of edge affine [20] invariants as follows:

$$E_0 = \frac{1}{\mu_{00}^2} \left(\mu_{20}\mu_{02} - \mu_{11}^2 \right) \qquad (3)$$

$$E_1 = \frac{1}{\mu_{00}^7} \left(\mu_{30}^2 \mu_{03}^2 - 6\mu_{30}\mu_{12}\mu_{21}\mu_{03} + 4\mu_{30}\mu_{12}^3 + 4\mu_{21}^3 \mu_{03} - 3\mu_{21}^2 \mu_{12}^2 \right) \qquad (4)$$

$$E_2 = \frac{1}{\mu_{00}^7} \left[\mu_{20} \left(\mu_{21}\mu_{03} - \mu_{12}^2 \right) - \mu_{11} \left(\mu_{30}\mu_{03} - \mu_{21}\mu_{12} \right) + \mu_{02} \left(\mu_{30}\mu_{12} - \mu_{21}^2 \right) \right] \qquad (5)$$

$$E_3 = \frac{1}{\mu_{00}^7} (\mu_{20}^3 \mu_{03}^2 - 6\mu_{20}^2 \mu_{11} \mu_{12} \mu_{03} - 6\mu_{20}^2 \mu_{02} \mu_{21} \mu_{03}$$
$$+ 9\mu_{20}^2 \mu_{02} \mu_{12}^2 + 12\mu_{20} \mu_{11}^2 \mu_{21} \mu_{03} + 6\mu_{20} \mu_{11} \mu_{02} \mu_{03} \mu_{30}$$
$$- 18\mu_{20} \mu_{11} \mu_{12} \mu_{21} \mu_{02} - 8\mu_{11}^3 \mu_{30} \mu_{03} - 6\mu_{20} \mu_{02}^2 \mu_{30} \mu_{12} \tag{6}$$
$$+ 9\mu_{20} \mu_{02}^2 \mu_{21}^2 + 12\mu_{11}^2 \mu_{02} \mu_{12} \mu_{30} - 6\mu_{11} \mu_{02}^2 \mu_{30} \mu_{21} + \mu_{02}^3 \mu_{30}^2)$$

$$E_4 = \frac{1}{\mu_{00}^6} \left(\mu_{40} \mu_{04} - 4\mu_{13} \mu_{31} + 3\mu_{22}^2 \right) \tag{7}$$

$$E_5 = \left(\mu_{40} \mu_{04} \mu_{22} + 2\mu_{31} \mu_{13} \mu_{22} - 4\mu_{40} \mu_{13}^2 - 4\mu_{04} \mu_{31}^2 - \mu_{22}^3 \right) \tag{8}$$

where μ_{pq} is the edge center moment.

3.3 Algorithm Flows

In order to clearly express the texture feature extraction process proposed in this paper, we draw the actual application process shown in Fig. 3.

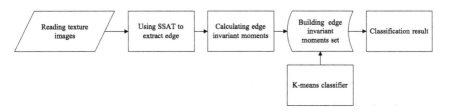

Fig. 3. Flow chart of our proposed scheme

When the texture image is read, our proposed scheme will call SSAT algorithm to extract the corresponding edge image. However, the SSAT itself needs to provide the detection threshold to determine whether it is an edge point. For uniformity, the edge detection threshold is fixed to 0.5. After calculating six EAIM, a set of feature vectors ($E0$, $E1$, $E2$, $E3$, $E4$, $E5$) can be arranged and added to the EAIM sets. And then, the classified recognition results will be obtained by K-means classifier.

4 Simulation and Experiments

In order to test the validity and robustness of the proposed method, we choose Brodatz and KTH-TIPS texture databases. Although the texture images in the above two kinds of texture libraries have changes in rotation, scale, and so on in the acquisition process, they need to be tested for robustness and brightness of the current algorithm. So, a certain degree extension had been added to texture databases. Figure 4 shows a partially expanded texture image.

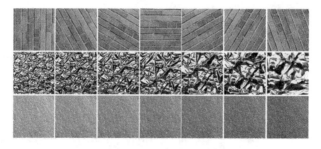

Fig. 4. Some samples in the extended texture database (The first row shows the rotation of the brick. The second row describes the scale change of aluminium foil. The third row is the brightness change of orange peel)

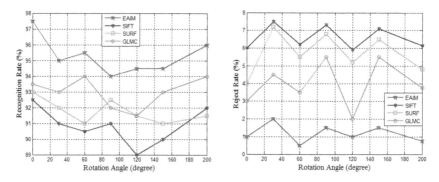

Fig. 5. Comparison of texture feature recognition results during image rotation

Figure 5 shows that the texture recognition rate based on edge affine invariant moment is higher than the other three feature extraction methods while the reject rate is the lowest. The relative error of reject rate of our proposed scheme only reaches 2% and the changing range of recognition rate is from 94% to 97.5%. At the same time, we notice that the recognition and the reject rate are periodic due to the symmetry of rotation.

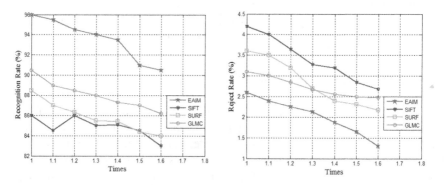

Fig. 6. Comparison of texture feature recognition results during image scale change

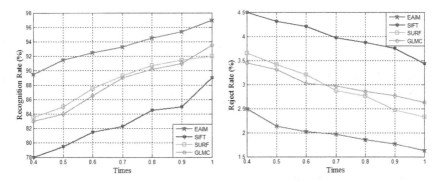

Fig. 7. Comparison of texture feature recognition results during light change

We fix image center and increase the scale of the original image in turn. It can be seen from Fig. 6 that the larger the scale, that is, the more concentrated on local detail, the more similar samples will be obtained. So, it also results in lower reject rate. But the overall loss of information is higher, and thus the recognition rate is lower.

At last, we reduce the brightness of the original image, and use different algorithms to obtain the features of classification and recognition. It can be seen from Fig. 7 that the smaller the brightness, that is, the more difficult to distinguish the local details, the greater the reject rate and because of higher loss of information, the recognition accuracy is low.

It can be seen from the above simulation experiments that the edge affine invariant moment can not only overcome the interference of rotation and scale change, but also is not sensitive to the change of brightness. It is a worthy of generalization of texture feature extraction method.

5 Conclusion and Further Research

In this paper, a new approach is proposed for texture image feature extraction from edge affine invariant moment. The performance of our proposed approach is evaluated by applying EAIM on tow important texture data sets and the results are compared to other well-known descriptors for texture analysis. The algorithm is very simple and possesses less complexity. The proposed approach achieved significant improvements for all tested datasets. To further enhance texture classification performance, some good classifier, such as SVM, will be included in our future research.

Acknowledgments. This work was supported in part by the Major Projects of Nature Science Research in Universities of Anhui (No. KJ2015ZD06), the Key Projects of Nature Science Research in Anhui Universities (No. KJ2015A311, KJ2015A353, KJ2016A802), and Provincial Nature Science Research Project of Anhui Province Higher Education Promotion Plan (No. TSKJ2014B06, TSKJ2015B16).

References

1. Shrivastava, V.K., et al.: Computer-aided diagnosis of psoriasis skin images with HOS, texture and color features: a first comparative study of its kind. Comput. Methods Programs Biomed. **126**, 98–109 (2016)
2. Zheng, X., et al.: Study on image retrieval based on image texture and color statistical projection. Neurocomputing **215**, 217–224 (2016)
3. Song, C., et al.: Bayesian non-parametric gradient histogram estimation for texture-enhanced image deblurring. Neurocomputing **197**, 95–112 (2016)
4. Junior, J.J.D.M.S., Backes, A.R.: ELM based signature for texture classification. Pattern Recogn. **51**, 395–401 (2016)
5. Min, H., et al.: An intensity-texture model based level set method for image segmentation. Pattern Recogn. **48**, 1547–1562 (2015)
6. Cernadas, E., et al.: Influence of normalization and color space to color texture classification. Pattern Recogn. **61**, 120–138 (2016)
7. Casaca, W., et al.: Combining anisotropic diffusion, transport equation and texture synthesis for inpainting textured images. Pattern Recogn. Lett. **36**, 36–45 (2014)
8. Raghuwanshi, G., Tyagi, V.: Texture image retrieval using adaptive tetrolet transforms. Digit. Signal Proc. **48**, 50–57 (2015)
9. Pang, Z.F., Yang, Y.F.: A projected gradient algorithm based on the augmented Lagrangian strategy for image restoration and texture extraction. Image Vis. Comput. **29**, 117–126 (2011)
10. Liu, L., et al.: Local binary features for texture classification: taxonomy and experimental study. Pattern Recognit. **62**, 135–160 (2017)
11. Yong, X., et al.: Scale-space texture description on SIFT-like textons. Comput. Vis. Image Underst. **116**, 999–1013 (2012)
12. Jayaraman, U., Prakash, S., Gupta, P.: An efficient color and texture based iris image retrieval technique. Expert Syst. Appl. **39**, 4915–4926 (2012)
13. Siqueira, F.R., Schwartz, W.R., Pedrini, H.: Multi-scale gray level co-occurrence matrices for texture description. Neurocomputing **120**, 336–345 (2013)
14. Dou, Y., Hao, K., Ding, Y.: A short step affine transformation Sobel algorithm based image edge detection in low illumination. In: Proceedings of 2015 Chinese Automation Congress, IEEE, Wuhan, China, November, pp. 594–597 (2015). doi:10.1109/CAC.2015.7382569
15. Zhao, L., et al.: Fault condition recognition based on multi-scale texture features and embedding prior knowledge k-means for antimony flotation process. IFAC Papersonline **48**, 864–870 (2015)
16. Lenc, L., Král, P.: Automatic face recognition system based on the SIFT features Comput. Electr. Eng. **46**, 256–272 (2015)
17. Kashif, M., et al.: Feature description with SIFT, SURF, BRIEF, BRISK, or FREAK? A general question answered for bone age assessment. Comput. Biol. Med. **68**, 67–75 (2015)
18. Yang, P., Yang, G.: Feature extraction using dual-tree complex wavelet transform and gray level co-occurrence matrix. Neurocomputing **197**, 212–220 (2016)
19. Honarvar, B., Paramesran, R., Lim, C.L.: Image reconstruction from a complete set of geometric and complex moments. Sig. Process. **98**, 224–232 (2014)
20. Yamashita, Y., Wakahara, T.: Affine-transformation and 2D-projection invariant k-NN classification of handwritten characters via a new matching measure. Pattern Recogn. **52**, 459–470 (2015)

Intelligent Private Fitness System Based on ARM and Hybrid Internet of Things

Zihao Wang[1], Zhengnan Yuan[2], He Xu[1,3(✉)], and Caleb Eghan[4]

[1] School of Computer Science,
Nanjing University of Posts and Telecommunications, Nanjing 210023, China
1390424429@qq.com
[2] University of Electronic Science and Technology of China, Chengdu, Sichuan, China
916260629@qq.com
[3] Jiangsu High Technology Research Key Laboratory for Wireless Sensor Networks,
Nanjing 210003, China
xuhe@njupt.edu.cn
[4] Overseas Education College,
Nanjing University of Posts and Telecommunications, Nanjing 210023, China
calebeghan@yahoo.com

Abstract. With the purpose of being fit, slim and active, a popular trend of gym culture is sweeping the whole current society. However, some drawbacks have gradually surfaced. On top of that, facing some of the common barriers, those new styles of different body-building activities could even do more harm then good to the individuals where these negative effect on the long-time training is not visible until the individual is facing physical injuries. For those reasons, this paper proposed a novel personal fitness system based on the ARM which attempts to match the requests of environmental friendly. Specifically, inventing a more scientific option of body building than the traditional gym to prevent incorrect ways of training and guide the individuals to do healthy exercises by utilizing visual personal training system and internet to design a distributed mobile application.

Keywords: Private fitness system · ARM · Energy conservation · IoT system

1 Introduction

The gym culture is affecting our daily life with pros and cons. Firstly, exercising in poor ventilated gym will lead to the inhaling of hazardous particles such as carbon dioxide which could cause damage to the respiratory system [1]. Secondly, the demand of equipment and coaches enlarge the usage of fake and inferior supply. Some poorly-funded gyms choose equipment with safety problems. For common people, weekends are their only time of going to the gym while they tend to get no chance of doing proper exercise since these gyms are already full of people. Last but not the least, commercials in the public media and

© ICST Institute for Computer Sciences, Social Informatics and Telecommunications Engineering 2017
F. Chen and Y. Luo (Eds.): Industrial IoT 2017, LNICST 202, pp. 91–101, 2017.
DOI: 10.1007/978-3-319-60753-5_10

commercialize operational system lure consumers to go to the gyms with a low cost performance but a high threshold [2]. As a result, some of them are not qualified as a high standard gym.

This idea is inspired by the research we conduct about smart home. Since a lot of research is poured in improving the environment of gymnasiums such as "The new public gymnasium air purification intelligent control system" [3] and "Unhealthy factors in the gym" [4], we began to wonder if there is an alternative way of working out. Combined IoT technology, we present a personal fitness system which is highly innovative, because the latest paper we can find that is similar to our project is "Virtual intelligent fitness system based on embedded ARM" [5] from 9 years ago. Meanwhile, scattered research achievements like Heart Rate Monitoring Systems in Groups for Assessment of Cardiorespiratory Fitness Analysis or "Smart shoes design with embedded monitoring electronics system for health-care and fitness applications" [6] and "Healthy Together: exploring social incentives for mobile fitness applications" [7] have enabled us to build a multi-functional integrated fitness system as a substitute which has not been taken into account of by sales market despite of such sophisticated R&D environment.

This paper proposes the idea of personalizing the fitness activities so that each person could exercise with the guidance of the 'personal coach' and tailor-made equipment in the form of applications. As a result, the quality of the equipment and coaches, exercising environment, scientific methods of exercising and a low cost performance could be ensured. According to the feedbacks collected by the sensors of pressure, visual, gravity and so on by the equipment to the consumers, those processed information could guide consumers intelligently to do healthy exercise. Individuals do not have to stand in the lines for the treadmills, bench press equipment and exercise bicycles. Apart from that, the lack of resources and misleading problem could be settled.

2   System Designation

The core part of our proposed system is based on the ARM (Acorn RISC Machine) which presents a high cost performance, code density, excellent real-time interrupt response and low electricity consuming with a small piece of silicon chip. Specifically, ARM is an ideal option for the embedded system that could assume more significant functions other simple SCM (Single Chip Micyoco) cannot, for instance, micro control system 51 Series and Arduino. It also has enough pins of GPIO and ADC (Digital Analog Conversion) that can be connected to the number of sensors. Additionally, its external RAM and ROM could strengthen the ability of algorithms and memories. External screens have the ability of making the operations more humanized. Built-in value-set registers enable the system to update the data from the cloud. All those advantages make the ARM the best choice of completing the fitness system.

The basic design is built on the entire integral fitness equipment. As Fig. 1 shows, energy conversion and storage system on the bottom layer of the fitness

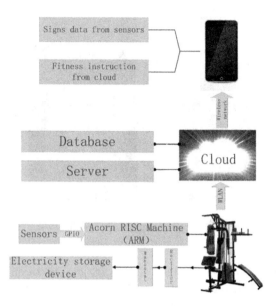

Fig. 1. System structure.

equipment is an innovation of this project. First of all, small-scale generators are installed on each body-building module and stored in the storage devices after adjustment to reduce or even avoid the power loss. Secondly, several sensors (the processor is ARM) are embedded to construct the base of the feedbacks to the mobile terminal. Moreover, data are sent by the ARM through Wi-Fi to Cloud services and database to be integrated with those are already in the cloud before sending to the mobile terminal app. Eventually the consumers are able to gain intuitive results of exercising with processed data from sensors.

3 System Realization

3.1 Energy-Saving System

Considering energy-saving and emission reduction, several small-scale generators with a common output are installed on the bottom layer of the highly integrated fitness equipment. Since different means of exercises would generate various kinds and scales of currents, the rectified module is added to transform all the DC (directive current) and AC (alternative current) into DC output. To protect the energy storage module from breaking down by the high voltage and ensure a stable output, a module of adjusting voltage is designed by choosing capacitors as a snuffer in the energy storage module. After this adjustment, the time of charging and discharging is reduced and the circuits of charging is becoming more simple by the use of capacitance which is more suitable for the centralized fitness system with proper control circuit rather than battery.

Fig. 2. Energy-saving system realization.

In the stimulating system as shown in Fig. 2, The AC terminal and its diagonal position of KBPC3510 (diode rectifier) are connected to the anode and cathode of the generator respectively. Likewise, the positive terminal and its diagonal position is connected to the anode and cathode of the load which is corresponding to the LM2596 in this system. As for LM2596, the part with completed function of protecting circuit and current limitation, is the output module of the step-down power source control chip with a fixed frequency oscillator (150 kHz) and reference voltage regulator (1.23 V). Utilizing this module and several peripheral components, an efficient circuit with adjusted voltage could be built.

3.2   Data Collecting on ARM

The sensors, such as pressure sensor and pulse sensor, with a carrier of ARM are the basic neurons of the intelligence. For instance, the system could use pressure sensor to estimate if the gesture is standard, pulse sensor to estimate if the amount of exercise has reached the consumer's max physical limit. Also, a speed sensor can be introduced on the chain to detect if users are moderately operating the equipment. Those data could then be shown to the users through WAP browser to ensure a proper gestures and sports intensity which could even be more thorough than the coaches of the gym. Take the pulse sensor (Fig. 3) as an example to set the ARM register: Pulse Sensor measures human being's heart beat by various light transmittance of the human tissue in the veins followed by the process of ARM to transform the stimulate signals into digital signals [8]. Finally, the signals are transformed into electric signals and amplified for an easier calculation.

```
Part of pseudo-code:
rTSADCCON1  |= (1<<16); // resolution set to 12bit
rTSADCCON1  |= (1<<14);      // enable clock prescaler
rTSADCCON1  &= ~(0xFF<<6);
rTSADCCON1  |= (65<<6);// convertor clock=66/66M=1MHz, MSPS=200KHz
rTSADCCON1  &= ~(1<<2);// normal operation mode
rTSADCCON1  &= ~(1<<1);// disable start by read mode
rADCMUX     &= ~(0x0F<<0);
rADCMUX     |= (1<<0);       // MUX choose ADCIN1
while (external interrupt){
    rTSADCCON1  |= (1<<0);           //open ADC
    while (!(rTSADCCON1 & (1<<15))); //wait for opening
      val = rTSDATX1;                    //data from pulsesensor
        upload( val & (0xFFF<<0));
        delay();
}
```

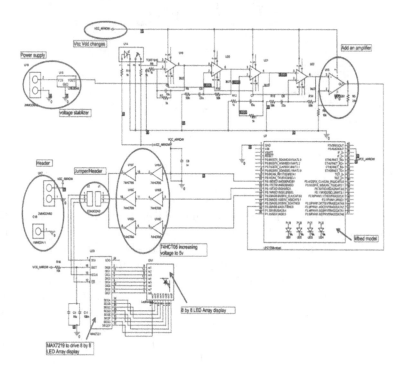

Fig. 3. Pulse sensor circuit realization.

3.3 System Realization Based on Arduino

By presenting a simulated embedded back muscles trainer we can intuitively understand the feasibility of this project. Back muscles trainer is a rather complicated equipment which can demonstrate most of the interfaces needed in this system. So once this part is tackled, we can finish the rest rapidly. The simulated system is based on Arduino, which is more affordable for students and can perform as well as ARM in simple development.

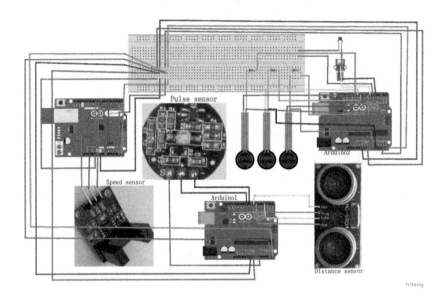

Fig. 4. Schematic of intelligent back muscles trainer based on Arduino.

As initially intended, the sensors are introduced for motion correcting. The schematic is showed in Fig. 4. Sensors are placed on 3 Arduinos to avoid interrupts set for the sensors interfering each other. THD11 is added on Arduino2 to judge the need for warm-up by reading the room temperature. There are also three pressure sensors on Arduino2. Two of them are to detect which part of the bar is held, because which part users hold determines which part of muscles users exercise. The third pressure sensor serves as counter with an external interrupt set. Pulse sensor and range sensor (HC-SR04) are placed on Arduino1. A FIFO queue is used on data from HC-SR04 to acquire the shortest distance which can be combined with users' height gathered from application to calculate if users pull the bar low enough. Timer interrupts are introduced on pulse sensor and speed sensor on Arduino BT (Arduino3) to fulfill the security needs. I2C serial communication technique is applied for data transmission between Arduinos and Bluetooth is used to connect mobile terminal.

```
Key Code:
  Wire.requestFrom(2, 6);
  while(Wire.available())
  {
    count = Wire.read()*256 + Wire.read();
    Serial.print(count); Serial.print('/');
    which = Wire.read()*256 + Wire.read();
    Serial.print(which); Serial.print('/');
    temp = Wire.read()*256 + Wire.read();
    Serial.print(temp); Serial.print('/');
  }

  Wire.requestFrom(3, 6);
  while(Wire.available())
  {
    heart = Wire.read()*256 + Wire.read();
    Serial.print(heart); Serial.print('/');
    cmH = Wire.read()*256 + Wire.read();
    cmL = Wire.read()*256 + Wire.read();
    cm[0] = cm[1]; cm[1] = cm[2];
    cm[2] = (double)cmH+(double)cmL/100;
  }
  if(cm[1]<=cm[0]&&cm[1]<=cm[2])
    mc = cm[1];
  Serial.print(mc); Serial.print('/');
  Serial.println(speet);
  delay(300);
}
```

3.4   Communication Module on ARM

Wi-Fi, a technology that normally uses the radio frequency of 2.4G UHF or 5G SHF ISM, allows the electronic devices connected into the WLAN (Wireless Local Area Network). One of the most significant features of the WLAN is that the internet terminals do not need to be connected by the internet cable, which makes the construction of the internet and the mobile of terminals more flexible.

This system updates the data directly to the cloud without utilizing the traditional sports sensors link between cells and sensors. One of the reasons is that the function of building the base station through the ARM could update the data directly through WLAN. On the other hand, the data that are processed in the cloud could be more accurate than those from ARM terminals. Moreover, the information that state in front of the consumers could be more variable.

The flowchart of the structure of Wi-Fi devices with the software of Linux is shown as Fig. 5. (including WLAN and SPI port drives). In other words, WLAN drive is the interface of the whole process of receiving the data flow from the first stage applications and emitting information through the SPI to the Wi-Fi

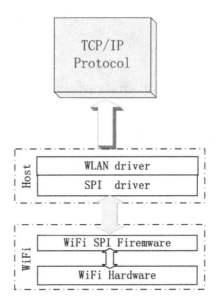

Fig. 5. The structure of Wi-Fi devices.

hardware device. Additionally, if the response from the Wi-Fi hardware devices is cut off, it would read the data from the snuffer region and send them to the first stage applications by the protocol function registered by the programmer [9].

3.5   Feedback Interface and Cloud Server

The cloud and mobile terminals demonstrates the mechanized data and information in front of us in a mimic way as demonstrated in Fig. 6. The cloud data has two parts: first of all, storage of the information from the ARM with the basic information of the consumers forms a view history where people could keep a trace on their effect of body building. Secondly, all kind of recommendation in the cloud could be shared to different groups of people by analyzing their information in cloud. An algorithm is expected to offer them a more scientific way of doing exercise, for instance, share motivating articles about keeping fit to the over-weight groups, and advanced articles that contain more professional guidance to consumers who are already fit and doing exercise regularly.

Nowadays, the methods of cloud storage and transmission are rather sophisticated. Apart from that, mobile application programming has been mastered by a growing number of people. Mysql, thanks to the application of WEB that could be easily used because of the compatibility for most of the programming languages, can customize databases on cloud according to the need of users. On top of that, Apache, an admirable choice of WEB server of WAMP or LAMP is often chosen by most of developers. The PHP (Professional hypertext Preprocessor) is a free open-source scripting language for the service terminal of learning

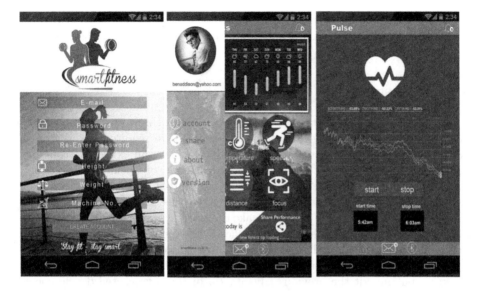

Fig. 6. Mobile App.

```
mysql> select * from userinfo
    -> ;
+----+----------+----------+
| id | username | password |
+----+----------+----------+
|  1 | do       | 4        |
|  2 | GG       | 44       |
|  3 | q        | 1        |
+----+----------+----------+
3 rows in set (0.08 sec)

mysql> select * from sportinfo;
+----+----------------------+-----------+----------+-----------+---------
---+----------------+------------+-------------+------------+
| id | uid                  | heart_mes            | tmp_mes | sport_mes | light_m
es | generation_mes | sport_time | calorie_mes | date       |
+----+----------------------+-----------+----------+-----------+---------
---+----------------+------------+-------------+------------+
|  1 | <!DOCTYPE HTML PUBLI | 91.4                 | 37.2 C  | 1968J     | 20.4min
   | 4.2?           | 00:15      | 203k        | 2016-11-10 |
| 45 | <!DOCTYPE HTML PUBLI | 46.75                | 37.2 C  | 2232J     | 21.2min
   | 4.2°C          | 00:14      | 213K        | 2016-11-12 |
```

Fig. 7. Data stored on cloud server.

construct dynamic interactive stage. It can also be used cross-platform such as between a Windows or Linux on cloud (Fig. 7). Those kinds of platforms are becoming more and more common, the obstacles in the exploration of the cloud and mobile terminal are barely seen in the current network environment [10].

Along with the development of IoT, the interaction between human and computer becoming more diversified, which means once the interface is provided, technically, we can communicate with one another. Cloud storage enable us to share experience to others, and this feature cater the basic need of being listened. This is the point of this project and the reason it can outperform gym culture.

We focus more on matching fitness with the daily requirement. With a friendly interface shown to users, it is a more effective way to overcome the obstacles mentioned above.

4   Conclusions

A foundation of an industry is not that easy to be overthrown by several experimental experiments. A large quantities of capitals are required if this fitness system is coming onto the market. However, to achieve an expected economic benefit, one of the idea is to match the rigid demand of consumers to attract more users and to sell more entities to gain more profit. A set of sophisticated system after R&D can be manufactured at market price of approximately $1300. The match of hardware and software make the training more scientific and safer. Likewise, facing the shortage on the coaches in the gym, the matching application could enable users to have a personal area to work out with professional instructions. As the replacement of the gym culture, it not only gets rid of the weakness but inherit the previous advantages. In the skyrocketed development IoT industry, our lifestyle is supposed to have more changes than ever by getting rid of the out-of-date methods and choosing the more scientific ones.

Acknowledgments. This work is financially supported by the National Natural Science Foundation of P. R. China (No. 61373017, No. 61572260, No. 61572261, No. 61672296, No. 61602261), the Natural Science Foundation of Jiangsu Province (No. BK20140886, No. BK20140888), Scientific & Technological Support Project of Jiangsu Province (No. BE2015702, BE2016185, No. BE2016777), Natural Science Key Fund for Colleges and Universities in Jiangsu Province (No. 12KJA520002), China Postdoctoral Science Foundation (No. 2014M551636, No. 2014M561696), Jiangsu Planned Projects for Postdoctoral Research Funds (No. 1302090B, No. 1401005B), Natural Science Foundation of the Jiangsu Higher Education Institutions of China (Grant No. 14KJB520030), Jiangsu Postgraduate Scientific Research and Innovation Projects (SJLX15_0381, SJLX16_0326), Project of Jiangsu High Technology Research Key Laboratory for Wireless Sensor Networks (WSNLBZY201509), NUPTSF (Grant No. NY214060, No. NY214061) and the STITP projects of NUPT (No. XZD2016032 and No. XYB2016532).

References

1. Chan, G.S.H., Middleton, P.M., Lovell, N.H., Celler, B.G.: Extraction of photoplethysmographic waveform variability by lowpass filtering. In: 27th Annual International Conference of the Engineering in Medicine and Biology Society, pp. 5568–5571. IEEE Press, New York (2005)
2. Lu, D.J., Shen, Y.L.: Research and analysis of body-building environment of gymnasium. J. Sports Sci. **196**, 9–17 (2012)
3. He, J.M., Zhang, N.: The new public gymnasium air purification intelligent control system. Electron. Prod. **14**, 41–42 (2014)
4. Li, D.S., He, Y.Z.: Investigation of quality and safety risks for outdoor body-building equipments. Risk Manage. **35**, 40–43 (2014)

5. Li, L.Y.: Virtual Intelligent Fitness System Based on Embedded ARM. Kunming University of Science and Technology, China (2007)
6. Hwang, P.Y., Chou, C.C., Fang, W.C., Hwang, C.M.: Smart shoes design with embedded monitoring electronics system for healthcare and fitness applications. In: IEEE International Conference on Consumer Electronics-Taiwan (ICCE-TW), pp. 1–2. IEEE press, New York (2016)
7. Chen, Y., Pu, P.: HealthyTogether: exploring social incentives for mobile fitness applications. In: Proceedings of the Second International Symposium of Chinese CHI, pp. 25–34. ACM (2014)
8. Zhu, Y.P.: ARM bare metal the use of ADC, Wuhan, China (2014)
9. Liu, F.H.: Research and Implementation of WiFi Wireless Communication Terminal Based on ARM. Wuhan University of Science and Technology, China (2010)
10. Xuan, H.: The Interaction Design Research of Mobile Social App Based on User Needs Take "Renren Android" as Example. Jangnan University, China (2013)

Research and Application of Security and Privacy in Industrial Internet of Things Based on Fingerprint Encryption

Cong Xie[✉] and Shu-Ting Deng

School of Information Engineering, Guangxi University of Foreign Languages,
Nanning 530222, China
ningjianfeng123@126.com

Abstract. Industrial Internet of things is developing with a high speed, but it also faces the threat from all sides. In order to deal with the security applications of industrial Internet of things, this paper summarizes the security and privacy issues of industrial Internet of Things, then analyzes the common security threats and attacks, and draws on several kinds of fluent security measures, putting forward the security program of Fingerprint encryption. The program combines the fingerprint identification technology, PDF417 code and RC4 encryption method, matching through the fingerprint data to be decoded out. Because the fingerprint information is unique, whether the success of the match can determine whether the operation is by itself, and then decides the next step, protects the user's security and privacy in a great degree.

Keywords: Industrial Internet of Things · Fingerprint technology · PDF417 code · RC4 encryption

1 The Development of Industrial Internet of Things

With the development of industrial technology and intensify of market competition, in order to improve efficiency and product quality, making full use of resources, reducing labor intensity, meeting the needs of mass production, industrial automation came into being. Then, with the development of information technology, industrial automation broke through the limitations of LAN, enterprise information system will be extended to the Internet, achieving the fifth generation of Internet-based industrial automation technology–industrial networking technology.

Industrial Internet of things is related to the traditional things for a few different things: the Internet of Things architecture has a perception layer, transport layer and application layer, but industrial Internet of Things applications are closed-loop, while the other is open-loop; Internet of Things is not so strict to the real-time of the network, but industrial networking has strict requirements of the time synchronization and stable communication; Internet of things is not demanding on the equipment working environment, but industrial Internet of Things is not only in a high temperature, humidity

© ICST Institute for Computer Sciences, Social Informatics and Telecommunications Engineering 2017
F. Chen and Y. Luo (Eds.): Industrial IoT 2017, LNICST 202, pp. 102–110, 2017.
DOI: 10.1007/978-3-319-60753-5_11

and vibration and other harsh environment, but also maintaining smooth in complex network interference.

At present, the industrial Internet of Things is still at the early stage of development, but because of its broad application prospects and huge revenue potential, many large multinational corporations, governments and international organizations have invested heavily in industrial Internet of Things. Such as the second Internet of Things Forum Cisco hosted, Cisco exhibited more than 250 industrial applications case; in 2014, General Electric achieves 1 billion in revenue increase for its global customers through industrial Internet of Things technology and services; Huawei is the acquisition of Neul which is a company of industrial Internet of Things British startups. At the national level, the Chinese and German governments have had a high-level dialogue about jointly promoting the development of "Industrial 4.0", developing two strategy that major manufacturing countries deepen cooperation in the Internet of things and cloud computing and other related technologies.

In addition, international organizations such as Industrial Internet Consortium (IIC), AllSeen Alliance and Open Interconnect Consortium (OIC) 6 have been set up in the world.

According to Accenture research report, the global industrial Internet of Things market size in 2012 reached 20 billion US dollars, expected in 2020 will be more than 500 billion US dollars in recent years will have a high growth. At the same time, based on the current level of input, by 2030, industrial Internet of things is expected to bring at least \$10 trillion to the world economy, while investment based on sustained increases suggests that by 2030, Reaching 14 trillion dollars.

At present, Chinese industrial Internet of things is in the initial formation of the industrial chain, which's main gainers of industrial profits, are the equipment manufacturers and system integrators. As the industry matures, the market demand for services will become stronger, network operators and platform providers will rapidly rise in profits, and will become the industry's main profit earners. With the implementation of 《Made in China 2025》 , the next decade, Chinese manufacturing industry will greatly enhance the overall level of information technology, manufacturing digital, network, intelligent will make significant progress. Digital Research and development design tools, key processes manufacturing equipment NC will be used as the basis of industrial Internet of Things and in the above-scale enterprises will be widely used also.

Industrial Internet of Things develops in China fast, but the overall level is not as good as abroad. The development of industrial Internet of Things in China basically has the following characteristics: small-scale enterprises, low level of technology Research and development; technical standards behind the application development; the number of application level is low; lack of industry talent, industrial development environment needs to be further improved, the industry management system to be improved. Therefore, at present, foreign enterprises have monopolized the industrial Internet of things in China. Although technology import substitution has promoted the development of local enterprises, foreign enterprises have monopolized industries such as smart grid, railway, oil and gas, etc. It has a large potential threats to information security, which requires us to make breakthroughs in the field of industrial Internet of Things. With

Chinese enterprises to gradually replace foreign enterprises, it also greatly promote the development of domestic industrial Internet of Things.

2   The Security and Privacy of Industrial Internet of Things

Enterprise users and individual users in the enjoyment of industrial Internet of things personalized service, at the same time, will also face their own privacy information which may be leaked because of "ubiquitous" network environment and "get in by every opening" hackers. In addition, the industrial Internet of things project is completed by a number of network nodes, collaborative data output during the node will also cause privacy leaks. Therefore, how to protect the privacy of users is an urgent problem to be solved.

From the industrial Internet of things point of view, the perception layer is mainly based on the sensor field devices; at present, the specific potential attacking against the industrial Internet of things are mainly the following:

(1) Attacks on the node. Mainly on the node control and node capture. Node control is due to the network attacker access to the network node within the Shared secret or gateway nodes and remote information processing platform between the Shared secret leaked; Node capture not involves the secrets of network nodes, but can block nodes to compromise network connectivity, or to obtain network privacy by identifying the type of sensor and inferring the mode of operation of the network.

(2) Attacks on RFID systems. RFID, also known as radio frequency identification, is a communications technology that allows radio signals to identify specific targets which can read and write related data without establishing a mechanical or optical contact between the system and a specific target. Companies prevent theft, improve inventory management, easy inventory of stores and warehouses. Besides, the use of RFID technology, which can greatly reduce consumer waiting time in front of the checkout counter. However, with the development of RFID technology and the increasing popularity of RFID tags, security issues, especially user privacy, are becoming more and more serious. If a user uses a product with an insecure label, which is read by a nearby reader without the user's perception, thereby disclosing personal sensitive information such as money, drugs (associated with a particular disease), a book (Which may contain personal preferences), etc., in particular, may expose the user's location privacy, so that users are being tracked.

In addition, due to the introduction of industrial control systems of the industrial network, there are some forms of attack that are not available in other fields, such as resonance attacks: In the implementation of this attack, the network attacker will force the existing physical system to produce resonance near the specific frequency through the illegal control of the sensor or controller, which will destroy the normal operation of the system. Clock synchronization attack: for strict industrial control system, it belongs to the timing system, the network attacker can spread the false clock message to destroy the unified system clock, so as to achieve the purpose of attack; Control system attacks. In this attack, the network attacker will influence the correct evaluation of the current network state through the interference control system, and forge or replay the control command to implement the forgery attack, the tampering attack of the sensing data and the control network DOS attack.

3 Industrial Internet of Things System Security and Privacy Solutions

At current protection technologies and measures, mostly concentrated in the industrial application of things level, the application of technology are: data dissemination, data mining and wireless sensor networks. Specific privacy protection methods are:

(1) Anonymization method: it is the most important one kind of technical means of privacy protection in data mining. It protects privacy by blurring sensitive information.

(2) Encryption method: this method is the original plaintext file or data by an algorithm to deal with, making it unreadable code, usually referred to as "ciphertext", so that it can only be entered after the corresponding key to show the original content, in such a way to achieve the protection of data from unauthorized persons to steal, the purpose of reading. The reverse process of this process is decryption, that is, the process of converting the encoded information into its original data.

(3) Routing protocol method: This method is generally used for wireless sensor network node location privacy protection, generally based on random routing strategy, that is not every packet transmission from the source node to the convergence layer, a certain probability of the packet away from the convergence layer in the direction of transmission, while the transmission path will change. Each data packet transmission path will be randomly generated, which makes the attacker to obtain accurate location information on the node becomes difficult, so as to achieve the purpose of security.

In summary, to the current level of industrial networking, a lot of industrial networking security system is built on the existing mobile network based on the industrial sensing network and industrial application platform integration, gathered together. In addition, in the traditional network architecture, the network layer and the business layer are separated from each other in the security and protection level and independent, while the industrial Internet is due to constitute the specific way and specificity. At the same time, although the industrial Internet of things referred to the Internet information network model, the industrial Internet of things for industrial production, reliability, data integrity, real-time and security requirements are high. Therefore, the security mechanism needs to be supplemented and adjusted according to its characteristics.

4 Fingerprint Recognition Overview

Biometrics is the combination of computer and optical, acoustic, biosensor and biostatistics principles, using the inherent physiological characteristics of the human body (such as fingerprints, face images, iris, etc.) and behavioral characteristics (such as handwriting, Voice, gait, etc.) for personal identification. According to the IBG (International Biometric Group) statistics, the market has a variety of applications for different physiological characteristics and behavioral characteristics. Among them, the highest share is the fingerprint identification. Fingerprint recognition is currently the most widely used one. Fingerprinting technology to a person with his fingerprints, by comparing his fingerprints and pre-stored fingerprints to compare, you can verify his true identity. Each person (including the fingerprints) is different in pattern, breakpoint, and intersection point, that is, unique, and remains unchanged.

Two fingerprints often have the same general characteristics, but the details are not exactly the same. Fingerprint lines are not continuous, smooth straight, but often interrupted, fork or transition. These breakpoints, bifurcation points and turning points are called "feature points".

The feature points provide the fingerprint identification information, the most typical is the end point and bifurcation point, the other also includes bifurcation point, isolated point, ring point, short lines etc. The parameters of feature points (including the direction of node can toward a certain direction) and curvature (description of pattern direction change speed), position (the position of the node is described by x/y coordinates can be absolute, can also be compared to the triangulation points or feature points). The typical fingerprint feature points are shown (Fig. 1):

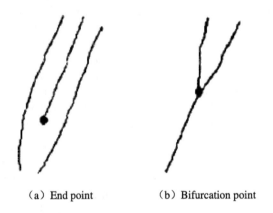

(a) End point   (b) Bifurcation point

Fig. 1. Typical fingerprint feature points

Fingerprint identification to achieve a variety of ways. Some of which are modeled after traditional methods used by the public security department to compare local details of fingerprints; some are identified directly by all features; and others are more unique, such as corrugated edge patterns of fingerprints and ultrasound. Some devices can instantly measure finger fingerprints, while others do not.

5   The Concrete Application of PDF417 Two-Dimensional Code

PDF417 two-dimensional bar code is a stacked two-dimensional bar code, currently the most widely used. PDF417 bar code is invented by the US company SYMBOL, PDF (Portable Data File) means "portable data files". Each bar code composed of bar code by the four and four empty 17 modules, it is called PDF417 bar code. PDF417 bar code need to have 417 decoding function of the bar code reader to identify. PDF417 bar code biggest advantage lies in its huge data capacity and strong error correction capability. The following Fig. 2 shows the PDF417 two-dimensional code:

Fig. 2. PDF417 two-dimensional code

Because fingerprints are the key to identity recognition, fingerprint encryption provides a strong fence for user security and privacy. Fingerprint information is encrypted to generate PDF417 bar code. It Can effectively protect the user's security and privacy. In addition, the fingerprint can also be encrypted to prevent forgery of fingerprints to enhance the security of identification.

The workflow of a typical fingerprint identification system is as follows (Fig. 3):

(1) Acquisition of the required fingerprint image through the fingerprint acquisition device.
(2) The collected fingerprint images are processed as follows:
   • Image quality judgment
   • image enhancement
   • Fingerprint region detection
   • Fingerprint pattern and frequency estimation
   • Image two value (the gray value of each pixel in the fingerprint image is set to 0 or 255)
   • Image thinning
(3) From the preprocessed image, the ridge line data of the fingerprint is obtained.
(4) The required feature points of the fingerprint identification are extracted from the ridge data of the fingerprint.
(5) The extraction of fingerprint features (feature points) in the database and the preservation of the fingerprint feature matching one by one, to determine whether the same fingerprint.
(6) After the completion of the fingerprint matching process, the output of the fingerprint identification processing results.

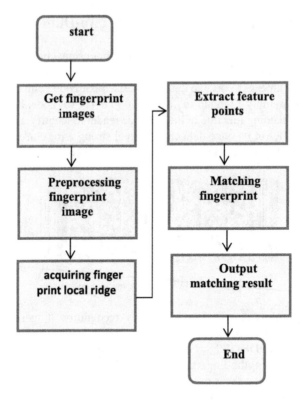

Fig. 3. Fingerprint identification process

Through the above process of fingerprint identification can be seen, the fingerprint identification system does not take the form of encryption, which makes criminals easily illegal access to fingerprint information, which has a negative effect on the security and privacy of users, thereby undermining the production safety. The structure of the current fingerprint identification system is shown in the following Table 1:

Table 1. Structure of fingerprint identification system

Upper application system		
Fingerprint classification	Recognition and Matching	Fingerprint compression
Fingerprint acquisition device		

In this paper, the use of RC4 algorithm for encryption and decryption. RC4 algorithm is a kind of electronic information in the field of encryption technology, for wireless communication network, is an electronic password, only authorized (to pay the corresponding fee) users can enjoy the service. RC4 algorithm characterized by the algorithm is simple, fast, and the key length is variable, variable range of 1–256 bytes (8–2048 bits), in today's technology support, when the key length is 128 bits, it is not feasible to use the violent method to search for the key. Therefore, it is expected that the key range of RC4 can still resist the attack of violent search key for a long time. The structure of the data encryption system is shown in the following Fig. 4:

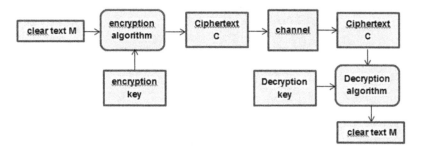

Fig. 4. Structure of data encryption system

In fact, there is no effective attack method for RC4 encryption algorithm with 128 bit key length.

6 Concluding Remarks

Industrial Internet of things in the traditional Internet of things based on the integration of the Internet, WSN and field bus network and other related technologies, and then have the environmental awareness of various types of terminals, cloud computing model, mobile communications, real-time communication into industrial production Link network, in today's industrial environment, the application prospects are very good.

In order to adapt to the security applications of industrial Internet of things, this paper mainly studies the industrial objects networking to strengthen the protection of users' security and privacy through the combination of fingerprint identification technology, PDF417 code and RC4 encryption methods, to promote the industrial networking and industrial networking security. The reference role. Industrial Internet of Things technology is rapid progress in all directions, but in the long run, industrial production and management of the demand continues to increase, the requirements of security technology also continue to put forward new challenges.

References

1. Yang, Y.: Ning executive loop. Research on the security and protection technology of industrial object networking. Intell. Process. Appl. 65–66 (2015)
2. Liu, D.: Fingerprint encryption two-dimensional code in the file management system application research. Zhejiang University of Technology, Zhejiang (2015)
3. Chen, H.: Entropy analysis based on fingerprint identification and encryption algorithm application research. Xidian University, Xi'an (2012)
4. Liang, T.: PDF417 two-dimensional code of the fingerprint encryption and identification. Liaoning University of Science and Technology, Liaoning (2015)

5. Wang, H., Li, Y., Mi, M., Wang, P.: A method of data fusion based on supervisory mechanism for industrial Internet of Things Safety. J. Instrum. Instrum. 817–824 (2013)
6. Ji, J.: Industrial Internet of Things security technology. Jiangnan University, Wuxi (2012)

Improved Reversible Data Hiding Scheme Based on AMBTC Compression Technique

Shan Sun, Zhaoxia Yin[✉], Jin Tang, and Bin Luo

Key Laboratory of Intelligent Computing and Signal Processing, Ministry of Education,
Anhui University, Hefei 230601, People's Republic of China
yinzhaoxia@ahu.edu.cn

Abstract. As the compression technique spread on the Internet, data hiding combining with compression techniques is a hot property in recent years. In this paper, a reversible data hiding (RDH) scheme for Absolute Moment Block Truncation Coding (AMBTC) compressed image is proposed. In the proposed scheme, according to the four kinds of situations which the secret data combine with the bitmap value, we provide some rules to embed data by use the mean value and the absolute moment. Experimental results and analysis demonstrate that, the proposed method can achieve high capacity with low distortion. Besides, the proposed method is very simple and can be easily applied to real-time transmission due to its lower computational complexity.

Keywords: AMBTC · Reversible data hiding · High capacity

1 Introduction

Reversible data hiding (RDH) is a technique which embeds secret data into a cover medium and can extract the embedded data and recover the original medium with lossless. The technique is used in some special applications, which the exact recovery of the original cover medium is required, such as military images, medical images and forensics. The difference expansion (DE) scheme is one of the popular RDH schemes which first compute the error of pixel groups and expand it to adjust additional secret data [1]. The histogram shifting (HS) is another classic method which hides secret data by shifting the histogram of pixel values [2]. And other RDH schemes also have a very good ascension in embedding effect [3–5].

The compressed domain image data hiding schemes embed secret data in encrypted images. As is known to all, Joint Photographic Experts Group (JPEG) [6], Vector Quantization (VQ) [7] and Block Truncation Coding (BTC) [8–11] are the most well-known lossy compression techniques, and the relevant schemes have been proposed. In 1979, BTC was proposed by Delp and Mitchell [12]. Lema and Mitchell improve the BTC method by proposing an Absolute Moment Block Truncation Coding (AMBTC) scheme [13] which compute low mean pixel value, high mean pixel value and bitmap or absolute moment, mean pixel value and bitmap in each block. When receiver get the triple, it can easily reconstructed image block by replacing each '0' of bitmap with the low mean value and each '1' of bitmap with a high mean value. Hong et al. presented a reversible

© ICST Institute for Computer Sciences, Social Informatics and Telecommunications Engineering 2017
F. Chen and Y. Luo (Eds.): Industrial IoT 2017, LNICST 202, pp. 111–118, 2017.
DOI: 10.1007/978-3-319-60753-5_12

data hiding method based on AMBTC-compressed images without extra keeping cost [14]. In 2010, Chen et al. [9] proposed a novel scheme to achieve reversible data embedding in the AMBTC compression by interchanging of the two quantization levels accompanied by the bitmap flipping. Ou et al. [15] presented a reversible secret sharing method generated AMBTC-compressed shadows in 2014. And proposed two ways to extract the secret data and achieve decoding according to whether the light-weight computational devices are obtainable. If they are obtainable, the stego image can be completely decoded and recover the original image without error, otherwise, the decoded image is very similar to primitive image. In 2015, Lin et al. [16] utilized the redundancy of the block in the AMBTC-compressed images to decide whether the block can embed the secret data. Then the scheme created four incompatible situations in the embeddable blocks to embed data. Lin et al.'s method used four hiding strategies to deal with four different cases in the embeddable cover blocks. This achieves low image distortion and high payload, but if the to-be-embedded data are continuous 0 or 1 accidentally, the rest blocks can't continue embed. So the embedding capacity is extremely instable. In order to solve this problem, we make improvement based on Lin et al.'s method.

In this paper, we proposed a reversible data hiding method for AMBTC-image base on Lin et al.'s method and have a great improvement in hiding capacity. Section 2 describes the details of the proposed scheme. Section 3 offers the experimental results. Finally, the conclusions are shown in Sect. 4.

2 Proposed Method

This section presents our new data hiding scheme, includes data embedding, data extraction and image recovery.

2.1 Data Embedding

Choose an AMBTC-compressed image as the cover, and each $m \times n$ size block including a $m \times n$ size bitmap, the mean pixel value AVG_i and the absolute moment a. There are four kinds of situations which the to-be-embedded secret data combine with the bitmap value. For example, if the secret data is '0' and the bitmap value is '1', and it is situation 01. According to the number of the case type t, we can embed the secret data by using the following strategies.

If $t = 1$, we will discard the block.

If $t = 2$, it must meet the conditions that all of the secret data are '0' or '1'. What's more, if all of the secret data are '0' and the number of '0' in the bitmap is more than or equal to 2, the number of '1' in the bitmap is more than or equal to 3, and then could embed the data. Here are the embedding rules:

Situation 00: The to-be-embedded data is '0' and the bitmap is '0'. If first time pertains to situation 00, the relevant pixel value is $AVG - a - 1$ in the cover block. If second time pertains to situation 00, the relevant pixel value is $AVG - a$ in the cover block. Else, the relevant pixel value is $AVG - a$ in the cover block.

Situation 01: The to-be-embedded data is '0' and the bitmap is '1'. If first time pertains to situation 01, the relevant pixel value is $AVG + a + 2$ in the cover block. If second time pertains to situation 01, the relevant pixel value is $AVG + a + 1$ in the cover block. If third time pertains to situation 01, the relevant pixel value is $AVG + a$ in the cover block. Else, the relevant pixel value is $AVG + a$ in the cover block.

It's important to note that $AVG - a$ is must greater than 0, and $AVG + a$ is must lesser than 254 in order to prevent overflow.

If $t = 2$ and all of the to-be-embedded data are '1' and the number of '0' in the bitmap is more than or equal to 3, the number of '1' in the bitmap is more than or equal to 3, and then could embed the data. Here are the embedding rules:

Situation 10: The to-be-embedded data is '1' and the bitmap is '0'. If first time pertains to situation 10, the relevant pixel value is $AVG - a - 2$ in the cover block. If second time pertains to situation 10, the relevant pixel value is $AVG - a - 1$ in the cover block. If third time pertains to situation 10, the relevant pixel value is $AVG - a$ in the cover block. Else, the relevant pixel value is $AVG - a$ in the cover block.

Situation 11: The to-be-embedded data is '1' and the bitmap is '1'. If first time pertains to situation 11, the relevant pixel value is $AVG + a + 2$ in the cover block. If second time pertains to situation 11, the relevant pixel value is $AVG + a + 1$ in the cover block. If third time pertains to situation 11, the relevant pixel value is $AVG + a$ in the cover block. Else, the relevant pixel value is $AVG + a$ in the cover block.

It's important to note that $AVG - a$ is must greater than 1, and $AVG + a$ is must lesser than 254 in order to prevent overflow.

If $t = 3$ or 4, it could embed secret data using the following strategies:

Situation 00: The to-be-embedded data is '0' and the bitmap is '0'. The relevant pixel value is $AVG - a$ in the cover block.

Situation 01: The to-be-embedded data is '0' and the bitmap is '1'. The relevant pixel value is $AVG + a$ in the cover block.

Situation 10: The to-be-embedded data is '1' and the bitmap is '0'. The relevant pixel value is $AVG - a - 1$ in the cover block.

Situation 11: The to-be-embedded data is '1' and the bitmap is '1'. The relevant pixel value is $AVG + a + 1$ in the cover block.

It's important to note that $AVG - a$ is must greater than 0, and $AVG + a$ is must lesser than 255 in order to prevent overflow.

2.2   Data Extraction and Image Recovery

Having received the stego image that embeds secret data, the receiver could extract the secret data and recover the original image with lossless. The specific steps are shown below.

Step 1:   Scan each $m \times n$ size stego-block. Count the number of the different pixel values num in the current block.

Step 2:   If $num = 1$ or 2, then go to Step 3. Else if $num = 3$, then go to Step 4. Else if $num = 4$, then go to Step 8. Else if $num = 5$, then go to Step 9. Else, go to Step 10.

Step 3: *num* = 1 or 2 suggested that it is a non-embeddable block, the block same as the original block. If don't scan all blocks, then go to Step 1.

Step 4: *num* = 3, the number is three. Sort the three different values as x_1, x_2 and x_3 from high to low. Calculate $x_1 - x_2$ and $x_2 - x_3$.

Step 5: Compare $(x_1 - x_2)$ with $(x_2 - x_3)$. If $(x_1 - x_2) > (x_2 - x_3)$, then go to Step 6. If $(x_1 - x_2) < (x_2 - x_3)$, then go to Step 7. $(x_1 - x_2)$ could not be equal to $(x_2 - x_3)$ according to our embedding strategies.

Step 6: Because $(x_1 - x_2) > (x_2 - x_3)$, x_2 belongs to Situation 00 and x_3 belongs to Situation 10. According to the parity of x_1 could ensure the case. If the parity of x_1 is the same as x_2, x_1 belongs to Situation 01. We could get $AVG = (x_1 + x_2)/2$, $a = AVG - x_2$. Else, x_1 belongs to Situation 11. We could get $AVG = (x_1 + x_3)/2$, $a = AVG - x_2$. If don't scan all blocks, then go to Step 1.

Step 7: Because $(x_1 - x_2) < (x_2 - x_3)$, x_1 belongs to Situation 11 and x_2 belongs to Situation 01. According to the parity of x_3 could ensure the case. If the parity of x_3 is the same as x_2, x_3 belongs to Situation 00. We could get $AVG = (x_3 + x_2)/2$, $a = AVG - x_3$. Else, x_3 belongs to Situation 10. We could get $AVG = (x_1 + x_3)/2$, $a = AVG - x_3 - 1$. If don't scan all blocks, then go to Step 1.

Step 8: *num* = 4. Sort the four different values as x_1, x_2, x_3 and x_4 from high to low. x_1 belongs to Situation 11, x_2 belongs to Situation 01, x_3 belongs to Situation 00 and x_4 belongs to Situation 10. We could get $AVG = (x_3 + x_2)/2$, $a = AVG - x_3$. If don't scan all blocks, then go to Step 1.

Step 9: *num* = 5. Sort the five different values as x_1, x_2, x_3, x_4 and x_5 from high to low. x_1, x_2, x_3 belongs to Situation 01, x_4 and x_5 belongs to Situation 00. We could get $AVG = (x_3 + x_4)/2$, $a = AVG - x_4$. And all of the data embedded is '0'. We could get the bitmap value according to the position corresponding case. If don't scan all blocks, then go to Step 1.

Step 10: *num* = 6. Sort the six different values as x_1, x_2, x_3, x_4, x_5 and x_6 from high to low. x_1, x_2, x_3 belongs to Situation 11, x_4, x_5, x_6 belongs to Situation 10. We could get $AVG = (x_3 + x_4)/2$, $a = AVG - x_4$. And all of the data embedded is '1'. We could get the bitmap value according to the position corresponding case. If don't scan all blocks, then go to Step 1.

So far, each $m \times n$ size block including a $m \times n$ size bitmap, the mean pixel value AVG_i and the absolute moment a_i. The triple is same as the block's triple of the original AMBTC-compressed image. And we completed the data extraction and image recovery.

3   Experimental Results

In order to evaluate the proposed method, we use six test grayscale images as shown in Fig. 1. There are Lena, Jet, Sailboat, Baboon, Man, Woman. Each of them has the size of 512 × 512. The secret data are generated by employing a pseudo random number generator. We perform several experiments to instruct the proposed method superiorly of hiding capacity (CAP) and stability compared with Lin et al.'s method. In all the experiments, the block of AMBTC-compression size is 4 × 4.

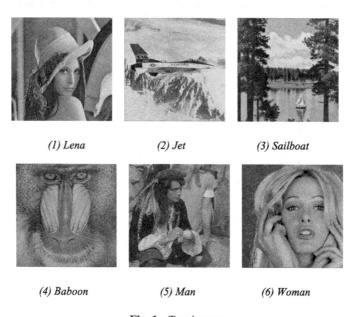

(1) Lena   (2) Jet   (3) Sailboat

(4) Baboon   (5) Man   (6) Woman

Fig. 1. Test images

In order to prove the proposed method superiorly of the hiding capacity (bits), we test each image by embedding the secret data in ten times using the proposed method and Lin et al.'s method [16]. Table 1 shows average of the hiding capacity (bits) and compare with Lin et al.'s method in ten times test.

Table 1. The PSNR values and CAP and compare with Lin et al.'s method

Image	Lena	Jet	Sailboat	Baboon	Man	Woman
Proposed method CAP (bits)	262101	256173	262072	262141	260045	258891
Lin et al.'s method CAP (bits)	198395	205171	176277	221394	248544	246723
Improvement (bits)	63706	51002	85795	40747	11501	12168

As shown in Table 1, the proposed method performs significantly better than Lin et al.'s method in hiding payload. In order to prove the proposed method superiorly of the embedding stability, we use each image by embedding the secret data in ten times by the proposed method and Lin et al.'s method. Figure 2 shows the hiding capacity (bits) of Lena by using proposed method and Lin et al.'s method. All of the binary data embedded in the first experiment are "0" and in the second experiment are "1". Then in the following eight experiments, the to-be-embedded data are generated by employing a pseudo random number generator which using the same seed in the same experiment ID, ensuring using the same to-be-embedded data in the same experiment ID.

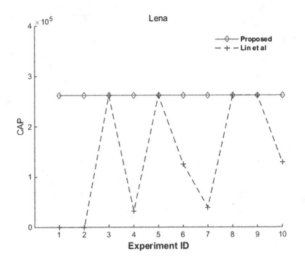

Fig. 2. Experimental results of Lena in ten times (Color figure online)

The horizontal axis represents the experiment index, and the vertical axis represents the hiding capacity in Fig. 2. Red solid curve represents the proposed method hiding capacity in different test and has changed little. Blue dotted curve represents Lin et al.'s method hiding capacity in different test and has almost changed dramatically. And it is obvious that the movements of the blue dotted curve are almost identical. This is because that the defects of this method which can't continue to embed data when the embedded data are continuous 0 or 1 accidentally. But the proposed method is almost unaffected. Compare with the proposed method, the curve with no fluctuations suggest that our method is more settled. Obviously, our proposed scheme can embed much more secret data and the embedding capacity is much more stable.

4   Conclusion

In this paper, a reversible data hiding in encrypted AMBTC-compressed image is proposed. With the combination of the bitmap and secret data, creates four situations. According to the four situations, a quite simple calculation method be provided. We make the improvement when the to-be-embedded data are continuous "0" or "1" that

Lin et al.'s method can't embed data. So the proposed method makes use of the redundant space of encrypted AMBTC-compressed image without any additional information. In addition, the stego image is not easily discovered by attacker, because it looks the same as the common image. When receiver gets the image with the secret data, he can extract the secret data and recover the original image. Experimental results and analyses demonstrate that compared with prior works, the proposed method improve the embedding capacity, and also enhance the stability of embedding.

Acknowledgments. This research work is partly supported by the National Natural Science Foundation of China (61502009, 61671018, 61472002), China Postdoctoral Science Foundation (2016M591650), Anhui Provincial Natural Science Foundation (1508085SQF216), Key Program for Excellent Young Talents in Colleges and Universities of Anhui Province (gxyqZD2016011), Quality Engineering Program for Colleges and Universities in Anhui Province (2015jyxm042) and Undergraduates Training Foundation of Anhui University (J10118515631, J18520229).

References

1. Tian, J.: Reversible data embedding using a difference expansion. IEEE Trans. Circuits Syst. Video Technol. **13**(8), 890–896 (2003)
2. Ni, Z., Shi, Y., Ansari, N., et al.: Reversible data hiding. IEEE Trans. Circuits Syst. Video Technol. **16**(3), 354–362 (2006)
3. Luo, L., et al.: Reversible image watermarking using interpolation technique. IEEE Trans. Inf. Forensics Secur. **5**(1), 187–193 (2010)
4. Li, X.L., Yang, B., Zeng, T.Y.: Efficient reversible watermarking based on adaptive prediction-error expansion and pixel selection. IEEE Trans. Image Process. **20**(12), 3524–3533 (2011)
5. Zhang, X.: Reversible data hiding with optimal value transfer. IEEE Trans. Multimed. **15**(2), 316–325 (2013)
6. Qian, Z., Zhang, X.: Improved anti-forensics of JPEG compression. J. Syst. Softw. **91**(4), 100–108 (2014)
7. Chang, C.C., Nguyena, T.Y., Lin, C.C.: A novel VQ-based reversible data hiding scheme by using hybrid encoding strategies. J. Syst. Softw. **86**(2), 389–402 (2013)
8. Chuang, J.C., Chang, C.C.: Using a simple and fast image compression algorithm to hide secret information. Int. J. Comput. Appl. **28**(4), 329–333 (2006)
9. Chen, J., Hong, W., Chen, T.S., Shiu, C.W.: Steganography for BTC compressed images using no distortion technique. Imaging Sci. J. **58**(4), 177–185 (2010)
10. Hong, W., Chen, J., Chen, T.S., Shiu, C.W.: Steganography for block truncation coding compressed images using hybrid embedding scheme. Int. J. Innov. Comput. Inf. Control **7**(2), 1–11 (2011)
11. Ou, D., Sun, W.: High payload image steganography with minimum distortion based on absolute moment block truncation coding. Multimed. Tools Appl. **74**(21), 9117–9139 (2015)
12. Bai, J., Chang, C.C.: A high payload steganographic scheme for compressed images with hamming code. Int. J. Netw. Secur. **18**(6), 1122–1129 (2016)
13. Delp, E.J., Mitchell, O.R.: Image compression using block truncation coding. IEEE Trans. Commun. **27**(9), 1335–1342 (1979)
14. Hong, W., Chen, T.S., Shiu, C.W.: Lossless steganography for AMBTC-compressed images. Int Congr Image Signal Process **2**, 13–17 (2008)

15. Ou, D., Sun, W.: Reversible AMBTC-based secret sharing scheme with abilities of two decryptions. J. Vis. Commun. Image Represent. **25**(5), 1222–1239 (2014)
16. Lin, C.C., Liu, X.L., Tai, W.L., Yuan, S.M.: A novel reversible data hiding scheme based on AMBTC compression technique. Multimed. Tools Appl. **74**, 3823–3842 (2015)

Link-Based Privacy-Preserving Data Aggregation Scheme in Wireless Sensor Networks

Kai Zhang[1,2], Haiping Huang[1,2,3(✉)], Yunqi Wang[1,2], and Ruchuan Wang[1,2]

[1] College of Computer, Nanjing University of Posts and Telecommunications,
Nanjing 210003, China
hhp@njupt.edu.cn
[2] Jiangsu High Technology Research Key Laboratory for Wireless Sensor Networks,
Nanjing 210003, China
[3] College of Computer Science and Technology,
Nanjing University of Aeronautics and Astronautics, Nanjing 210016 ,China

Abstract. Data privacy-protection is of great importance during data aggregation in Wireless Sensor Networks. A distinctive data aggregation scheme based on data link is proposed in this paper. To be specifically, the data link is formed according to energy consumption and distance. For each round of the data aggregation, nodes within a certain cluster perform data aggregation together by subtracting the base value(given by cluster head) from its real value, and then add the random number (generated by itself) for privacy protection. The cluster head will form the information matrix according to the data from the link, and then perform homomorphic transformation. Finally, the data reach the base station which will feed back the aggregation results effectively. Compared with previous work, our scheme can effectively protect data privacy and cause low computation overhead and energy consumption. Meanwhile, the base station can acquire the correlation between nodes in certain clusters.

Keywords: Wireless sensor networks · Data aggregation · Privacy · Data link · Homomorphic transformation

1 Introduction

Being composed by various tiny sensing nodes, Wireless Sensor Network (WSN) is used to monitor the environment nearby. It has greatly changed how people focus on and interact with the environment. However, energy of these sensors are strictly limited, data generated by neighbor nodes are relatively overlapped and redundant. Therefore, it is more meaningful to transfer those processed and essential data than raw ones during the data aggregation in WSN. The goal of data aggregation is to reduce computation overhead and energy consumption by all nodes processing the data together, and it can be used to do sum, average and min/max operation in WSN.

The data privacy owns the highest priority in data aggregation. For example, medical data like blood sugar and blood oxygen which concern the patients' privacy should be protected in Smart Medical System based on WSN. However, these sensitive data are

© ICST Institute for Computer Sciences, Social Informatics and Telecommunications Engineering 2017
F. Chen and Y. Luo (Eds.): Industrial IoT 2017, LNICST 202, pp. 119–129, 2017.
DOI: 10.1007/978-3-319-60753-5_13

being transferred through wireless channels which will be easily attacked and thus exist the high risk that the private data may be exposed.

Some traditional solutions, like complicated encryption algorithm and data mining are not suitable for the special environment of WSN. In addition, sensor nodes in WSN are resource-restricted, so certain schemes that can protect data privacy and meanwhile reduce energy consumption are needed.

In this paper, we propose a link-based privacy-preserving data aggregation scheme (LPDA). Compared with previous work, our scheme presents the following advantages: (1) By introducing the base value, the amount of data is greatly reduced. (2) The data link can be used effectively and repeatedly. (3) The base station can acquire the correlation among nodes in certain cluster.

The paper is organized as follows: Sect. 2 summarizes the related work; Sect. 3 briefly introduces the models in this paper; Sect. 4 describes the procedures of our proposed scheme LPDA in detail; Sect. 5 evaluates LPDA and the paper is concluded in Sect. 6.

2   Related Work

Aiming at the data aggregation in WSN, many effective schemes have been proposed by researchers. Madden put forward the classic TAG scheme [1], Intanagonwiwat [2] and Bista [3] also proposed relevant data aggregation schemes. However, these schemes are all based on trusted environments. In reality, the WSN is probably being deployed in open environment, the attackers will capture and manipulate the nodes. In addition, sufficient privacy protections are not involved in these schemes.

Feasible schemes for privacy protection in WSN can be divided into data perturbation, secure multi-party computation, homomorphic encryption and polynomial regression. Among these four categories, secure multi-party computation has the advantage of low energy consumption and high level of privacy-preserving. W. He put forward two effective privacy-preserving schemes: CPDA and SMART [4]. CPDA, characterized by complicated inter-cluster computation, is in fact secure multi-party computation. It can effectively protect data privacy, but nodes have to interact with each other frequently and thus causing high computation overhead and energy consumption. SMART is based on data-slicing. Each node will slice its data into several pieces, encrypt these pieces and send them to its neighbors. And finally each node will pass data pieces to its parent along the tree structure. It has to be noticed that this scheme is also of high consumption. Sheikh R. put forward a k-sum secure protocol [5] to protect data privacy through secure multi-party computation. Shi J. proposed a privacy-preserving scheme PriSense [6] which uses city sensing as its background, defends conspiracy attacks through data-slicing and mixing techniques and thus provides sound privacy-preserving abilities. Shi E. put forward a privacy-preserving data aggregation scheme by using time series [7]. This scheme is carried forward through the encrypted data uploaded by nodes, but a trusted key manager is needed. Jung T. suggested several data aggregation algorithms to perform sum operation [8] based on the hypothesis that all the channels and nodes cannot be trusted. But the polynomials are partly public in this scheme, causing information leakage during computation and communication. Wang proposed an efficient data aggregation scheme [9] with secure channel and data-slicing as its main techniques. Zhang [10] is the first to put forward the data aggregation scheme through data link. Compared with previous work, this scheme has the advantage of low computation overhead. For each round of the data aggregation, the cluster head will generate a random number and carries this number along this link to perform sum operation, and finally the cluster head subtract the random number from the results to get actual aggregation results. But this scheme fails to make the best use of the natural advantage of data link.

3 Models

3.1 Network Model

In this paper, the network model is a connected graph. Sensor nodes can be divided into three categories: base station that at the top of the entire network, cluster head and leaf node which gather data and upload data. Being different from the traditional data structure—tree, the plane structure—data link is used in our proposal. And this paper mainly focuses on sum operation, but other operations like average and variance can be done through some modifications.

The network model in this paper has the following features: (1) N sensor nodes are randomly distributed in the entire area. (2) All the nodes have the same communication range R and sensing abilities. (3) All the nodes have the sufficient initial energy to support the proposed scheme. (4) The base station is aware of the location of each node.

3.2 Security Model

This paper is based on the semi-honest model that each node executes the protocol strictly and correctly but it will try to capture or reveal others' private data. And meanwhile, the attackers will attempt to eavesdrop the raw data, capture nodes and tamper with the message.

We use the key distribution scheme in [11], which has three phases: key pre-distribution, shared-key discovery and key-pairs formation. For the key pre-distribution phase, a large key pool with K keys will be generated. Each node in the WSN will select k keys from the key pool randomly to form a key ring. For the shared-key discovery phase, nodes will discover neighbors with the same keys through the share of information. If two neighbors have the same key, a secure channel will be formed between them. And for the key-pairs formation phase, if there is no same keys between neighbors but they can reach each other through several hops, a channel key will be generate between them.

The data aggregation in WSN must satisfy the following requirements: (1) Privacy. (2) Accuracy, that no packages loss occur during aggregation and communication. (3) Efficiency, to reduce computation overhead and energy consumption.

4   Link-Based Privacy-Preserving Data Aggregation Scheme

4.1   Clustering

The clustering procedure can be described as follows: (1) Information is stored as set for each node. (2) Node will become the cluster head according to the probability Pc. (3) The base station will divide the entire network into layers according to the distance between each node and the base station, which is a significant factor that affects Pc.

The information set of *Nodei* can be described as <*NL, C, PPi, PDi, Er, Ec, P*>, *NL* is the neighbor set of *Nodei*, which is { *'Nd':distance, 'Nc':cluster*} in detail; *Nd* is the distance between the neighbor node and *Nodei*; *Nc* is the ID of a cluster that the neighbor belongs to; *PPi* stands for the random number for privacy-preserving for *Nodei*; *PDi* stands for the real value of *Nodei*; *Er* and *Ec* are the remaining energy and communication cost of *Nodei*, respectively; and *P* is the parent of *Nodei*.

Before clustering, the base station will divide the entire area into several layers, shown in Fig. 1. Since the base station is aware of the location of each node, so layers can be defined as:

$$L = \frac{d_{max}}{R} \qquad (1)$$

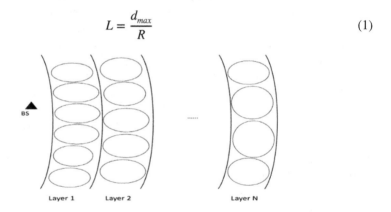

Layer 1   Layer 2   Layer N

Fig. 1. Layers of the network

Where d_{max} stands for the furthest distance against the base station and R is the communication radius. The probability Pc is defined as:

$$P_c = \frac{1 - \dfrac{E_c}{E_r}}{L} \qquad (2)$$

To be specifically, for the clustering, the base station will trigger a CLUSTER message to perform one query Q = (class = CLUSTER) ∩ (attribute = NONE). The message is described as <*NL0, C0, P0*> and for the base station, *NL0* = *C0* = *P0*. When receiving the CLUSTER message, node becomes the cluster head according to the probability Pc and when it becomes the cluster head, it will forward the CLUSTER message, or it will wait CLUSTER message from other nodes and select one cluster to join in. For each node, upon receiving the CLUSTER message, it will update its neighbor set and if it joins a certain cluster, it will update its C and P. For example, node a sends the CLUSTER message to node b and node b decides to join in. It will update the neighbor set NL, update C to be the cluster that b belongs to and P to be node a. The process above will be done repeatedly and finally several clusters will be formed.

After the clustering, we may focus on the following issues:

(1) Nodes within each cluster should be no less than three. If there is only one node, apparently, the data aggregation operation cannot be performed, so it will join the cluster of its parent node. And if there is only two nodes, such cluster is too small in size and has low level of privacy and under such circumstance, we have one cluster head and one none-head node, so both of them will join the cluster of the parent node of the cluster head.

(2) Layer L should be inversely proportional to the probability Pc. This means that those nodes that are closer to the base station will have higher probability to become the cluster head for the closer the distance is, the more the amount of data, communication overhead and energy consumption. So more cluster heads around the base station shall bear more stress in the entire network.

(3) The less the energy ratio Ec/Er, the more $1 - Ec/Er$. This means those nodes who become cluster nodes have the feature of low energy consumption.

The pseudo code of clustering are as follows:

```
L = dmax/R;
for each node Nodei do
    Pc = (1-Ec/Er)/L;
    if receives CLUSTER message form Nodej
            update NL;
            if Nodei elect itself as cluster head with Pc
                    construct    CLUSTER    message    and
            broadcast;
            else if join the cluster
                    Ci = Cj;
                    Pi = Pj;
            end if
    else
            wait for next CLUSTER message;
    end if
    if node within a cluster < 3
            join the cluster of head's parent;
    end if
end for
```

4.2   Formation of Data Link

The meaning of constructing data link lies: forming a link to perform data aggregation which can be used effectively and repeatedly, and accomplishing initialization and information storage before data aggregation. All the nodes within a certain cluster have received the CLUSTER message from the cluster head, so in the neighbor set of the cluster head, the exact locations of each node are stored. The energy ratio Ec/Er computed during clustering will be sent to the cluster head before the formation of data link.

It is obvious that the one significant feature of data link is that the last few hops in the link shall take responsible for more data packages and thus consuming more energy. So based on that, the cluster head will search for those nodes that are far away from it (greater than a threshold that has been previously set). And for the area nearby, the cluster head will choose the routes according to the energy ratio in the descending order. Here the less the energy ratio Ec/Er, the less communication cost and the more remaining energy a node has, and these are the exact nodes that are suitable to be the last few hops within the data link. The cluster head keeps above procedures repeatedly until it reaches the last node within its cluster.

Subsequently, a link that starts from the cluster head, goes through all the modes and finally goes back to the cluster head will be formed. All the none-head nodes within in certain clusters will generate a random number PPi, and then use the key between itself and the base station to encrypt the number and send it to the cluster head. Upon receiving these encrypted data, the cluster head will sort these data in the sequence as the data link, and send the data to the base station along with the ID of these nodes. The base station will decrypt these data and store them locally. And then the base station is able to query the random number of none-head nodes within a certain cluster according to the mark of the cluster.

The pseudo code of formation of data link are as follows:

```
generate a list called List1
generate a list called List2
for each Nodei do
   if distance between head and Nodei > threshold
         join List1;
   else
         join List2;
   end if
end for
for each Nodei in List2 do
   sort the list according to energy ratio;
   join List1;
end for
generate PPi and send it to base station;
```

4.3 Aggregation Within Clusters

Different from the traditional data aggregation technique that each node within the cluster uses their complete sensing data, in this paper, we require the data that each node uploaded is the one that subtract the base value from its real value. The benefit of doing this is that the amount of data is greatly reduced and thus both communication overhead and energy consumption are decreased. So the base value for each round of aggregation obtains the priority because extreme results will occur if the base value given is too small, too large or not reasonable, and the data in the link will show signs of left-skewed or right-skewed.

We will take the example of a common sensing data item in WSN—temperature to show how the base value is given. The key to choose base value is to modeling the history data. Temperature is the kind of data that changes frequently, but take a long-term view, it is relatively stable. That is to say, the temperature fluctuate against a certain mean value, which obviously has the horizontal pattern statistically. So we model the temperature data by using the exponential smoothing.

The equation for exponential smoothing can be described as:

$$F_{t+1} = \frac{1}{n-1}Y_t + \left(1 - \frac{1}{n-1}\right)F_t \tag{3}$$

where F_{t+1} is the base value for time series $t + 1$, Y_t is the mean value (the mean of real values for all nodes) and F_t is the base value for time series t, n stands for the number of nodes within a cluster.

Before the data aggregation, the nodes within the cluster will sense and gather data in advance and send the data to the cluster head. The cluster head will do a mean operation on these data so as to give the first base value for the first round of data aggregation. After the aggregation, the cluster head will calculate the mean value, and according to Eq. (3), it gives the base value for second round of the aggregation and so on.

The packages in the data link is an array in the shape of $1 * (n - 1)$. Each node will subtract the base value from its real sensing value PDi and then add its private random number PPi, denoted as X, send it to the next hop along the link until it reaches the cluster head.

4.4 Aggregation Among Clusters

Take a cluster of five nodes as an example, after the cluster head receives the data package, it will do further processing on the data. It computes the subtraction between each X, and fill them into the following matrix:

$$\begin{matrix} 0 & X_1 - X_2 & X_1 - X_3 & X_1 - X_4 \\ X_2 - X_1 & 0 & X_2 - X_3 & X_2 - X_4 \\ X_3 - X_1 & X_3 - X_2 & 0 & X_3 - X_4 \\ X_4 - X_1 & X_4 - X_2 & X_4 - X_3 & 0 \end{matrix}$$

It can be seen that this matrix consists two triangular matrixes, so the cluster head only computes one triangular matrix, and then fill the negatives in corresponding positions.

Furthermore, we may get the adjacency matrix of the topological graph for the correlation of the nodes within the cluster by subtracting random numbers of each node, and this will be done by the base station. To take the security to a higher level, we can conduct the homomorphic transformation to raw topological graph, and transfer the processed graph in the network. The simplest homomorphic transformation can be finite exchange of rows and columns in the matrix. Each cluster head shares the information of its own homomorphic transformation with the base station.

After the transformation, the cluster head finds the parent node according to its information set and sends the processed matrix. Finally, the base station restores the matrix. To do that, the base station will query and subtract the private data PPi of each node through the mark of the cluster and solve some simple equations to get the value x(the real value being subtracted by the base value).

If it is just to perform aggregation operation, the base station has no need of restoring original sensing value (real value) for each node. Through (4) the sum of a certain cluster can be acquired and through (5) the mean value rb can be computed. And the base station will feed these data back to each cluster head.

$$sum = \sum_{i=1}^{n-1} x_i + b * (n-1) \tag{4}$$

$$rb = \frac{\sum_{i=1}^{n-1} x_i}{n-1} + b \tag{5}$$

where b stands for the base value in a certain round of aggregation.

5   Analysis and Evaluation

In this section, we will compare our scheme LPDA with the classic TAG in [1], CPDA in [4] and RPDA in [10], so as to analyze the advantages of our scheme from different perspectives.

5.1   Privacy

For the key-distribution phase, we selected k keys from the key pool of K keys, for any pair nodes, the probability that they have common keys, namely the connectivity $P_{connect}$:

$$P_{connect} = 1 - \frac{((K-k)!)^2}{(K-2k)!K!} \tag{6}$$

In addition, we define the probability that a certain node can eavesdrop encrypted message as $P_{overhear}$, which means there is a third party that obtains the same key:

$$P_{overhear} = \frac{k}{K} \tag{7}$$

We suppose that there are 1000 keys in the key pool, and we have selected 200 keys from the key pool in the key-distribution phase. So $P_{connect} = 98.3\%$ and $P_{overhear} = 0.2\%$, which means that the probability that encrypted message being eavesdropped is relatively low. In the following, we will analyze the ability for resisting such attacks of our proposed scheme:

(1) LPDA can effectively resist eavesdrop attack: the data being transferred in the link have been encrypted. Even the attacker somehow obtains the plaintext, the private data in the plaintext are mixed with random numbers, so the attacker cannot acquire the private data.

(2) LPDA can effectively resist conspiracy attack: suppose there are two nodes in one cluster attempt to strike conspiracy attack over a third node. If these two nodes are none-head nodes, as illustrated above, the private data cannot be acquired; and if one of these two nodes is the cluster head, though it has the key to the third node, it still cannot obtain the private data for the data is protected by the random number of the third node which is only known to itself and the base station.

Furthermore, the cluster head has performed homomorphic transformation on the information matrix which makes it harder for attackers to acquire the raw data.

5.2 Communication Overhead

Figures 2 and 3 describe the changes of communication overhead against the network size and epoch duration. TAG has the lowest communication cost for it has no security protection. Nodes in TAG generally send two messages: one for constructing aggregation tree and the other for data aggregation. CPDA has the highest communication overhead which increases dramatically as the network size expands. This is because the cluster head has to send at least four messages and nodes within the cluster have to send at least three massages for the complicated computation. RPDA has relatively low communication overhead for the cluster head sends two messages and nodes within the cluster send one message. As for LPDA, none-head nodes only perform light-weight computation like subtraction and cluster head only performs computing base value and homomorphic transformation, thus greatly reducing the communication overhead. Overall, the communication overhead of LPDA increases as the network size expands, it is relatively low and slightly over TAG, and the epoch duration has low effects on LPDA.

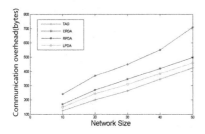 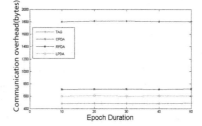

Fig. 2. Communication overhead against network size

Fig. 3. Communication overhead against epoch duration

5.3 Energy Consumption

Figure 4 reveals the trends of average remaining energy with the increase of query times. TAG has the lowest energy consumption for it has no security protection. The average remaining energy drops significantly because it has to perform complicated computation and nodes have to frequently exchange messages. The performance of RPDA is better than CPDA. And the average remaining energy of LPDA is more than RPDA and relatively less than TAG, because the cluster head is chosen wisely, and the burden of data packages are bear by those nodes with better performance according to our strategy, and furthermore, the size of the data being transferred as relatively small.

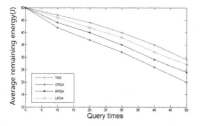 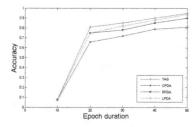

Fig. 4. Remaining energy against query times   **Fig. 5.** Accuracy against epoch duration

5.4 Accuracy

Figure 5 shows the changes of accuracy against epoch duration. Under the ideal circumstances, without packages loss, the base station should have the 100% accurate results. Here we define accuracy as the ratio of the aggregation data against actual results from all nodes. We may see that the accuracy increases together with the epoch duration, this is because the larger the epoch duration, the less probability of data collision through data aggregation. Overall, the accuracy of LPDA is slightly less than TAG, for the base station can acquire the correlation of nodes and calculates the aggregation results through light-weight computation.

6 Conclusion

We propose the LPDA scheme to address the privacy-preserving in data aggregation and meanwhile focus on energy consumption. LPDA is based on data link and the data being transferred through the link is relatively light. The cluster head provide further security protection by performing homomorphic transformation on the data. And finally the base station can acquire abundant and accurate data. The simulation results show that our scheme is feasible, secure and effective. Our future works include: (1) Provide data integrity protection. (2) Dynamically form the data link according to the remaining energy in real time.

Acknowledgement. The subject was sponsored by the National Natural Science Foundation of P.R. China (No. 61373138, 61672297), the Key Research and Development Program of Jiangsu Province (Social Development Program, No. BE2015702), Postdoctoral Foundation (No. 2015M570468, 2016T90485), the Sixth Talent Peaks Project of Jiangsu Province (No. DZXX-017), the Fund of Jiangsu High Technology Research Key Laboratory for Wireless Sensor Networks (WSNLBZY201516), Science and Technology Innovation Fund for Postgraduate Education of Jiangsu Province (No. KYLX15_0853).

References

1. Madden, S., Franklin, M.J., Hellerstein, J.M., et al.: TAG: a tiny aggregation service for ad-hoc sensor networks. ACM SIGOPS Oper. Syst. Rev. **36**(SI), 131–146 (2002)
2. Intanagonwiwat, C., Estrin, D., Govindan, R., et al.: Impact of network density on data aggregation in wireless sensor networks. In: Proceedings of the 22nd International Conference on Distributed Computing Systems, pp. 457–458. IEEE (2002)
3. Bista, R., Kim, Y.K., Chang, J.W.: A new approach for energy-balanced data aggregation in wireless sensor networks. In: Ninth IEEE International Conference on Computer and Information Technology, 2009 (CIT 2009), vol. 2, pp. 9–15. IEEE (2009)
4. He, W., Liu, X., Nguyen, H., et al.: PDA: privacy-preserving data aggregation in wireless sensor networks. In: 26th IEEE International Conference on Computer Communications (INFOCOM 2007), pp. 2045–2053. IEEE (2007)
5. Sheikh, R., Kumar, B., Mishra, D.K.: Privacy preserving k secure sum protocol. arXiv preprint arXiv:0912.0956 (2009)
6. Shi, J., Zhang, R., Liu, Y., et al.: Prisense: privacy-preserving data aggregation in people-centric urban sensing system. In: Proceedings of IEEE INFOCOM 2010, pp. 1–9. IEEE (2010)
7. Shi, E., Chan, T.H.H., Rieffel, E., et al.: Privacy-preserving aggregation of time-series data. In: Proceedings of NDSS, vol. 2, pp. 1–17 (2011)
8. Jung, T., Mao, X.F., Li, X.Y., et al.: Privacy-preserving data aggregation without secure channel: multivariate polynomial evaluation. In: Proceedings of IEEE INFOCOM 2013, pp. 2634–2642. IEEE (2013)
9. Wang, T., Qin, X., Liu, L.: An energy-efficient and scalable secure data aggregation for wireless sensor networks. Int. J. Distrib. Sens. Netw. **9**, 843485 (2013)
10. Zhang, X., Chen, H., Wang, K., et al.: Rotation-based privacy-preserving data aggregation in wireless sensor networks. In: 2014 IEEE International Conference on Communications (ICC), pp. 4184–4189. IEEE (2014)
11. Eschenauer, L., Gligor, V.D.: A key-management scheme for distributed sensor networks. In: Proceedings of the 9th ACM Conference on Computer and Communications Security, pp. 41–47. ACM (2002)

Reversible Authentication of Wireless Sensor Network Based on Prediction-Error Histogram and CRC

Guangyong Gao[✉], Caixue Zhou, Zongmin Cui, Shimao Yao,
and Zhijun Chong

School of Information Science & Technology,
Jiujiang University, Jiujiang 332005, China
gaoguangyong@163.com

Abstract. In this paper, a reversible authentication scheme for wireless sensor network (WSN) is proposed. Firstly, the WSN data stream is divided into some authentication groups, and each authentication group is composed of a generator group and a carrier group. Then the cyclical redundancy check (CRC) code of generator group is produced as the authentication information. In the carrier group, using the prediction-error-based histogram shifting algorithm, the authentication information is reversibly embedded into the fluctuation region of prediction-error histogram (PEH), not the smooth region. Experimental results and analysis demonstrate that compared with previous schemes, the proposed scheme achieves better performances on computation complex, false tampering alarm and attraction to attackers.

Keywords: Wireless sensor network (WSN) · Reversible authentication · Prediction-error histogram (PEH)

1 Introduction

The data integrity authentication is a core issue of wireless sensor network (WSN). Traditionally, encryption technology is applied to maintaining the security of WSN [1, 2]. But due to the limitation of sensor node resource, it is not fit to apply encryption technology to WSN.

Later, the information hiding technology applied to image security is used for the data authentication of WSN. Compared to encryption, the information hiding is more lightweight on resource consumption. In [3], an information hiding scheme is firstly proposed. The scheme utilize the property of micro-errors of sensor data to embed information, and so long as the introduced error is within a limited scope, the WSN data can be used normally. In [4], a fragile chain-watermarking scheme is developed. This scheme regarded the WSN data as a stream chained by many groups, and generate watermarking by the repeated use of hash function for different groups. The experimental results indicated the fragile chain-watermarking scheme can verify the integrity of WSN data. It is noted that above information hiding schemes is not reversible.

© ICST Institute for Computer Sciences, Social Informatics and Telecommunications Engineering 2017
F. Chen and Y. Luo (Eds.): Industrial IoT 2017, LNICST 202, pp. 130–139, 2017.
DOI: 10.1007/978-3-319-60753-5_14

In some special applications such as medical and military fields, the authenticated data is not allowed to be modified. Therefore, for these applications, only the reversible information hiding technology [5, 6] is adopted. In [7], Shi et al. proposed a reversible authentication scheme based on group strategy. Each authentication group is determined dynamically by synchronization points, and the data stream can be totally recovered after the authentication information composed of hash value of authentication group is extracted. In [8], a reversible authentication scheme is achieved based on the cyclical redundancy check (CRC) and odd-even invariability, but this scheme has a high false tampering-alarm rate.

In this paper, a novel reversible authentication scheme for WSN is proposed. The authentication information is generated by calculating the CRC code of generator group. In the fluctuation region of prediction-error histogram (PEH) of carrier group, the authentication information is reversibly embedded by applying the PEH shifting algorithm. Experimental results and analysis demonstrate the proposed scheme achieves better performances than previous reversible authentication schemes.

2 Proposed Scheme

2.1 System Model

A simple WSN system model is provided in Fig. 1, where there are three types of nodes such as sensor node, transmission node and convergence node. The sensor node is responsible to collect periodically the environmental data and embed the authentication information. The embedded WSN data is then sent to convergence node by transmission node. The convergence node, as the central node of WSN, has rich computation resources and strong energy, where the data group is authenticated with extracted embedded-information.

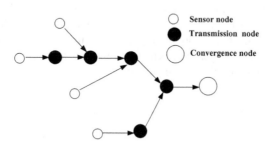

Fig. 1. Diagram of WSN data transmission

In proposed scheme, the WSN data stream collected by sensor node is denoted by V, which is divided into a series of authentication groups. An authentication group consists of a generator group and a carrier group that is shown in Fig. 2. Each element in an authentication group is presented by v_i. The CRC code of each generator group, as authentication information, is embedded reversibly into the corresponding carrier group

Generate group				Carrier group			
v_1	v_2	•••	v_M	v_{M+1}	v_{M+2}	•••	v_{M+N}

Authentication group

Fig. 2. An example of authentication group

using the prediction error-based histogram shifting algorithm [9]. In the decoding end, the integrity of each authentication group is judged in terms of the comparison between the extracted hidden-information from each carrier group and the CRC code of the corresponding generator group.

2.2   Prediction Error-Based Histogram Shifting Algorithm

2.2.1   Encoding Phase

Let v_i be an element of a carrier group, v_{i+1} *and* v_{i+2} are two neighbor elements of v_i. The prediction value of v_i is denoted by $\hat{v}_i$, which is calculated using Eq. (1).

$$\hat{v}_i = \left\lfloor \frac{v_{i+1} + v_{i+2}}{2} \right\rfloor \tag{1}$$

Then the prediction error between v_i and $\hat{v}_i$, denoted by e_i, is counted using Eq. (2).

$$e_i = v_i - \hat{v}_i \tag{2}$$

An example of PEH is shown in Fig. 3, where the middle part of PEH is smooth region, the two sides of PEH is called as fluctuation region. If the authentication information is embedded into the smooth region, then the smooth property of this region will be destroyed, which may attract the attention of attackers. In contrast, embedding the authentication information into the fluctuation region can not change its fluctuation property. Therefore, the fluctuation region is a better choice to embed the authentication information than the smooth region.

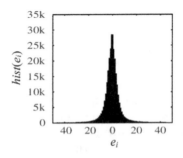

Fig. 3. An example of the prediction-error histogram

Since the prediction errors e_is at two sides of PEH are different, an initial parameter T_m with lower absolute value is selected by Eq. (3).

$$T_m = \min(|\min(e_i)|, \max(e_i))$$ (3)

Then the end parameter T_p is selected in terms of Eq. (4), which should satisfy the capacity demand of embedded authentication information.

$$\begin{cases} \text{maximize } T_p \in (0, 1, 2, \ldots, T_m) \\ \text{subject to } (\sum_{E=-T_m}^{-T_p} hist(E) + \sum_{E=T_p}^{T_m} hist(E)) > capacity \end{cases}$$ (4)

In Eq. (4), $hist(E)$ denotes the pixel number with the prediction error of E, and *capacity* means the bit number of the embedded authentication information.

A bit of authentication information, denoted by b, is embedded into the fluctuation region of PEH by Eq. (5).

$$D_i = \begin{cases} e_i + 1, & e_i > E \\ e_i - 1, & e_i < -E \\ e_i + b, & e_i = E \\ e_i - b, & e_i = -E \\ e_i, & else \end{cases}$$ (5)

where D_i is the modified prediction error. It is observed from Eq. (5) that the prediction errors larger than E or less than $-E$ are shifted by increasing 1 or decreasing 1, and the prediction errors in the smooth region remain unchanged.

Finally, the marked element value V_i is calculated using Eq. (6).

$$V_i = D_i + \hat{v}_i$$ (6)

It is noted that the prediction errors of the neighbor elements v_{i+1}, v_{i+2} *and* v_{i+3} of v_i are not counted and not used to embed information. In addition, in order to recover the original authentication group in the receiving end, the parameters T_m and T_p need to be embedded into the first thirty LSBs of carrier group. Together with the authentication information, the first thirty LSBs of carrier group are embedded the fluctuation region of PEH by Eq. (5).

2.2.2 Decoding Phase

In the receiving end, firstly, the first thirty LSBs of carrier group are extracted to obtain the parameters T_m and T_p. Then the modified prediction error D_i is calculated using Eq. (7).

$$D_i = V_i - \hat{v}_i$$ (7)

The hidden information is extracted using Eq. (8), where f_i changes from 0 to $f_{max} - 1$, H_i changes from T_p to T_m, and $f_{max} = T_m - T_p + 1$.

$$b = \begin{cases} 0, & D_i = H_i + f_i \quad or \ D_i = -H_i - f_i \\ 1, & D_i = H_i + f_i \ + 1 \ or \ D_i = -H_i - f_i - 1 \end{cases} \tag{8}$$

The original prediction error e'_i is recovered using Eq. (9)

$$e'_i = \begin{cases} D_i - f_i, & D_i = H_i + f_i \\ D_i + f_i, & D_i = -H_i - f_i \\ D_i - f_i - 1, & D_i = H_i + f_i + 1 \\ D_i + f_i + 1, & D_i = -H_i - f_i - 1 \\ D_i, & D_i > -H_i - f_i \ and \ D_i < H_i + f_i \end{cases} \tag{9}$$

The original prediction error larger than T_m is recovered using Eq. (10).

$$e'_i = \begin{cases} D_i - f_{max}, & D_i > T_m + f_{max} \\ -D_i + f_{max}, & D_i < -T_m - f_{maxi} \end{cases} \tag{10}$$

The original WSN data element is restored by Eq. (11).

$$v_i = \hat{v}_i + e'_i \tag{11}$$

Finally, the first thirty LSBs of carrier group extracted by Eq. (8) is written back, so that all elements of a carrier group are completely restored.

2.3   Generation of Authentication Information

The CRC code of each generator group is calculated as authentication information using Algorithm 1.

Algorithm 1: Generation of authentication information

Input: Generator group element v_i
Output: CRC code
Step1. The generator group element v_i is translated to binary expression, which is denoted by bv_i, then bv_i is represented as a polynomial. For example, '1011001' is expressed as $x^6 + x^4 + x^3 + 1$.
Step 2. bv_i is shifted left l bits and regarded as dividend, where l is a parameter controlling the length of CRC code. The polynomial $x^l + x^{l-2} + x^{l-3} + 1$ is taken as divisor.
Step 3. The module-2 division between the dividend and divisor polynomials is used to obtain l-bits remainder cv_i, which is CRC code of v_i.
Step 4. XOR operation among the CRC codes of all elements of current generator group is performed to generate the authentication information W, as shown in Eq. (12) where $\oplus$ indicates XOR operation.

$$W = cv_1 \oplus cv_2 \oplus \cdots \oplus cv_{M-1} \oplus cv_M \tag{12}$$

2.4   Embedding of Authentication Information

From Sects. 2.2 and 2.3, it is known that the information to be embedded is composed of the authentication information W and the first thirty LSBs of carrier group with a length of $(l + 30)$ bits. In order to keep the description compact, we still adopt W to represent all information to be embedded, and call W as authentication information. To assure the total embedding of W, the length of carrier group is set as $(l + 30) \times 9 + 30$. Moreover, for the convenience to detect carrier group in receiving end, an element as a string "000000" is added as last element of carrier group, and the notation EOC is used to denote the element. Therefore, each carrier group includes $(l + 30) \times 9 + 31$ elements. The embedding procedure of authentication information W may refer to Algorithm 2.

Algorithm 2: Embedding

---

1.   while (stream V is not over) do //V is the WSN data stream
2.   while (stream V is not over, and $i \leq M$) do
3.   Buffer(v_i); //buffer current data element
4.   calculate cv_i; // get CRC code of v_i according to Algorithm 1
5. $CRC = CRC \oplus cv_i$; //calculate CRC code of current generator group
6.   end while
7.   if (stream V is not over) do
8.   Buffer(carrier group); // buffer $(l + 30) \times 9 + 30$ elements as current carrier group
9. $W = CRC \cup LSBs$ //W includes the first thirty LSBs of carrier group
10.   embed W according to the embedding method given in Section 2.2.1
11.   Insert EOC as last element of carrier group
12.   end if
13.   end while

2.5   Information Extraction and Authentication

In receiving end, the receiver can extract the embedded authentication information, and confirm if a transmitted data group is tampered in terms of the comparison between the generated authentication information by generator group and the extracted authentication information. If a group is intact, then the group will be restored to its original state. The concrete procedure may refer to Algorithm 3.

Algorithm 3: Extraction and authentication

---

1. while (stream V is not over) do // V is the WSN data stream
2.   buffer(G); //buffer current authentication group
3.   while (group G is not over, and $i \leq M$) do
4.   buffer(v_i);
5.   calculate cv_i; // get CRC code of v_i according to Algorithm 1
6. $CRC = CRC \oplus cv_i$; //calculate CRC code of current generator group
7.   end while
8.   if (group G is not over) do
9.   buffer(carrier group);
10.   extract W according to the information extraction method given in Section 2.2.2;
11. $C R C$ is obtained by separating W;
12.   if ($CRC == CRC'$) do
13. G passed the authentication;
14.   restore G according to the recovery method given in Section 2.2.2;
15.   else
16.   authentication on G failed;
17.   end if
18.   end if
19. end while

---

3 Experimental Results and Analysis

3.1 Experimental Data

The original WSN data in the experiments is from the real WSN deployed in Intel Berkeley Lab [10]. In this network, a series of sensor nodes collect periodically four types of data such as temperature, humidity, light and voltage. The experimental data used in each experiment consists of the information of 10000 times collection by a node, i.e., each experimental data stream includes 10000 elements. As shown in Fig. 4,

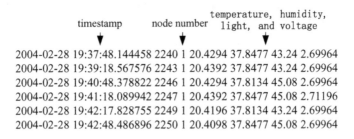

Fig. 4. Original WSN data from Intel Berkeley Lab

every element is composed of eight columns data, involving time stamp, node number and four types of collected data. For simplicity, we only consider to authenticate the integrity of four types of collected data. The verification experiments for the performance of proposed scheme are performed by MATLAB simulation.

3.2   Integrity Authentication Test

The integrity authentication tests for six common tampering attacks are performed and the test results are listed in Table 1. The six attacks involve randomly inserting, deleting and modifying an element or several elements in generator group and carrier group. If the tampering attack is not detected, then the integrity authentication is failing. Each kind of attack adopts 100 random samples. It is indicated from Table 1 that the unsuccessful detection number is zero for all kinds of attacks, and the successful authentication rate is 100%, which demonstrate the proposed authentication scheme is reliable.

Table 1. Integrity authentication test

Tampering type	Number of detection failure	Authentication succeed rate
Insert an element or several elements in generator group	0	100%
Insert an element or several elements in carrier group	0	100%
Delete an element or several elements in generator group	0	100%
Delete an element or several elements in carrier group	0	100%
Modify an element or several elements in generator group	0	100%
Modify an element or several elements in carrier group	0	100%
Average	0	100%

Furthermore, for the authentication group not being tampered, the comparison test between the recovered group after extracting the embedded information and the corresponding original group shows they are consistent, namely, the authentication group can be completely restored.

3.3   Complexity Analysis

Firstly, the space complexity is analyzed. In the sensor node, the buffer size containing carrier group at the most is needed to finish the embedding of authentication information. Comparison with the buffer size containing total authentication group demanded by the traditional WSN authentication methods, the proposed method has some advantages. In the convergence node, the buffer size containing total current authentication group is needed to achieve information extraction and authentication. Since the convergence node has rich resource, the demand for buffer size is easy to satisfy. For the side information, only two additional parameters, T_m and T_p, are needed to transmit.

Next, the analysis for time complexity is given. In the proposed scheme, the time consumption mainly involves the group division of data stream, the calculation of CRC code, and the embedding and extraction of authentication information. Assume the length of data stream is L, then the time complexity for the group division of data stream is $O(L)$. The time consumption for the calculation of CRC code is closely related with the number of generator group elements M and the controlling parameter of CRC code length l, so the time complexity is $O(M \times l)$. Moreover, in terms of the Algorithms 2 and 3, it is known that the time complexities for embedding and extraction are $O(l \times L)$ and $O(M \times l) + O(L)$, respectively. Therefore, the total time complexity is $O(l \times L)$.

3.4   Detection Efficiency

The false negative rate is adopted to measure the detection efficiency of the proposed scheme, and is analyzed under three kinds of attacks such as inserting, deleting and modifying an element. Assuming inserting an element in generator group, the position probability of this inserted element is $1/M$. Meanwhile, the probability to let the CRC code after inserting be consistent with that before inserting is $1/2^l$. Therefore, the false negative rate is $1/(M \times 2^l)$. If an element is inserted in carrier group, then the analysis for the false negative rate is more complex. But surely the false negative rate in this case is less than $1/(M \times 2^l)$. For other two attacks such as deleting and modifying an element, the false negative rates are similar to that of inserting attack. It is concluded from the above analysis that the probability to make a false judgement for tampering attack will be very low if the values of M and l are big enough.

3.5   Comparisons Among Several Schemes

The comparisons among Shi's scheme [7], Wu's scheme [8] and the proposed scheme are conducted. In Shi's scheme, the hash values of generator group are used as authentication information. In comparison to CRC code, the computation complex of hash function is higher. In Wu's scheme, an authentication group insists of current data group and former data group, and the sizes of the current data group and former data group are fixed, i.e., the division of authentication group is based on fixed length. So when an element is inserted, all authentication groups will be changed so that the false tampering alarm may be induced. In the proposed scheme, the authentication group is divided according to the end notation, hence the situation similar to Wu's scheme does not occur. In addition, Shi's scheme and Wu's scheme do not distinguish the smooth and fluctuation regions when the authentication information is embedded. However, the proposed scheme only embeds the authentication information into the fluctuation region, which may attract less the attention of attackers.

4 Conclusion

Based on CRC code and prediction-error histogram, this paper proposes a reversible authentication scheme for WSN. For decreasing the computation complexity, the CRC code replacing the hash function is adopted to produce the authentication information. To increase the imperceptibility of embedding information into the carrier group, the fluctuation region of prediction-error histogram is used to hide the authentication information. In the future work, degrading further the time complexity will be considered.

Acknowledgments. This work is supported in part by the National Natural Science Foundation of China (Grant No. 61662039, 61362032, 61462048), the Natural Science Foundation of Jiangxi Province, China (Grant No. 20171BAB202004, 20151BAB207003, 20161BAB202036), and the State Scholarship for Overseas Studies (Grant No. 201408360019).

References

1. Seo, S.H., Won, J., Sultana, S., Bertino, E.: Effective key management in dynamic wireless sensor networks. IEEE Trans. Inform. Forensics Secur. **10**(2), 371–383 (2015)
2. Marzi H.: A security model for wireless sensor networks. In: IEEE International Conference on Computational Intelligence and Virtual Environments for Measurement Systems and Applications, pp. 64–69. IEEE Press (2014)
3. Wong J.L, Feng J., Kirovski D.: Security in sensor networks: watermarking techniques. In: Wireless Sensor Networks, pp. 305–323 (2004)
4. Guo, H., Li, Y., Jajodia, S.: Chaining watermarks for detecting malicious modifications to streaming data. Inform. Sci. **177**(1), 281–298 (2007)
5. Thodi D.M., Rodriquez J.J.: Prediction-error-based reversible watermarking, In: IEEE International Conference on Image Processing, pp. 1549–1552. IEEE Press (2004)
6. Li, X., Zhang, W., Gui, X.: Efficient reversible data hiding based on multiple histograms modification. IEEE Trans. Inform. Forensics Secur. **10**(9), 2016–2027 (2015)
7. Shi, X., Xiao, D.: A reversible watermarking authentication scheme for wireless sensor networks. Inform. Sci. **240**(10), 173–183 (2013)
8. Wu, H., Chen, Y., Ji, Z.: Wireless sensor networks authentication algorithm based on CRC and reversible digital watermarking. Comput. Appl. Softw. **33**(6), 294–298 (2016)
9. Yang, Y., Zhang, W., Hou, D., Wang, H.: Research and prospect of reversible data hiding method with contrast enhancement. Chin. J. Net. Inform. Secur. **2**(4), 12–19 (2016)
10. http://db.lcs.mit.edu/labdata/labdata.html

Heterogeneous Component Model for Architecture of Community Medical Internet of Things

Cheng Zhang, Fulong Chen[✉], Jie Yang, Junru Zhu, Ziyang Zhang,
Chao Liu, and Chuanxin Zhao

Department of Computer Science and Technology, Anhui Normal University,
Wuhu 241002, Anhui, China
{zhangcheng,long005,yangjie_7,jrzhu_study,zzy000,lcahnu,
zhaocx}@ahnu.edu.cn

Abstract. As a kind of medical services around people, community health care is closely related to people's lives, and thus it has also been placed higher requirements. In the face of growing community medical needs, the construction and development of community medical Internet of things is imminent. Through analyzing the existing construction of medical Internet of Things, combined with the community application environment, a heterogeneous component model for the community medical Internet of things is designed to be applied to the actual community situation. The model includes three parts such as heterogeneous components for medical Internet of things, their flat physical structure and hierarchical logical structure. Related model description is presented meanwhile to make the whole system architecture more perfect and also make the system architecture meet the needs of different users.

Keywords: Community health · Internet of things · Component · Heterogeneity · Model

1   Introduction

As a basic unit of society, community is a group of life which is formed in a certain field by several social groups and social organizations. Therefore, to strengthen the quality of community health service is an important part of health care reform. Community health is the most front end of the entire health system. Establishing community personal health records, analyzing health status and health risk factors, establishing community health self-detection mechanism, the formulation of corresponding health care plan, providing personalized health services, strengthening community medical institutions with the hospital, reducing the risk of community members, and alleviating the pressure of large hospitals are the main contents of community health services.

In community medical Internet of things (CMIoT), some Internet of things technologies are used. In CMIoT, the general practitioners are taken as the backbone, focusing on the health of community residents, mainly for the elderly, children, women, patients with chronic diseases and disabilities, etc., its main tasks are disease prevention, health

© ICST Institute for Computer Sciences, Social Informatics and Telecommunications Engineering 2017
F. Chen and Y. Luo (Eds.): Industrial IoT 2017, LNICST 202, pp. 140–151, 2017.
DOI: 10.1007/978-3-319-60753-5_15

care and medical services, and its main content is the treatment and rehabilitation of the common diseases, mild symptoms and chronic.

Using various means of communication and the Internet of things (IoT) technology to achieve multi-level contact among large medical institutions - community medical institutions - community masses, improving the circulation speed and real-time performance of health information, this will not only save medical resources, but also enhance the quality of service in the medical industry.

No matter that the CMIoT application system is mixed with heterogeneous components or oriented to information processing, when the system is complex to a certain extent, if we disign it with directly programming, it will increase the likelihood of errors or even failures.

In view of the complex collaborative design task of different components of CMIoT, in order to meet the requirements of good performance, low cost and high reliability, and improve the quality and efficiency of the system development, the design needs to be carried out under the description for completing the design cycle [1], and therefore, the first step in collaborative design of all kinds of components should be to establish the model of the system, that is to say, to get the abstract description of the system.

2 Related Works

Since the emergence of the IoT, many scholars and research institutions have designed the architecture of the Internet of things according to their characteristics, and for the specific application domain, a lot of reference architectures for building the Internet of things have been put forward. Chen [2] pointed out that up to now, no one has made a unified comparison and analysis of many Internet of things architectures, no one has a hierarchical induction of its implementation method, and no one correspond the system structure to the implementation method, all those make it difficult for designers to choose what kind of architecture and implementation method in the development of the Internet of things. In his paper, the analysis of the system structure and implementation methods of the predecessors is very thorough. However it is still based on the abstract level, and it is lack of a practical model. At present, many scholars have carried on the related researches on the system structure of the Internet of things and also proposed some architectures, e.g., World Wide Web Architecture of things (WOT) [3], IoT autonomic architecture, EPC network architecture [4], Architecture based on Wireless Sensor Networks (WSN), M2 M (machine-to-machine) architecture [5].

Many scholars build up the hierarchy of the Internet of things from the vertical perspective, e.g., the USN [6] (5 layers including the sensing, access, network infrastructure, middleware, and application platform layer) of International Telecommunications Union (ITU), Physical-net [7] (4 layers including service provider, gateway, coordination, and application layer), OT-A [8] (4 layers including application, IP, API M2 M, and wireless communication protocol layer), SENSEI [9] (3 layers including communication services, resources, applications layer), Networked Auto-ID [10] (3 layers including RFID identification and reading, information transmission network and identity analysis and services layer), uIDIoT [11], M2 M [12] (3 layers including the core network, service capabilities and application layer), AOA [13] (4 layers including data, passive intelligence, knowledge and management layer), SOA [14] (4 layers including sensing, network, service and interface). Ma [15] sets up a model of 4 layers of IoT architecture, which is composed of object layer, data exchange layer, information integration layer and application service layer, and abstracts the Internet of things from the functional level. It has better scalability and mobility, and has better adaptability in the large-scale and dynamic characteristics of IoT. However, how to achieve the specific implementation of structured protocol package is still a problem.

However, most of the existing IoT application systems are based on different protocols and mechanisms. Their composition has strong heterogeneity used in different industries and fields. Therefore, it is needed to build the flat IoT architecture so as to solve the problem of mutual connection and communication between different components. Xie [16] proposes a physical model driven software architecture of IoT, composed of 3 layers such as application model, the sensing/executing model and the physical model, in which vertical physical applications are interconnected in a unified framework and implementation method and the architecture of the proposed IoT is verified with Wright and other methods of formal description and proof. But it does not take into account the interaction between social groups in the user model and the factors that affect the overall stability of the model. IoT-A model unifies the different wireless communication protocol stack as a material communication interface, combine the interconnection communication protocol to support the interconnection between large scale and heterogeneous devices, and support a large number of different components and their applications without specific scheme in the support of behavior model.

In the specific application, Cao [17] proposes the architecture of information system for the smart grid development from the perspective of information technology, including 3 layers such as the infrastructure layer, platform layer, and application layer. It realizes the integration and interaction of physics, information and application system. Since the structure is designed for smart grid, it lacks the extensible support for the heterogeneous components of the IoT applications. From the trend of the integration of human and vehicle, and the coordination needs of human, vehicle and environment, for vehicle networking, Li [18] proposes the object collaboration model and the architecture model, so that these models can meet the requirements of global information sensing, control and sustainability of vehicle networking services. However, because the structure is very high to the multi dimension group collaborative computing and evaluation, there are still some needs to study new theories and models to support it.

3   Heterogeneous Components in CMIoT

Component technology is a new idea of software development, in which the complex large-scale system is decomposed into several independent modules, and a unified connection standard between the components is established, in order to realize the connection between components or between components and users. Component technology packages details which users can operate directly without needing to fully understand. The research of component technology makes the process of system development have a very big change, at the same time, the maintenance cost of the system is greatly reduced, the flexibility of the development is increased, and the most important is that it can greatly enhance the scalability of the system. Therefore, we introduce the design idea of the component to the architecture of CMIoT. In the heterogeneous component model of CMIoT, a variety of different functional entities in the community medical Internet of things are abstracted into some objects with independent attributes and methods, and then, according to the different needs of each application, designers select the desired object so that objects can work together, and ultimately achieve the desired function.

3.1 Heterogeneity of Components in CMIoT

It is mainly manifested as follow:

- **Heterogeneity of network transmission**
  It shows the diversity of transmission modes. Data or control commands in the transmission process, possibly reach the destination through different networks. Common network transmission modes include 2G/3G/4G and other mobile communication networks, wireless sensor networks, wireless local area networks and large-scale data transmission network.
- **Heterogeneity of component functionality**
  It shows that each component has a different job content. In IoT, the functionalities of the components are usually divided into data acquisition, data transmission, data processing and data services. Each component achieves its respective functions and all components work together.
- **Heterogeneity of component behavior**
  It shows different information processing methods of different components. For the components of the hardware modules, they process signal information, and for the components of the software modules, they process data information.
- **Heterogeneity of component structure**
  It shows that different components have different internal structures and there are different connection structures between components. For the sensing/executive component, it mainly consists of the sensing or executive module. For the data processing component, it mainly consists of data processing module.

3.2 Composition of Components in CMIoT

According to the functionalities of CMIoT, it can be divided into the following several major components.

- **Sensing components**
  They are sensing nodes in CMIoT. Their functions are different, and they are used to sense various physical sign data and environmental data. They are to help users to collect their own physiological parameters, and monitor their health status.
- **Executive components**

They are executer nodes in CMIoT. Their role is to receive the decision information which is determined by the analysis of the computing component, and to act on the decision.

– **Computing (information integration) components**
They include two kinds such as microprocessors with the computing function and the related equipment and health care workers who participant in medical activities.

– **Transmission components**
They are a kind of components with information transfer functionalities. They include Wi-Fi, ZigBee, 3G, 4G, and wired Ethernet, etc.

– **Storage components.**
They are the storage containers for system information. They are embodied in the sensing components, executive components, computing components, etc.

4   Flat Physical Structure of CMIoT

A big difference between IoT and Internet is that the members of the Internet of things are the objects in reality, not the abstract concept. Therefore, according to the application environment of CMIoT, its physical structure of the component model needs to be given. This structure is flat in intuition. It is divided according to the space region and role in CMIoT. It mainly includes community resident unit, community care unit and medical support unit. Through this structure, as shown in Fig. 1, we can clearly understand the physical composition of CMIoT and the interaction between the constituent elements.

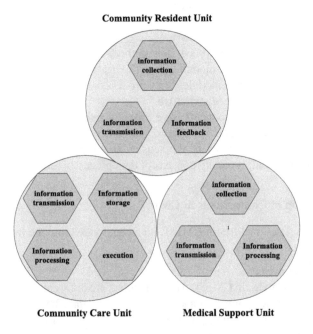

Fig. 1. Physical structure of CMIoT.

4.1   Community Resident Unit

In CMIoT, all sources of information at the beginning are community resident units, which constitute the most front ends of the whole physical structure, and usually contain information collection part, information transmission part and information feedback part.

4.2   Community Care Unit

It is the data processing and decision making unit of the whole physical system and at the same time is also the executive unit of the decision-making unit, and constitutes the back-end of the physical structure. Its composition includes information transmission part, information storage part, information processing decision part and executive part.

4.3   Medical Support Unit

Although the community medical unit has certain medical decision-making ability and is also capable of providing medical care for mild conditions and known chronic diseases, when faced with a serious illness, its ability is slightly less. At this point, the community medical unit will be able to turn to the medical support unit (generally refers to large medical institutions) for help. The medical support unit mainly includes information transmission part information processing decision part and executive part.

5   Hierarchical Logical Structure of CMIoT

In addition to the division according to the space region and role, designers can also be to establish the hierarchical model of the heterogeneous components of CMIoT in accordance with the logic level of components. As shown in Fig. 2, it mainly consists of four layers: sensing/executing layer, data transmission layer, information integration layer and application system layer.

5.1   Sensing/Executing Layer

Sensing/executing layer is divided into two sub layers such as physical sub layer and device sub layer. The physical sub layer is composed of some physical components, e.g., machine, house, electric appliance, vehicle, watch, even air or human body, etc., which are composition elements of the physical environment, and used to receive some controlling signals from controllers and send feedback signals to sensors. The device sub layer includes some device components connected with physical components so as to make the latter run in more smart way.

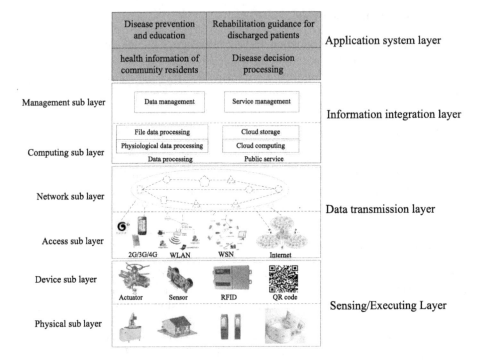

Fig. 2. Hierarchical logic structure of CMIoT.

5.2 Data Transmission Layer

This layer is the connection and information transfer layer of CMIoT. The main task is to build a bridge for the sensing/executing layer and the information integrated layer and transfer information between them. This layer can also be divided into two sub layers including access sub layer and network sub layer. The access sub layer contains a variety of access components such as 2G/3G/4G/5G, IEEE 801.11, IEEE 802.3, ZigBee, Bluetooth, infrared and so on. The network sub layer is used to establish the connection of heterogeneous network, e.g., IPv6 is the most suitable choice for the future.

5.3 Information Integration Layer

The information integration layer is a middleware layer which provides common service components for the system application layer. It includes computing sub layer and management sub layer. For the computing sub layer in CMIoT, there is a kind of public service components such as cloud storage, cloud computing, and also there is a kind of data processing components such as physiological data processing, file data processing (sorting, computing, etc.), encryption/decryption, and so on. For these two kinds of components, in the information integration layer, their management components are provided in the management sub layer so that the latter can manage them.

5.4 Application System Layer

CMIoT takes the health of community residents as the central service. The main service objects are the elderly, children, women, patients with chronic diseases and disabilities, etc. Its main task is disease prevention, health care, medical treatment, and so on. The main content is the treatment and rehabilitation of common diseases, mild symptoms and chronic diseases. Therefore, this layer should include the following contents such as disease prevention and education, health information of common residents, rehabilitation guidance for discharged patients, and disease decision processing.

5.5 Model Description

In order to facilitate the visual description of the heterogeneous component model of CMIoT, some graphic elements are introduced as shown in Fig. 3. The rectangle represents a component, and its interior is composed of attributes and behaviors. The triangle represents an interface connected different components. The line indicates the direction of information transfer.

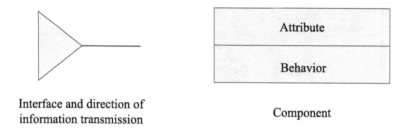

Interface and direction of
information transmission

Component

Fig. 3. Component graphics.

Through the analysis of flat physical structure and hierarchical logical structure of CMIoT, its model is built as shown in Fig. 4. The whole model consists of user component, sensing component, transmission component, storage component, computing component and so on which form a closed loop. In this model, first, the sensing component senses the monitoring data from the user side, and is uploaded to the storage component through the transmission component. Second, the data is saved by the storage component. Third, the computing component can extract the relevant information from the storage components, and through the method of data mining, cloud computing and artificial identification, the information is processed and fused, and the decision information is generated. Finally, the decision information is transmitted to the executing component through the transmission component, and finally the user component is affected.

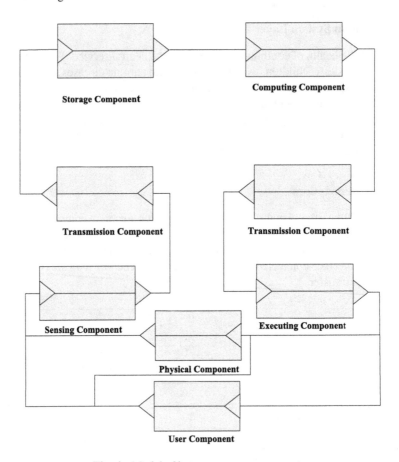

Fig. 4. Model of heterogeneous components.

6   Prototype System of CMIoT

6.1   Network Structure

In the prototype System of CMIoT, the transmission part adopts ZigBee + Wi-Fi wireless transmission mode, and at the same time, wired Ethernet is taken as an auxiliary transmission mode. The network structure is shown in Fig. 5.

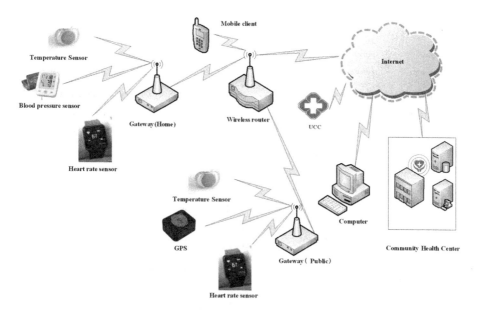

Fig. 5. Prototype system of CMIoT.

The transmission component of sensor and actuator side adopts the ZigBee transmission mode. A large number of ZigBee terminal nodes communicate with the gateway in their respective regions and form their own ZigBee network. The sink gateway of different regions is connected with the converged wireless router which is distributed in the fixed area through the Wi-Fi mode. Wireless router can choose wired or wireless way to connect to the Internet network. According to the actual situation, computing components select the apt access network, and due to the high requirements of data transmission speed and stability, storage components (data server) adopt wired access mode.

6.2   Deployment Structure

The whole prototype system is divided into three blocks, which are three different areas such as home, public area and community hospital as shown in Fig. 6. Among them, in the home, there is a sink gateway and two sensing/executing nodes, in which the sensing component is a temperature sensor for measuring the temperature value of the user, the executing component is a buzzer connected with the sink gateway. The configuration of the public area is similar to the home. In the community hospital, there is a desktop as a storage component (which is the role of the system server), a laptop as a computing component (system client), and a wireless router as information transmission component.

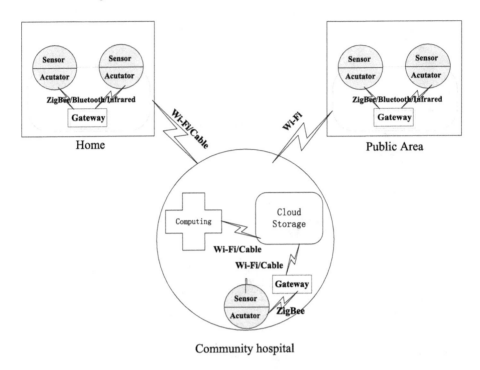

Fig. 6. Deployment structure diagram.

7   Conclusion

This paper takes CMIoT as a standpoint. We first analyzes the main tasks of community medical Internet of things, and based on these tasks and the actual situation of the community medical environment, a heterogeneous component model is proposed. The definition, composition, flat physical structure and hierarchical logical structure are given. The graphical description of the model is provided. All above lay the foundation for the next step to build a prototype system for CMIoT.

Acknowledgement. The authors would like to thank our colleagues and students in Engineering Technology Research Center of Network and Information Security at Anhui Normal University. We thank National Natural Science Foundation of China under Grant No. 61572036, University Natural Science Research Project of Anhui Province under Grant No. KJ2014A084, Anhui Province University Outstanding Youth Talent Support Program under Grant No. gxyqZD2016026 and Anhui Provincial Natural Science Foundation under Grant No. 1708085MF156.

References

1. Chen, F., Ye, H., Yang, J., et al.: A standardized design methodology for complex digital logic components of cyber-physical systems. Microprocess. Microsyst. **39**(8), 1245–1254 (2015)
2. Chen, H., Cui, L., Xie, K.: A comparative study on architectures and implementation methodologies of internet of things. Chin. J. Comput. **36**(1), 168–188 (2013)
3. Yan, B., Huang, G.: Supply chain information transmission based on RFID and internet of things. In: Proceedings of ISECS International Colloquium on Computing, Communication, Control, and Management (CCCM 2009), pp. 166–169 (2009)
4. Bauer, M., Bui, N., Loof, D., et al.: IoT reference model. In: Enabling Things to Talk, pp. 113–162 (2013)
5. Lo, B., Thiemjarus, S., King, R., Yang, G.: Body sensor network–a wireless sensor platform for pervasive healthcare monitoring. In: Proceedings of the 3rd International Conference on Pervasive Computing, pp. 77–80 (2005)
6. Muthanna, A., Prokopiev, A., Koucheryavy, A.: The mixed telemetry/image USN in the overload conditions. In: Proceedings of 16th IEEE International Conference on Advanced Communication Technology (ICACT2014), pp. 475–478 (2014)
7. Vicaire, P., Xie, Z., Hoque, E., et al.: Physicalnet: A generic framework for managing and programming across pervasive computing networks. In: Proceedings of 2010 16th IEEE Real-Time and Embedded Technology and Applications Symposium (RTAS 2010), pp. 269–278 (2010)
8. Ruther, S.: Assistive Systems for Quality Assurance by Context-Aware User Interfaces in Health Care and Production. Bielefeld University (2014)
9. Presser, M., Barnaghi, P., Eurich, M., et al.: The SENSEI project: integrating the physical world with the digital world of the network of the future. IEEE Commun. Mag. **47**(4), 1–4 (2009)
10. Sarma, S., Brock, L., Ashton, K.: The Networked Physical World–Proposals for Engineering The Next Generation of Computing, Commerce & Automatic Identification. MIT Auto-ID centre White paper(2000)
11. Koshizuka, N., Sakamura, K.: Ubiquitous ID standards for ubiquitous computing and the internet of things. IEEE Pervasive Comput. **9**(4), 98–101 (2010)
12. ETSI. Machine-to-Machine Communications (M2 M): Functional Architecture. ETSI. Technical Specification:102 690V1.1.1 (2011)
13. Pujolle, G.: An autonomic-oriented architecture for the internet of things. In: Proceedings of IEEE International Symposium on John Vincent Atanasoff Modern Computing, pp. 163–168 (2006)
14. Li, H., Dimitrovski, A., Song, J., et al.: Communication infrastructure design in cyber physical systems with applications in smart grids: a hybrid system framework. IEEE Commun. Surv. Tutorials **16**(3), 1689–1708 (2014)
15. Ma, H., Song, Y., Yu, S., et al.: The research of IoT architecture model and internetworking mechanism. Sci. Sinica **43**(10), 1183–1197 (2013)
16. Xie, K., Chen, H., Li, C.: PMDA: a physical model driven software architecture for internet of things. J. Comput. Res. Dev. **50**(6), 1185–1197 (2013)
17. Cao, J., Wan, Y., Tu, G., et al.: Information system architecture for smart grids. Chin. J. Comput. **36**(1), 143–167 (2014)
18. Li, J., Liu, Z., Yang, F.: Internet of vehicles: the framework and key technology. J. Beijing Univ. Posts Telecommun. **37**(6), 95–100 (2014)

A Novel Grouping-Based WSN Clustering Data Transmission Protocol

Jiequ Ji, Xianjin Fang$^{(\boxtimes)}$, Dai Chen, Yafei Xiao, and Yanting Wu

School of Computer Science and Engineering,
Anhui University of Science and Technology, Huainan, China
xjfang@aust.edu.cn

Abstract. The Grouping-based Clustering Data Transmission (GCDT) protocol is proposed in this paper, which aims at the problem of data loss easily during transmission process and the defects of transmission path after clustering on wireless sensor network (WSN). By calculating the reach probability of data packets, the original data packets are grouped to guarantee data integrity before transmission. Creating multipath between cluster heads and the base station is to ensure reliable delivery of packets. The simulation experiment results show that the packet loss ratio using GCDT protocol can decrease about 15% to 28% compared with the existing routing protocols. The GCDT protocol proposed in this paper improved the reliability of the data transmission and the network survivability effectively.

Keywords: Grouping-based clustering · Data transmission · Wireless sensor network

1 Introduction

With the development and integration of sensors, computers, wireless communication and micro-electromechanics in recent years, the Wireless Sensor Network (WSN) has been paid more and more attention. Its concept was put forward in the 1970s. Consisting of low-cost, low-power, multi-functional and wireless-capable sensor nodes that can be deployed in random form at any location and at any time, enabling new applications and services in a wide range of areas, including environmental monitoring, target tracking, natural disaster prediction, smart home, intelligent traffic control and military situations etc [1].

WSN usually includes sensor nodes, sinks and base stations (BSs) and management nodes. A large number of sensor nodes are usually deployed in a random manner, which can achieve data transmission of short distance, low power consumption and low rate. Sensor nodes are limited in battery, memory, computing power and communication bandwidth, and they often operate in harsh environments, which all lead to the failure of data transmission of sensor nodes easily. Therefore, the survivability has become a key issue in the study of WSN [2].

ARRIVE proposed by Karlof et al. [3] is a topology-based, tree-like probabilistic algorithm to achieve fault-tolerant routing to prevent link failure and

© ICST Institute for Computer Sciences, Social Informatics and Telecommunications Engineering 2017
F. Chen and Y. Luo (Eds.): Industrial IoT 2017, LNICST 202, pp. 152–162, 2017.
DOI: 10.1007/978-3-319-60753-5_16

node-mode failure. This method relies on periodic network flooding to prevent malicious or an orbiting nodes. Because flooding consumes a large amount of traffic and consumes a lot of resources, Braginsky et al. Proposed that the query-based route is no longer flooding the entire network, but uses a random path to send a query protocol to the target area [4].

The intrusion-tolerant wireless sensor network routing proposed by Deng et al. [5] adopts multi-path and combines the cryptographic mechanism to realize the WSN routing intrusion, it can achieve intrusion detection by bypassing the malicious nodes instead of intrusion detection. In order to facilitate the communication between the sensor nodes and the base station, INSENS constructs a forwarding table at each node.

Younis et al. Proposed a hybrid clustering protocol HEED (Hybird Energy-Efficient Distributed clustering) [6]. HEED points out that extending network life cycle, scalability and load balancing are the three most important requirements in WSN and extend the life cycle of the network by distributing the energy consumption evenly across the network. The disadvantage of HEED is that energy balance between cluster heads is not considered.

The survivability of the data transmission is studied by several algorithms above. In the wireless sensor network, all the data can not be lost in the transmission process [7]. In view of how to ensure the reliable transmission of data to establish multi-path between the CH and BS, this paper presents a grouping-based clustering data transmission protocol (GCDT) for WSN, and adopts distance based cluster head selection algorithms (DBCH) [8] to cluster each node. Under the premise of multi-path, the packets transmitted via WSN are divided into a series groups, then these are sent to the destination through multiple independent paths. In this paper, we propose a multi-path generation algorithm between cluster heads and base stations, which can ensure the transmission of cluster information in order, without loss or error, provide reliable data transmission services to the base station, and save some energy of the cluster head through multi-hop communication between cluster head and base station. Thus, the network's survival time is extended.

2   Model Building

2.1   Network Model

Reference [8,9], this paper on the wireless sensor network has the following settings.

(1) The nodes in the network remain the same location after the completion of the layout, and the nodes know themselves location information;
(2) A node can make damage around a small part of itself, but not the whole network;
(3) Prior to data transmission, there are already multiple-path established by the routing protocol throughout the network;
(4) Each path has its own key, which is independent of each other;

(5) Neighboring clusters can communicate with each other, and the cluster heads have data sent to the base station so that the base station can more accurately estimate whether the data is reliably transmitted to the destination;

(6) Base station is rich in resources, and can be trusted.

Based on the idea of divide and conquer, this paper divides the data transmission problem of large-scale network into small units of data transmission in the form of clustering. In the initial stage of the network, reference [10], using DBCH algorithm for cluster division and cluster head selection, and making the cluster head selection threshold $T(n)$ to the following improvements:

$$T(n) = \frac{p}{1 - p * [r \ mod(i/p)]} + (1 - p)\frac{D_{max} - D_{i \ to \ BS}}{D_{max} - D_{min}}(\frac{D_R}{D_0}) \tag{1}$$

Where, p is the optimal percentage of cluster heads, which determines the number of cluster heads per round; r is the election round number, $r \ mod \ 1 \ p$ represents the elected cluster head nodes in a round, D_{max} and D_{min} represent respectively the maximum and minimum distance from the base station, E_R is remaining energy of nodes in the current round, E_0 is the initial energy of nodes. This improvement needs to take the residual energy and distance factors into consideration, cluster to take the residual energy and distance factors into consideration, cluster head selection is based on the distance between the node and the base station, and the node near the base station will be elected as the cluster head.

2.2   Data Transmission Model

Wireless sensor network data transmission is usually to save energy as the goal, to maximize the extension of network life. The GCDT is a transmission protocol which makes data packet into groups and through multi-paths transmission to improve the transmission reliability, each node calculate the data packet reachable probability based on local channel bit error rate and hop count information. In this protocol, firstly it determines the expected successful transmission rate on the basis of the importance of the data packet before the source node sends a packet, and then determines the number of packets to be sent and the next cluster head node. The number of grouping N can be calculated from the locally estimated channel bit error rate, the number of hops from the source node to the cluster head node, and the expected success rate, which is calculated as follows [11]:

$$N = \frac{\log(1 - r)}{\log[1 - (1 - e)^h]} \tag{2}$$

Where, r indicates the expected successful transmission rate, e indicates the local channel bit error rate, h represents the hoc count of source node to the cluster head node. After the grouping is completed, the data packets in each group are transmitted to the base station through individual independent paths.

2.3   Energy Consumption Model

In this paper, only the energy consumption of communication is calculated according to the simple energy consumption model, and the energy consumption of nodes in the process of storage and calculation is neglected. The formula for the energy consumption of the transmitter is [12]:

$$E_{Tx}(ld) = E_{Tx\_elc}(k) + E_{Tx\_amp}(l,d) = \begin{cases} l \times E_{elc} + l \times \varepsilon f_s \times d^2, d < dl_1 \\ l \times E_{elc} + l \times \varepsilon amp \times d^4, d \geq dl_1 \end{cases} \quad (3)$$

The formula for the energy consumption of the receiver when acquiring information is:

$$E_{Rx}(1) = E_{Rx\_elec}(1) = 1 \times E_{elec} \quad (4)$$

$$dl_1 = \frac{\varepsilon_{fs}}{\varepsilon_{amp}} \quad (5)$$

Where, l is the number of bits of transmitted packets, d is the distance between transmitter and receiver, dl_1 is a distance threshold, E_{elec} is energy consumption of each bit data between transmitting circuit and receiving circuit, ε_{f_s} is the energy consumption which adopts the definition of free space model, ε_{amp} is the energy consumption of multi-path amplifying circuit.

3   GCDT Protocol Analysis

The goal of the GCDT protocol is to guarantee the reliability of data transmission in WSN. It has the following four assumptions [13]:

(1) Before the data transmission, the whole network has been divided into several clusters by clustering algorithm, CHs have been selected;
(2) Base station is rich in resources, and can be trusted;
(3) Reliable data transmission based on grouping can use NACK response mode;
(4) Before the WSN is configured, the base station and the cluster head node can send data according to the previous clustering algorithm, and send the CH_Msg message;
(5) In order to avoid data redundancy, the data packets sent by the common node to the cluster head node can be sent in groups. The transport layer uses the NACK packets for end-to-end packets loss recovery.

3.1   Data Packets Grouping Phase

The GCDT protocol first groups packets sent between nodes in each round [9], where the first three steps are performed at the sending node and the latter two steps at the receiving node. The procedure is as follows:

(1) The original data packets are divided into M blocks, and then re-assembled into N groups. N is the number of encryption algorithms that can be supported by the sensor node and is encrypted using a different encryption algorithm;

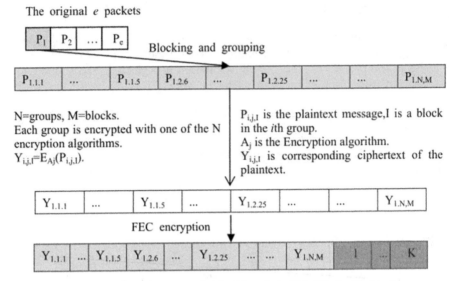

Fig. 1. GCDT protocol grouping process

(2) The data packets made up of M slices can be encrypted into M+K blocks using FEC error-correcting code before transmission, as shown in Fig. 1. It can be seen that only $M < K < M + K$, the packet can be used to reconstruct the encrypted data packet. The use of FEC error-correction codes allows the receiver to reconstruct the original packet even if several packets are lost during transmission;

(3) Packets encrypted with different encryption algorithms can be sent to the destination through multiple independent paths;

(4) When the receiver receives more than M encrypted blocks, and through the reliability of detection, the receiver will rebuild the packet, so you can save some of the energy and computing resources. The original packet can be obtained by decryption;

(5) If more than a certain period of time, or the last packet is not doing security and integrity testing, the data transmission system will re-request the transmitter to send a group desired by the receiver.

The pseudo-code for message receiving is described in Fig. 2.

3.2   Multi-paths Establishment Phase

According to the DBCH clustering algorithm, all the cluster heads of the network are generated, and then several transmission paths are established between the cluster head and the base station through the algorithm. Figure 3 is packet

```
1)  MsgHandle(msg) {
2)  switch(msg->type) {
3)    case Layer_Msg:
4) UpdateParents(msg);
5)      forward(msg);
6)      break;
7) case DATA:
8)      forward(msg);
9)      break;
10)   case Request_Msg:
11)     UpdateChildrens(msg);
12)     if(IsMychild){
13)       UpdateT(msg);
14)       SendNotify();
15)     }break;
16)   case Confirm_Msg:
17)     UpdateParents(msg);
18)     break;
19)   case Notify_Msg:
20)     UpdateChildrens(msg);
21)     if(IsMychild){
22)       UpdateT(msg);
23)       SendNotify();
24)     }break;
25)   )
26) }
```

Fig. 2. Message receiving part of the pseudo-code

format used for the establishment of multi-paths in the GCDT protocol between cluster head and base stations.

After the multi-path establishment between the cluster head and the base station and the data packet format is completed, the optimal path is selected for each data transmission, so as to avoid redundant data. The path generation algorithm is implemented in Fig. 4.

Type	Ows	Source_node	Path_Msg	Sig_Msg	Destination_Node

(a) Path request packet

Path_Msg | N_1 | N_2 | N_3 | ... |

(b) Path information

Sig_Msg | S_1 | S_2 | S_3 | ... |

(c) Signal strength information

Type	Ows	Source_Node	Forwarding_Table	Destination_Node

(d) Path feedback packet

Fig. 3. Packet format

```
Procedure Path Building
 Begin
  (1) Enter all the cluster head nodes into node V set,input one
node
to (2);
  (2) Calculates the number of all neighbor nodes of theinput
node,referred to as n;
  (3) If the number of neighbor nodes equals to 0, continue (4);
  Else repeat (3) .
End
  (4) The neighbor nodes are input to neigh V one by one;
Then do
Begin
 (4.1) While there is node vi do
If the node vi is the same as the parent node of the input node,
delete it;
  Else If energy of vi has been excessive consumed,delete it;
  Else If vi equals to Base node;
  Then outputs the path,de•lete the base node from
  neigh_V.
  End
 End
End
 (4.2) If neigh_V=0&&node_V=0, end the search;
Else turn to (1) ;
If neigh V≠0;
 Then the next node is taken from the set, repeat (2) .
End
End
```

Fig. 4. The steps of Path generation algorithm

4   Protocol Simulation and Result Analysis

4.1   Simulation Environment

In order to evaluate the performance of GCDT protocol, 100 nodes were set up by MATLAB7.0 to simulate ARRIVE, INSENS, HEED and GCDT under the same condition. The nodes were randomly generated in $500\,m \times 500\,m$ scene, and the energy consumption is respectively $1 \times 10 - 5\,J$, $5 \times 10 - 5\,J$ and $1 \times 10 - 4\,J$

Table 1. MATLAB network simulation parameters tables.

Parameter	Parameter description	Value
E_0	Initial energy of each node	50 J
l	Number of bits transmitted	20 bit
dl_1	Distance threshold	32 m
d	The distance between the transmitter and the receiver	18 m
Packet	Size Size of packet	10 bytes
n	Total number of nodes	100

for sensing, receiving and transmitting 1 byte data, and the other simulation parameters are shown in Table 1 [14].

4.2 Simulation Results Analysis

Figure 5 shows 100 nodes distributed randomly in the set area using MATLAB 7.0. Each node has the same initial energy E_0. Figure 6 shows the simulation of the selected 20 cluster head nodes (circle part) by the DBCH clustering algorithm.

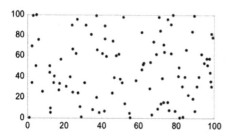
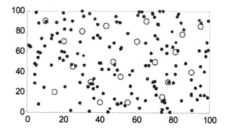

Fig. 5. Sensor node distribution diagram

Fig. 6. Cluster heads distribution of DBCH algorithm

In the simulation experiment, the number of packets transmitted in each cluster is counted, and a performance index equivalent to the network throughput is obtained. Figure 7 shows the network throughput of three algorithms, it can be seen, GCDT protocol network throughput is greater than ARRIVE and INSENS. Compared with ARRIVE and INSENS, the network throughput of GCDT is increased by about 18% and about 15% respectively when the data transmission rate is high (packet generation rate is more than 1 packet/s), which means that the effect of data aggregation is better after GCDT protocol grouping, and makes the network throughput had improved significantly.

We can get the packet loss rate after subtracting the total number of received packets from the total number of transmitted packets, divide by the total number

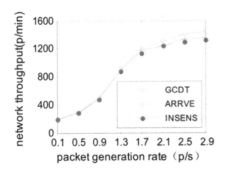

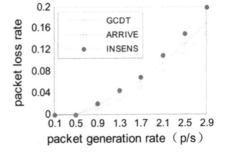

Fig. 7.   Comparison   of   network throughput

Fig. 8. Comparison of packet loss rate

of transmitted packets. Figure 8 shows the packet loss rate at different packet generation rates in each cluster [15]. It is calculated that, compared to ARRIVE and INSENS, the GCDT packet loss rate is reduced respectively by about 28% and about 15%, because the GCDT protocol determines the success rate according to the importance of the packet, and then determines the need to send the packet number of packets, reducing the probability of packet loss, better reliability

Figure 9 compares the effect of different paths on the rate of network adaptation under different node failure rate. GCDT protocol reduces the packet loss rate within the cluster, builds multi-path of energy more balanced, shares network load equally, without any external interference. The results show that with the increase of node failure rate, the network adaptation rate of GCDT decreases the most slowly, and the algorithm is more practical.

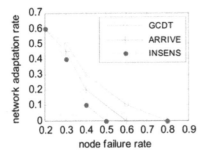

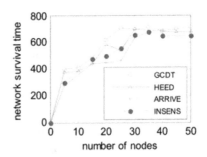

Fig. 9. Comparison of network adaptation rate

Fig. 10. Comparison of network survival time

Figure 10 shows the network survival time comparison of each algorithm [16]. Compared with the ARRIVE flooding method, which consumes a lot of traffic and much resources, the GCDT protocol establishes multi-path generation algorithm between the cluster head and the base station in the stable phase, and the cluster information can be reliably transmitted to the base station by multi-path. The multi-hop communication between the cluster head and the base station can save the energy of the cluster head, save the node's memory resources, thus prolong the network' s survival time.

5   Conclusion

In wireless sensor networks, the reliability of data transmission is the foundation of network performance. In order to achieve reliable transmission, this paper proposes a grouping-based wireless sensor network clustering data transmission protocol (GCDT), establishes a number of transmission paths before data transmission, access to the expected success rate of transmission and other parameters, determines the number of packet grouping, and then through the GCDT protocol for each round of the node to send the original packet between the packet, and finally these packets through multiple independent paths to send to the receiving end. Then grouping for the original data packets sent by nodes of each round through the GCDT protocol, and finally these groups are sent to the receiver through a number of independent paths. Through the GCDT protocol for each round of the node to send the original data packets are grouped, and finally these packets through a number of independent path to send to the receiver. Simulation results show that the GCDT protocol can effectively guarantee the communication reliability and improve the overall performance of the network compared with the existing survivable routing ARRIVE and INSENS.

Acknowledgement. The authors would like to thank our colluges and students in Anhui University of Science and Technology. This work is supported by the National Natural Science Foundation of China (Grant no. 61402012), and the National Natural Science Foundation of China (Grant no. 61572034).

References

1. Heinzelman, W.R., Balakrishnan, C.A.: Energy efficient communication protocol for wireless microsensor networks. In: Proceedings of the 33rd Annual Hawaii International Conference on System Science, Hawaii, pp. 10–15 (2000)
2. Huangfu, W., Zhang, Z.S., Chai, X.M., Long, K.: Survivability-oriented optimal node density for randomly deployed wireless sensor networks. Sci. China Inform. Sci. **57**(2), 1–6 (2014)
3. Karlof, C., Li, Y., Polastre, J.: Arrive: Algorithm for Robust Rounting in Volatile Environments. T R UCBCSD-03-1233, Computer Science Dept, Univ of California at Berkeley (2003)
4. Braginsky, D., Eslytin, D.: Rumor routing algorithm for wireless sensor networks. In: The First ACM International Workshop on Wireless Sensor Networks and Applications (WSNA 2002) (2002)
5. Deng, J., Han, R., Mishra, S.: Intrusion tolerance and anti-traffic analysis strategies in wireless sensor networks. In: IEEE International Conference on Dependable Systems and Networks(DSN 2004), Florence, Italy (2004)

6. Younis, O., Fahmy, S.: HEED. A hybrid, energy-efficient distributed clustering approach for adhoc sensor networks. IEEE Trans. Mobile Comput. **3**(10), 366–379 (2004)
7. Arumugam, G.S., Ponnuchamy, T.: EE-LEACH: development of energy-efficient LEACH Protocol for data gathering in WSN. Wireless Communications Networking, 76 (2015)
8. Papadimitratos, P., Haas, Z.: Secure data transmission in mobile Ad Hoc networks. In: ACM Workshop on Wireless Security (2003)
9. Cao, J., Chen, Y., Ren, Z., Li, Q.: Multi-round clustering based multi-hop clustering routing protocol for wireless sensor networks. Comput. Sci. **40**(7), 67–70 (2013)
10. Sharma, R., Mishra, N., Srivastava, S.: A proposed energy efficient distance based cluster head (DBCH) Algorithm: An Improvement over LEACH. Procedia Comput. Sci. **57**, 807–814 (2015)
11. Deb, B., Bhatnagar, S., Nath, B.: Reinform: reliable information forwarding using multiple paths in sensor networks. In: Proceedings of IEEELCN03, Bonn, Germany, pp. 406–415 (2003)
12. Kumar, N., Ghanshyam, C., Sharma, A.K.: Effect of multi-path fading model on T-ANT clustering protocol for WSN. Wireless Netw. **21**, 1155–1162 (2015)
13. Wan, C.-Y., Campbell, A.T., Krishnamurthy, L.: PSFQ: a reliable transport protocol for wireless sensor networks. In: Proceedings of ACM WSNA 2002, Atlanta, GA, pp. 1–11, September 2002
14. Mahadevaswamy, U.B., Shanmukhaswamy, M.N.: Delay aware and load balanced multipath routing in wireless sensor networks. Int. J. Wireless Inform. Networks **19**, 278–285 (2012)
15. Sun, B., Gui, C., Song, Y., Chen, H.: A novel network coding and multi-path routing approach for wireless sensor network. Wireless Pers. Commun. **77**, 87–99 (2014)
16. Luo, J., Di, W., Pan, C., Zha, J.: Optimal energy strategy for node selection and data Relay in WSN-based IoT. Mobile Netw. Appl. **20**, 169–180 (2015)

An Improved DV-Hop Localization Algorithm via Inverse Distance Weighting Method in Wireless Sensor Networks

Wenming Wang[1,2(✉)], Xiaowei Cao[1,2], Meng Qian[1,2], and Liefu Ai[1,2]

[1] College of Computer and Information,
Anqing Normal University, Anqing 246011, China
Wangwenming500@163.com
[2] The University Key Laboratory of Intelligent Perception
and Computing of Anhui Province, Anqing Normal University, Anqing 246011, China

Abstract. The node localization is an important problem in wireless sensor network (WSN). An improved algorithm is proposed by analyzing the deficiencies of random distribution in DV-Hop. Different from the previous results, minimum mean-squared error (MSE) and inverse distance weighting method are adopted to deal with the average one-hop distance in improved algorithm. Improved algorithm and DV-Hop are simulated by MATLAB R2015b, and the results of these two algorithms are analyzed and compared. The results show that the positioning accuracy is improved on the condition of no increasing complexity and cost.

Keywords: Wireless sensor networks · DV-Hop · Mean-squared error (MSE) · Inverse distance

1 Introduction

Wireless sensor network (WSN) [1] consist of many static and moving energy-autonomous microsensors distributed in a certain detection area. Its purpose is to perception, collection and processing of observed objects in the detection area [2–5]. At present, the WSN is mainly used in military, environmental testing and industrial fields.

Sensor node location information is very important to WSN, which can realize the monitoring of real-time monitoring and information acquisition [6]. How to achieve accurately node localization is a main concern for wireless sensor network, which plays a very important role in WSN. According to the distance between measurement nodes in the localization process, WSN node localization consists of range-based and range-free localization algorithms [7]. In this scheme, the nodes that are aware of their positions are called beacon nodes, while others are called unknown nodes. Range-Based positioning algorithm needs measure the distance, angle and other information between nodes, so the positioning accuracy is high relatively. Currently, typical Range-based localization

© ICST Institute for Computer Sciences, Social Informatics and Telecommunications Engineering 2017
F. Chen and Y. Luo (Eds.): Industrial IoT 2017, LNICST 202, pp. 163–168, 2017.
DOI: 10.1007/978-3-319-60753-5_17

algorithms included RSSI, TOA, TDOA, AOA [8,9], and so on. However, it is at the expense of increasing the cost and power consumption. Range-Free algorithm relies on network connectivity for localization, do not need range hardware support and are immune to range measurement errors. Several techniques based on Range-free included centroid location algorithm, DV-Hop, MSD MAP and APIT [10–12], and so on.

We discuss the DV-Hop algorithm, and propose two improvements about it in this paper. Improved algorithm can improve the positioning accuracy on the condition of without increasing complexity and cost. Compared with traditional DV-Hop algorithm, it is a simple and practical algorithm, and more available for WSNs.

This paper is organized as follows. The related work is presented in the next section. Section 3 analyzes the shortcoming of traditional DV-Hop algorithm and proposes our improved algorithm. Simulation results are shown in Sect. 4. Finally, we present our conclusions in Sect. 5.

2   Related Work

DV-Hop algorithm is one of the important Range-free localization algorithms, which is proposed by Niculescu and Badri [13] originally. The algorithm mainly consists of three steps [14–16].

In the first step, each beacon node broadcasts a packet, which includes its location information and initial hop value 0, to the neighboring nodes throughout the network. The receiving node retains the minimum hop count value of all received value from the beacon node, then adds 1 to the hop count and forwards it to the neighbor node. Then, each node will know the hop distances from itself to all anchors by the method.

In the second step, an beacon node can compute an average distance per hop (ADPH) according step 1, which is then flooded to the entire network. The average distance per hop can be calculated by the following formula (1).

$$C_i = \frac{\sum_{j \neq i} d_{i,j}}{\sum_{j \neq i} h_{i,j}} \tag{1}$$

where $d_{i,j} = \sqrt{(x_i - x_j)^2 + (y_i - x_y)^2}$, (x_i, y_i) and (x_j, y_j) are the location of anchor nodes i and j, $h_{i,j}$ is the hop value between anchor nodes i and j.

After calculating the ADPH of each beacon node, it is broadcasted to the whole wireless sensor network. Unknown nodes will only receive and save the information of ADPH from the nearest anchor node, then forward it to their neighbor nodes. After distance per hop and hops to the beacon nodes obtained, the distance between all unknown nodes and anchor nodes can be calculated.

In the third step, the trilateral medium [17] will be used to determine the position information of nodes.

3   Improved Algorithm

In this section, we analyze the shortcoming of traditional DV-Hop algorithm and improve it focus on step 2.

Firstly, the ADPH of the beacon node is calculated based on the unbiased estimation criterion at the step 2 of DV-Hop algorithm, and its measurement error mean is zero.

In fact, the errors are subject to Gaussian distribution normally. Therefore, the traditional DV-Hop algorithm has a strong dependence of the ADPH. If the ADPH value has error, the positioning accuracy will be inaccurate. So in order to improve the accuracy of location of unknown nodes, the mean square error method is more reasonable than that of using the variance or deviation. Consequently, the ADPH computed by the minimum MSE as the formula (3) in this paper.

$$f = \frac{\sum_{j \neq i}(d_{i,j} - C_i h_{i,j})^2}{N - 1}. \tag{2}$$

Let $\frac{\partial f}{\partial C_i} = 0$, then

$$C_i = \frac{\sum_{j \neq i}(h_{i,j} \cdot d_{i,j})}{\sum_{j \neq i} h_{i,j}^2}. \tag{3}$$

Secondly, using the ADPH information obtained by the unknown node from its nearest beacon node as the average on hop distance from the unknown node to beacon nodes in traditional DV-Hop algorithm. However, this method has the limitations where it can not fully take into account the random distribution of nodes in WSN. If just only a single beacon node is used to calculate the ADPH, it will generate a large deviation, and the localization accuracy of the unknown node will decreases.

In fact, different beacon nodes have different effects on unknown nodes. Therefore, in order to improve the positioning accuracy, we should take advantage of the information of beacon nodes in the network, and give a different weight to beacon nodes depending on the distance. So using inverse distance weighting to deal with the ADPH is another improvement in this paper. Assuming that the unknown node has saved the ADPH from the n beacon nodes, the weights Wi are given for each ADPH value of all beacon nodes respectively. In this paper, it is computed as follows:

$$W_i = \frac{h_{i,j}^{-1}}{\sum_{j=1}^{n} h_{i,j}^{-1}}. \tag{4}$$

$$C = \sum_{i=1}^{n}(W_i C_j) = \sum_{i=1}^{n}\left(\frac{h_{i,j}^{-1}}{\sum_{j=1}^{n} h_{i,j}^{-1}} \cdot C_j\right). \tag{5}$$

4   Simulation and Evaluation

To validate our improved method, DV-Hop and improved algorithm are simulated by MATLAB R2015b in this section. Both of the results are analyzed and compared (Fig. 1).

The simulation region is a square area with an area of 100 m 100 m, which is randomly produced by rand function. As shown in Fig. 2, there are 200 nodes in this area and the radius range of sensor nodes change from 15 m to 25 m. The number of anchor nodes increase from 5 to 25. Each experiment state is simulated 50 times, and takes the average value eventually.

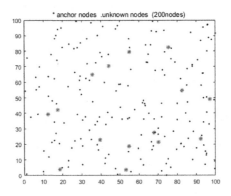

Fig. 1. Nodes distribution.

The average positioning error is defined as the ratio of the sum of the errors of all the successfully located unknown nodes to the communication radius. The formula is showed as follows:

$$\delta = \frac{\sum \sqrt{(x_i - x_i')^2 + (y_i - y_i')^2}}{R \cdot N}. \tag{6}$$

where, (x_i, y_i) and (x_i', y_i') are the real coordinates and positioning coordinates of unknown node i, respectively.

The curves showed in Figs. 2, 3 and 4 display the variation of the positioning error under different radius. Compared with the DV-Hop, the performance of improved algorithm is better in positioning accuracy with different radius range of sensor nodes. The experiment curve shows that the estimation accuracy is improved as increase of anchor node amounts, when the radiu reach a certain value. The localization error tends to be stable when the number of beacon nodes reach a certain value. When the beacon nodes share the same proportion, the localization error is obviously decrease as the increase of the radiu.

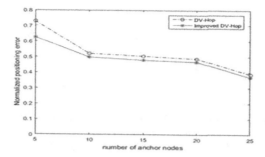

Fig. 2. The position error when the radiu is 15 m.

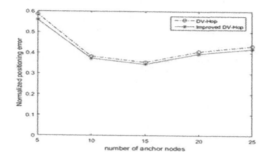

Fig. 3. The position error when the radiu is 20 m.

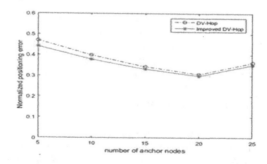

Fig. 4. The position error when the radiu is 25 m.

5   Conclusions

Unknown node localization in WSN has always been a research focus in WSN. To solve the deficiencies of random distribution in DV-Hop, an improved algorithm has been proposed in this paper. The simulation results show that the positioning accuracy is improved on the condition of no increasing complexity and cost. The improved algorithm is a simple and practical algorithm.

Acknowledgements. This work is supported by Youth Foundation of Anqing Normal University (KJ201406, KJ201303), Natural Science Foundation of Anhui Province (1608085MF144).

References

1. Tan, Z., Liu, Y.: An improved DV-Hop localization algorithm for wireless sensor networks. Int. J. Adv. Comput. Technol. **17**(4), 1–7 (2012)
2. Stefan, T., Ivan, M.: Improvements of DV-Hop localization algorithm for wireless sensor networks. Telecommun. Syst. **61**(1), 93–106 (2016)
3. Zhang, J., Cao, D., Fu, M.: Improvement on location error and coverage rate in DV-Hop algorithm. J. Comput. Appl. **31**(7), 1944–1947 (2011)
4. Liu, F., Zhang, H., Yang, J.: An average one-hop distance estimation algorithm based on weighted disposal in wireless sensor network. J. Electron. Inf. Technol. **30**(5), 1221–1225 (2008)
5. Doherty, L., Pister, K., Ghaoui, L.E.: Convex position estimation in wireless sensor networks. In: IEEE INFOCOM (2001)
6. Chen, J., Yao, K., Hudson, R.: Source localization and beamforming. IEEE Signal Process. Mag. **19**(1), 30–39 (2002)
7. Xu, C.H.X., Chen, J.Y.: Research on the improved DV-HOP localization algorithm in WSN. Int. J. Smart Home **9**(4), 157–162 (2016)
8. Yang, M., Qing, Q.Q.: Research on centroid localization algorithm for wireless sensor networks based RSSI. Comput. Simul. **28**(5), 163–166 (2011)
9. Ji, W.W., Liu, Z.: An improvement of DV-Hop localization algorithm in wireless sensor networks. Int. Conf. Wirel. Commun. **25**(10), 1–4 (2006)
10. Tao, X., Zou, G.H.: An improved DV-HOP localization algorithm based on beacon nodes at borderland of wireless sensor networks. Futur. Wirel. Netw. Inf. Syst. **143**(1), 147–154 (2012). Springer
11. Li, Y.F., Jiang, M., Lou, K., et al.: Improved DV-Hop localization algorithm in wireless sensor network. Comput. Eng. Appl. **50**(3), 79–81 (2014)
12. Gui, L., Val, T., Wei, A., Dalce, R.: Improvement of range-free localization technology by a novel DV-Hop protocol in wireless sensor networks. Ad Hoc Netw. **24**, 55–73 (2015)
13. Ji, W.W., Liu, Z.: Study on the application of DV-Hop localization algorithms to random sensor networks. J. Electron. Inf. Technol. **30**(4), 970–973 (2008)
14. Chen, H.Y., Sezaki, K., Deng, P.: An improved DV-Hop localization algorithm for wireless sensor networks. Int. Conf. Wirel. Commun. Netw. Mob. Comput. **9**(6), 2232–2236 (2010)
15. Tian, S., Zhang, X.M.: A RSSI-based DV-Hop algorithm for wireless sensor networks. In: International Conference on Wireless Communications Networking and Mobile Computing (2009)
16. Zhang, J.M., Guo, L.P., Zhang, X.D.: Effects of interpolation parameters in inverse distance weighted method on DEM accuracy. J. Geomat. Sci. Technol. **29**(1), 51–56 (2012)
17. Niculescu, D.: Positioning in ad hoc sensor networks. IEEE Netw. **18**(4), 24–29 (2004)

Study on Electromagnetic Scattering Characteristics of Bodies of Revolution by Compressive Sensing

Yanyan Zhu[1], Jie Fang[2(✉)], and Yun Shi[2]

[1] School of Electronic and Information Engineering, Anhui University,
111 Kowloon Road, Hefei 230039, Anhui, People's Republic of China
[2] School of Electrical and Optoelectronic Engineering, West Anhui University,
The Moon Island, Lu'an 237012, Anhui, People's Republic of China
63640193@qq.com

Abstract. Based on discrete wavelet transform (DWT), the discrete wavelet transform (DWT) is pre-processed on the basis of the Bodies of revolution-Method of Moments, and the underdetermined equation is constructed and solved by using the compressive perceptual method. In this method, non-zero lines are extracted from the sparse excitations of the wavelet coefficients, and a small-scale impedance matrix is formed to extract the impedance matrices, which reduce the memory consumption and improve the computational efficiency. This method of adding compression perception can systematically construct the corresponding underdetermined equations to ensure fast acquisition of the signal reconstruction solution.

Keywords: Bodies of revolution-method of moments · Discrete wavelet transform · Compressive sensing

1 Introduction

As a current numerical methods for solving electromagnetic scattering problems, the method of moments [1] is widely used because of its high accuracy. Its core is to describe the interaction between the source and the field by the Green function. The moment method is used to solve the electromagnetic scattering problem, and basic procedure is expand the functional equation by means of the basis function, then the weight function is used to form the matrix equation. Bodies of revolution-method of moments [2–5] to solve the problem of electrical large size problems, need involve the filling and inversion of large scale dense impedance matrix. The calculation process is complex, the computer occupies big memory, so the wavelet analysis tool is introduced. Discrete wavelet transform [6–9] is a sparse preconditioning matrix equation, the rotational symmetric moment method with the addition of wavelet sparse transform. In the premise of maintaining high accuracy, it can effectively reduce the amount of memory. Based on this, the paper introduces compressed sensing [10–12]. The threshold of the excitation vector in the wavelet domain is established and can get no-zero line. The no-zero line is used as a priori to extract the impedance matrix in the

F. Chen and Y. Luo (Eds.): Industrial IoT 2017, LNICST 202, pp. 169–175, 2017.
DOI: 10.1007/978-3-319-60753-5_18

wavelet domain to get the equation. The sparse current solution is recovered by the OMP recovery algorithm. Finally, the real current coefficient vector is obtained by inverse wavelet transform. Results show that the rotational symmetric moment method based on compressive sensing can effectively recover the signal in the field scattering problem. At the same time it reduces the amount of memory and improves the computational efficiency.

2 Theoretical Analysis

2.1 Bodies of Revolution-Method of Moments

The Bodies of Revolution-Method of Moments (BOR-MOM) is mainly used to deal with the electromagnetic scattering from the target of (Bodies), BOR and the target of rotational symmetry. The BOR has the characteristics of rotational symmetry of geometry and constitutive relation. Structural basis functions are constructed by using its structural characteristics. The vector integral equation is transformed into two scalar integral equations, which can reduce the dimension of the vector integral equations.

On the surface of BOR, if the exciting incident magnetic field H^i, then the induction current conductor surface for $\vec{J}$. According to the rotation symmetry property can be decomposed into:

$$\vec{J} = \vec{J}^t + \vec{J}^\varphi \tag{1}$$

Among them, $\vec{J}^t$ is the tangential component of current $\vec{t}$, $\vec{J}^\phi$ as a component of current azimuth $\vec{\varphi}$. By means of Fourier series expansion and the integral equation of the magnetic field into the surface of the component:

$$
\begin{aligned}
\vec{n} \times \vec{H}^{inc} = (&\sum_{n=-\infty}^{\infty}\sum_{i=1}^{N} I_{ni}^t \frac{T_i}{\rho} e^{jn\varphi}\vec{t} + \sum_{n=-\infty}^{\infty}\sum_{i=1}^{N} I_{ni}^\varphi \frac{T_i}{\rho} e^{jn\varphi}\vec{\varphi}) + \vec{n} \\
&\times \iint_S \{(\sum_{n=-\infty}^{\infty}\sum_{i=1}^{N} I_{ni}^t \frac{T_i}{\rho} e^{jn\varphi}\vec{t} + \sum_{n=-\infty}^{\infty}\sum_{i=1}^{N} I_{ni}^\varphi \frac{T_i}{\rho} e^{jn\varphi}\vec{\varphi}) \times \nabla G\}dS'
\end{aligned}
\tag{2}
$$

In which, $\nabla G = (\vec{r} - \vec{r}')[1 + jkr]\frac{e^{-jkr}}{4\pi r^3}$, I_{ni}^t, I_{ni}^φ said t and φ component to calculate the current coefficient, T^i for trigonometric function, ρ is the distance between the two segmentation points of subdivision surface.

This paper use the Galerkin's method, and according to the method of moments, the matrix can be used as follows:

$$ZI = V \tag{3}$$

Z is the impedance matrix, I is unknown current coefficient matrix, V is the excitation matrix.

2.2 Discrete Wavelet Transform Theory

To (3) carry on the wavelet transform, we can get:

$$\tilde{Z}\tilde{I} = \tilde{V} \tag{4}$$

Which, $\tilde{Z} = WZW^H$, $\tilde{I} = WI$, $\tilde{V} = WV$, and W is an orthogonal array constructed by the discrete wavelet transform. $WW^H = U$, U is a unit matrix, W^H is the conjugate transpose matrix of W.

In the wavelet domain, σ make the threshold. If the value of the matrix element is smaller than the threshold value is 0,

$$\sigma = \tau \|\tilde{Z}\|_1 / N = \tau \times \max_m \sum_n |\tilde{Z}(m,n)| / N \tag{5}$$

Among them, N is the dimension of the matrix, τ is the control variable to control the impedance matrix is sparse.

2.3 Compressive Sensing (CS)

Known (4) type $\tilde{V}$ is sparse in a wavelet domain excitation vector, $\tilde{V}$ and $\tilde{Z}$ also selected in the important position of the M line. The formation of small scale matrix $\tilde{V}_{M \times 1}^{CS}$ and $\tilde{Z}_{M \times N}^{CS}$ respectively into underdetermined equations:

$$\tilde{Z}_{M \times N}^{CS} \tilde{I}_{N \times 1} = \tilde{V}_{M \times 1}^{CS} \qquad (M < <N) \tag{6}$$

Which, $\tilde{I}_{N \times 1}$ is a sparse vector in wavelet domain, according to the theory of compressive sensing, $\tilde{V}_{M \times N}^{CS}$ can think of is known to be measured for sparse vector $\tilde{I}_{N \times 1}$ value, And $\tilde{V}$ in the position where the zero vector elements can be regarded as a priori knowledge, it's used to extract the specific location of the line in $\tilde{Z}$, the measurement matrix is constructed so as to form a fixed $\tilde{Z}_{M \times N}^{CS}$, underdetermined equations.

$\tilde{I}_{N \times 1}$ use OMP technology to reconstruct the recovery. Then the formula (7) inverse wavelet transform format to obtain the true coefficient of current vector $I_{N \times 1}$

$$I = W^H \tilde{I} \tag{7}$$

The computational complexity of the iterative solution of the traditional moment method is $O(PN^2)$, Where P is the number of iterations. The computational complexity of (6) is $O(SMN)$, which is S << P, M << N, and $\tilde{Z}_{M \times N}^{CS}$ build a sparse measurement matrix calculation will further reduce the complexity of OMP. Therefore, the method proposed in this paper can reduce the CPU memory loss and increase the speed of computation compared with the traditional method.

3   Instance Verification

Cases 1. The magnetic field integral equation calculation of radius R as the ideal conductor sphere 1 m, the current solution of the incident wave frequency is 300 MHz, the bus section sphere was divided into 257 segments. This example uses the Db8 wavelet to carry on the sparse processing, under the condition of selecting the excitation threshold 0.01, can get sparse excitation vector $\tilde{V}_{512 \times 1}$, the non-zero element number is K = 64, As shown in Fig. 1. According to the diagram (a) for no-zero position of the impedance matrix $\tilde{Z}_{512 \times 512}$. As a Fig. 2 extraction of M = K = 64 lines, the construction of a 64 × 512 small scale impedance matrix, Fig. 3. From the Figs. 4 and 5, we can see that the use of the traditional method of moments, wavelet sparse method and the CS method of the current solution is basically consistent, and the reconstruction error of CS is less than 1%. Using the method proposed in this paper, the current solution is obtained at 0° and 90° respectively.

nz = 64

Fig. 1. The non-zero element line

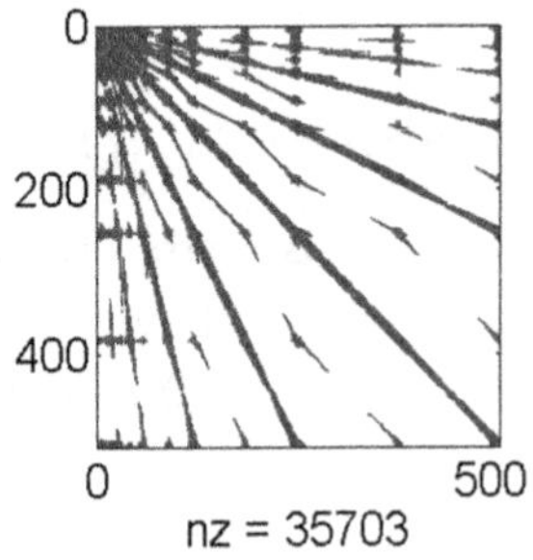

nz = 35703

Fig. 2. Non-zero elements position (shadows)

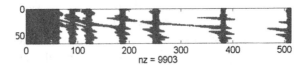

nz = 9903

Fig. 3. Non-zero elements in the row of extraction

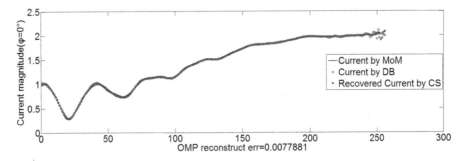

OMP reconstruct err=0.0077881

Fig. 4. When the incident angle is 0°, the current solution to the tangential direction of the plane

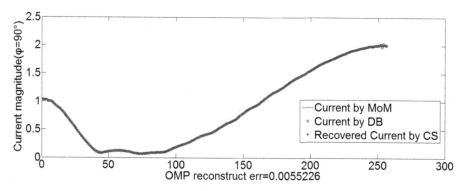

Fig. 5. When the incident angle is 90°, the current solution of the direction of the azimuthal direction of the plane.

Case 2. At a radius of 5 m, the cone angle is 60° on the ideal cone sphere of incident 300 MHz plane wave. The cone ball bus is divided into 257 sections, including angle bus into N1 = 128 segments, and spherical segment bus into N2 = 129 segments. This example also uses the DB8 wavelet sparse. After sparse extraction to get non zero line K = 245, M = K = 245 line extraction, it can construct a small scale impedance matrix of 245 × 512. Using the method proposed in this paper, the current solution is obtained at 0° and 90° respectively. The reconstruction error of the visible CS is less than 1%, as shown in Figs. 6 and 7:

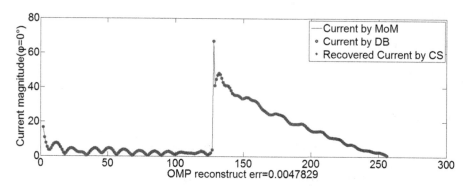

Fig. 6. When the incident angle is 0°, the current solution to the tangential direction of the plane

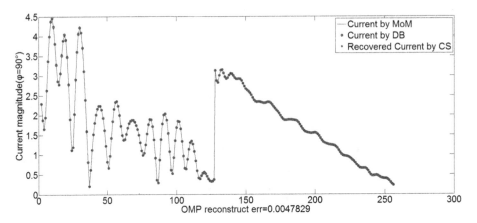

Fig. 7. When the incident angle is 90°, the current solution of the direction of the azimuthal direction of the plane.

4 Conclusion

In this paper, a rotational symmetry method based on compressive perception is presented. By analyzing the electromagnetic scattering properties of the two-dimensional half-targets, it is verified that the new method has more memory and higher precision than the traditional method, high probability reconstruction signal and other characteristics. The method is also applicable to the analysis of electromagnetic scattering properties of other large-scale rotationally symmetric targets.

Acknowledgement. We thank National Natural Science Foundation of China under Grant No. 61302179, for support of this research.

References

1. Gibson, W.C.: The Method of Moments in Electromagnetics, pp. 1–62. Chapman and Hall, USA (2007)
2. Wu, T.K.: Accurate PMCHWT solutions for scattering from arbitrarily-shaped penetrable bodies of revolution [Open Problems in CEM]. IEEE Antennas Propag. Mag. **56**(5), 315–320 (2014)
3. Mautz, J.R., Harrington, R.F.: Radiation and scattering from bodies of revolution. Appl. Sci. Res. **20**, 405–435 (1969)
4. Wu, T.K., Tsu, L.L.: Scattering from arbitrarily-shaped dielectric bodies of revolution. Radio Sci. **12**, 709–718 (1977)
5. Meincke, P., Jorgensen, E.: Efficient body of revolution method of moments for rotationally symmetric antenna systems with offset illumination. In: AP-S International Symposium (Digest) (IEEE Antennas and Propagation Society), pp. 1467–1468 (2014)
6. Wagner, R.L., Chew, W.C.: Study of wavelets for the solution of electromagnetic integral equations. IEEE Trans. Antennas Propag. **43**(8), 802–810 (1995)

7. Baharav, Z., Leviatan, Y.: Impedance matrix compression (IMC) using iteratively selected wavelet basis for MFIE formulations. Microw. Opt. Technol. Lett. **12**(3), 145–150 (1996)
8. Baharav, Z., Leviatan, Y.: Impedance matrix compression (IMC) using iteratively selected wavelet basis. IEEE Trans. Antennas Propag. **46**(2), 226–233 (1998)
9. Sokolik, D., Shifman, Y., Leviatan, Y.: Improved impedance matrix compression (IMC) technique for efficient wavelet-based method of moments solution of scattering problems. Microw. Opt. Technol. Lett. **40**(4), 275–280 (2004)
10. Peyre, G.: Best basis compressed sensing. IEEE Trans. Signal Process. **58**(5), 2613–2622 (2010)
11. Tsaig, Y., Donoho, D.L.: Extensions of compressed sensing. Signal Process. **86**(3), 549–571 (2006)
12. Duarte, M.F., Eldar, Y.C.: Structured compressed sensing: From theory to applications. IEEE Trans. Signal Process. **59**(9), 4053–4085 (2011)

An Inside Look at IoT Malware

Aohui Wang[1,3(✉)], Ruigang Liang[1,3], Xiaokang Liu[1,3], Yingjun Zhang[2,3], Kai Chen[1,3], and Jin Li[4]

[1] State Key Laboratory of Information Security, Institute of Information Engineering, CAS, Beijing, China
{wangaohui,liangruigang,liuxiaokang,chenkai}@iie.ac.cn
[2] Trusted Computing and Information Assurance Laboratory, Institute of Software, CAS, Beijing, China
yjzhang@tca.iscas.ac.cn
[3] School of Cyber Security, University of Chinese Academy of Sciences, Beijing, China
[4] Department of Computer Science, Guangzhou University, Guangzhou, China
jinli71@gmail.com

Abstract. It was reported that over 20 billion of Internet of Things (IoT) devices have connected to Internet. Moreover, the estimated number in 2020 will increase up to 50.1 billion. Different from traditional security-related areas in which researchers have made many efforts on them for many years, researches on IoT have just started to receive attentions in recent years. The IoT devices are exposing to many security problems, such as weak passwords, backdoors and various vulnerabilities including buffer overflow, authentication bypass and so on. In this paper, we systemically analyze multiple IoT malware which have appeared in the recent years and classify the IoT malware into two categories according to the way in which IoT malware infect devices: one is to infect IoT devices by brute force attacks through a dictionary of weak usernames and passwords; while the other one by exploiting unfixed or zero-day vulnerabilities found in IoT devices. We choose Mirai, Darlloz and BASHLITE as examples to illustrate the attacks. At the end, we present strategies to defend against IoT malware.

Keywords: Internet of Things · Malware · Botnet

1 Introduction

In recent years, the Internet of Things (short for IoT) which connect cyber devices embedded with software, electronics and sensors, have been developed prosperously. Traditional physical devices are offline, while IoT technologies push them online, making it possible to control these devices remotely by exchanging various data through Internet. This not only makes our life easier, but also increases the risk of malware infection on the IoT devices at the same time. According to the report from Symantec [1], IoT devices have been the target of lots of malware and have become one of the main sources of the distributed denial of service (DDoS) attacks. The dilemma is partially because of the design flaws in the IoT architecture [2], and also partially because of low quality of IoT software code. By taking the advantage of problems listed above,

© ICST Institute for Computer Sciences, Social Informatics and Telecommunications Engineering 2017
F. Chen and Y. Luo (Eds.): Industrial IoT 2017, LNICST 202, pp. 176–186, 2017.
DOI: 10.1007/978-3-319-60753-5_19

malware is created aiming at IoT devices. The IoT malware could steal users' private information, build botnets and even break the whole network infrastructure.

Discovering and analyzing software vulnerabilities and malware in IoT plays an important role in current security researches [3]. According to a report by Businessinsider [4], over 45 vulnerabilities in IoT devices are found in Defcon 2016, and totally 21 companies were impacted. Types of vulnerabilities found range from bad software design such as the use of weak and hard-coded passwords to flaws of coding like buffer overflows and command injection. And according to recent researches, more than 10% apps in 33 Android market and 6.84% apps in Google Play may contain malicious code [5].

There was not much systematic work to analyze IoT malware before. Motivated by this, we choose some typical malware to analyze. According to how malware affects IoT devices, we find that there are two major categories of IoT malware as described in Abstract. Although IoT malware based on brute-force attack plays the major role nowadays, this problem is easy to fix by vendors. However, fixing the vulnerabilities such as buffer overflow is very hard. Thus, code injection attack by exploiting the vulnerabilities could be the first choice for IoT malware in the near future. In this paper, we analyze these two kinds of IoT malware and give the examples of attacks. We also summarize the ways to defend them.

Section 2 describes IoT malware which are based on brute-force attack. We choose the Mirai to show details about this kind of malware. Section 3 describes IoT malware which is based on exploiting vulnerabilities in devices. We make a summary of popular vulnerabilities in the IoT devices manufacturer, and choose Darlloz and BASHLITE as examples to reveal the details. Section 4 describes some defense strategies to prevent IoT malware from spreading. Section 5 introduces the related work on IoT security. Section 6 gives the conclusion.

2   IoT Malware Based on Brute-Force Attack

2.1   Background

Using weak passwords is a security issue that has been present since the born of computers. According to a report by ESET, about 15% of the tested routers use weak or default usernames and passwords. It was reported that "admin" is the most common username. It is also discovered that nearly 20% of the tested routers expose their Telnet port to the Internet, which is a serious security implication [6].

Dyn is a cloud-based Internet Performance Management company in charge of many companies' internet domain name system (DNS) infrastructure. In October 2016, Dyn encountered an attack by more than one hundred thousand infected end devices [7]. Many of these devices got infected with a notorious malware called Mirai. This attack made websites such as Twitter, GitHub and Airbnb inaccessible to nearly half of Americans. We find that Mirai spread by brute-force attack and there are also some other IoT malware such as Remaiten and Aidra which affect devices in similar ways. In Sect. 2.2, we will make a complete analysis of Mirai.

2.2 Mirai

Mirai is malware that can compromise IoT devices which run Linux operating system and have Telnet (port 23) or port 2323 open remotely by brute-force attack. Those compromised devices are used as part of a botnet for large-scale DDoS attacks. It primarily targets online IoT devices such as cameras and routers that have at least ten architectures including ARM, MIPS and X86. The Mirai botnet played an important role in the recent destructive attacks, such as DDoS attacks on security journalist Brian Krebs's website in September 2016, and an attack on Dyn in October 2016. The source code of Mirai was publicly released on September 30, 2016 by Anna-senpai in the hacking community Hackforums. According to a report by IT world, after the Mirai source code is released, more IoT botnets are created by hackers [8].

Operating Principle
Mirai botnet consists of a Command and Control (short for CNC) server, a receiver for scanning results and a distributor (CB server for short), and an http or ftp server to store bot programs for downloading. The CNC server is used for managing the botnets and distributing commands to bot devices. CB server is used for receiving devices information which are just compromised and guides the devices to download bot program. The whole working network could be shown as (Fig. 1).

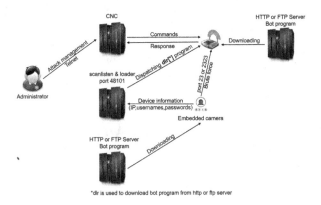

Fig. 1. The working principle of the Mirai botnet.

When a device is compromised, it will randomly select an IP address to scan. If the device being scanned has 23 port (or 2323 port) open, Mirai malware try to attack the device by brute-forcing through a dictionary of popular usernames and passwords, such as "admin", "password" and "root". If the username and password are right, the device's IP address, port, username and password will be transferred to the CB server. The CB server receives the compromised devices' details and tries to guide the device to download bot program. If the device finishes downloading the bot program, it becomes a bot device, continuing to scan other devices and waiting for commands from CNC server. An administrator can login on a CNC server to manage the bot devices and distribute commands to bot devices.

Distinguished features
There are some distinguished features which make Mirai powerful and different from precedent IoT malware. Mirai can disable devices' watchdog function to prevent them from restarting and kill competitor malware processes.

1. Monopolize devices. Mirai will disable watchdog function, and kill SSH, Telnet and HTTP daemons and occupy these ports to prevent others to access the device. Mirai will also kill other competitor malware such as Qbot [9], Zollard [10] and Remaiten [11].
2. Hide process name. Program name can be determined by the Linux command ps aux, or by reading the /proc/pid/cmdline. The running process's argument 0 is the process name, Mirai uses the random string to replace the argument 0 string. Also Mirai use the prctl system call with the PR_SET_NAME argument to make the process name to random string.
3. Unique infecting methods. Different from old methods to infect more devices directly through bot devices, a CB server is used for infecting devices specially. A CB server is used to receive feedback results from brute force attack, and distribute bot program to the compromised devices.
4. Advanced SYN scan technology. Bots brute working devices by scanning Telnet service using an advanced SYN scanner that is around 80 times faster than scanners in Qbot malware, and uses almost 20 times less resources [12].
5. Variety of attack methods. Mirai botnet can launch multiple attacks including straight UDP flood, DNS water torture, SYN flood, GRE IP flood and so on.

Detection and Defense
We made a study of the source code of Mirai that was released to public. From the analysis, we found there is an approach to locate the active infected devices and the attack infrastructure such as CNC servers. Also, we figured out a way to protect our devices from the infection of Mirai.

Detection. Internet Service Provider can locate the bot devices and CNC servers from the network traffic. To make a connection to a CNC server, bot devices will try to resolve the domain name of the CNC server by a DNS server 8.8.8.8. We can collect some features such as CNC domain name and look for the features in the network traffic. In this way, we were able to locate the infected devices. We also found that bot devices and CNC servers will send each other heartbeat packets every 60 s. Searching this pattern from the network traffic, we can locate the infected devices and the CNC server.

Defense. An infected device uses the port number 48101 to prevent multiple instances of bot program running together. The bot program will listen on the port when the device is first infected, as shown in Fig. 2. It will quit if another bot program connects this port which means two bot programs are running in the same device, as shown in Fig. 3. We create one defensive program which runs in the device forever and connects the port number 48101 every ten seconds. If Mirai infects the device, it suicides in 10 s, as shown in Fig. 5. We did experiments and the results shown that the malware exits right away after it infects the device (Fig. 4).

```
1.    addr.sin_family = AF_INET;
2.    addr.sin_addr.s_addr = local_bind ? (INET_ADDR(127,0,0,1)) : LOCAL_ADDR;
3.    addr.sin_port = htons(SINGLE_INSTANCE_PORT);  //bind to port 48101 when run the first time
4.    if (bind(fd_ctrl, (struct sockaddr *)&addr, sizeof (struct sockaddr_in)) == -1)
5.    { addr.sin_family = AF_INET;
6.      addr.sin_addr.s_addr = INADDR_ANY;
7.      addr.sin_port = htons(SINGLE_INSTANCE_PORT);
8.      //connect to port 48101 when the bot program run the second time
9.      if (connect(fd_ctrl, (struct sockaddr *)&addr, sizeof (struct sockaddr_in)) == -1){}
10.   }else
11.     if (listen(fd_ctrl, 1) == -1){}  //listen to socket when bot program first run
```

Fig. 2. When the bot program runs the first time, it will bind and listen to the port number 48101. When the bot program runs the second time, it will connect to port 48101.

```
1.    if (fd_ctrl != -1 && FD_ISSET(fd_ctrl, &fdsetrd))  another Mirai program connects to port 48101
2.    { struct sockaddr_in cli_addr;
3.      socklen_t cli_addr_len = sizeof (cli_addr);
4.      accept(fd_ctrl, (struct sockaddr *)&cli_addr, &cli_addr_len);
5.    #ifdef DEBUG
6.      printf("[main] Detected newer instance running! Killing self\n");
7.    #endif
8.    #ifdef MIRAI_TELNET
9.      scanner_kill();
10.   #endif
11.     killer_kill(); attack_kill_all(); kill(pgid * -1, 9);
12.     exit(0);  };
```

Fig. 3. When another Mirai instance connects to port 48101, the first Mirai instance will kill itself.

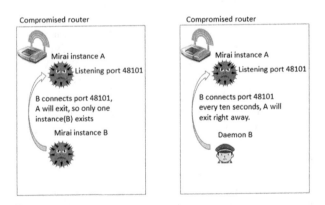

Fig. 4. Figure on the left shows how Mirai bot program prevents multiple instances running at the same time. Figure on the right shows how to protect device from Mirai infection.

3   IoT Malware Based on Exploiting Vulnerabilities

3.1   Background

More topics about the IoT security are shown on security conferences such as BlackHat, Defcon and GeekPwn in recent years with the increasing attention on IoT. Many topics about the IoT security are show on security conferences in recent years such as BlackHat, Defcon, Usenix, Pwn2Own and Geekpwn. For example, players are encouraged to crack IoT devices live in GeekPwn. In GeekPwn 2016, players from Chaitin exploit ten routers from Cisco, Huawei, Xiaomi, Asus and cameras from Xiaomi [13]. According to OWASP, the top IoT vulnerabilities include unencrypted services, poorly implemented encryption, buffer overflow, denial of service and so on. In Sect. 3.2, in order to learn the present situation and risks that IoT devices are facing, we make a statistics about the vulnerabilities in eight IoT manufacturers. In Sect. 3.3 we choose Darlloz and BASH-LITE as examples to illustrate how IoT malware use vulnerabilities to spread.

3.2   Statistics

According to the Common Vulnerabilities and Exposures (short for CVE) [14] databases, we make a statistics to vulnerabilities of IoT devices in Cisco, Huawei and other six companies, as shown in Figs. 5 and 6. From Fig. 5 we can learn that the IoT devices from Cisco have the most vulnerabilities through 2012 to 2015, which are 60, 136, 142, 178 respectively. It's not surprised that there are so many vulnerabilities in Cisco because of the big market of Cisco products. The number of vulnerabilities found in EMC's products is not a large number but increase each year through 2012 to 2015. And the number of vulnerabilities found in the rest of the companies is in a relatively stable state, with subtle increase.

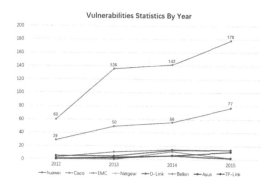

Fig. 5. Vulnerabilities grouped by company from 2012 to 2015

Figure 6 shows the number of vulnerabilities found in eight companies according to vulnerability type through 2012 to 2016(till November). From the figure, we can learn that DoS vulnerabilities take a large portion in most companies. Off all the vulnerability types, DoS takes 29.2%, while XSS and code execution take 15.2% and 11.5%, ranking

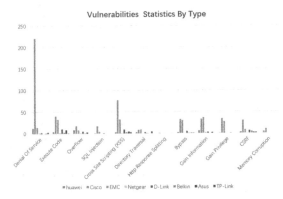

Fig. 6. Vulnerabilities grouped by type from 2012 to 2016 (till November).

the second and the third respectively. These vulnerabilities are the source of malware based on exploiting unfixed or zero-day vulnerabilities. On November 28, 2016, a variant of Mirai botnet is scanning IoT devices using a code execution vulnerability in TR069/TR064 that can hijack or crash the device. The attack caused about 900 thousands routers crash and affect over 20 million users in Germany [15]. IoT devices are facing great challenges because of the more vulnerabilities found in IoT. In the Sect. 3.3, in order to learn how malware based on exploiting vulnerabilities works, we select Darlloz and BASHLITE to illustrate.

3.3 Samples Analysis

Darlloz is a worm which targets at the IoT and infects cameras, routers and so on by exploiting a 'php-cgi' information disclosure vulnerability in PHP which is an old vulnerability that was patched in May 2012. The Darlloz was first discovered by Symantec in 2013 [16]. The whole working network can be shown as Fig. 7.

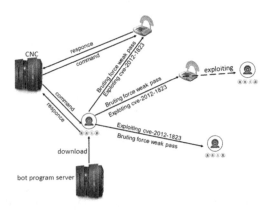

Fig. 7. The working principle of the Darlloz botnet.

When a device is compromised, it will randomly select an IP address to scan. If the Telnet port (port 23) in the device being scanned is open, it will be attacked by brute force. If the device is not vulnerable to weak passwords, the malware will try to exploit the target device using CVE-2012-1823. CVE-2012-1823 exists in PHP version before 5.3.12 and 5.4.x before 5.4.2, there is a fatal problem when cgi_main.c which is configured as a CGI script in PHP handles query strings that lack an equal sign character. This problem allows remote attackers to execute arbitrary commands in the query string [17]. If the device is exploited, it downloads the bot program from a malicious server. Then it connects to CNC server, waits for commands and tries to spread at the same time.

BASHLITE is another malware which affects IoT devices using ShellShock. Shell-Shock [18] is a family of severe security bugs in Unix Bash Shell. It was disclosed on 24 September 2014. The vulnerability exists in GNU Bash before version 4.3 and allows attackers to execute arbitrary commands. Vulnerable GNU Bash executes commands that are concatenated to the end of function definitions which are stored in various environment variables. IoT devices with busybox [19] installed have this vulnerability. When a device is compromised, it will download bot program from malicious server. The bot program is used to compromise other devices and waits for CNC server to launch DDoS attack.

4 Strategies for Defending

We find that most IoT malware attack devices by brute force methods or exploiting vulnerabilities in software or hardware in devices. So we come up some IoT malware defending strategies.

First, IoT devices producer should disable default or weak usernames and passwords. It's the reason that most of IoT malware exists.

Second, improving code quality in IoT devices' software. According to the statistics of the IoT vulnerabilities, we find that poor quality of code contributes to most of vulnerabilities.

Third, design secure IoT architecture that covers aspects from bottom up. Some aspects such as secure booting, access control, device authentication and updates & patches should be taken into consideration. Designing secure architecture can make the devices secure from the root level.

5 Related Work

IoT secure architecture, malware analysis, detection and prevention. A lot of efforts have been made to keep IoT devices secure. S. Chakrabarty et al. present a secure IoT architecture that contains four basic IoT architectural blocks to ensure a secure Smart City. The architecture can help mitigates cyber attacks at IoT nodes themselves [20]. A. Vimal Jerald et al. propose a novel security architecture that can help protect IoT devices from user and device authentication, sensor network, cloud and internet, applications and services [21]. Much of work propose detection and prevention methods for IoT malicious malware. Hao Sun et al. propose an anti-malware system called CloudEyes that provides efficient and secure services for resource-constrained IoT devices [22]. Android and IOS devices take the big part in all IoT devices. Ham et al. use linear support vector machine to detect Android malware code to ensure the safety of Android devices [23]. Chen et al. design a novel homology analysis method to detect application clones [24] on Android markets and malware on Android [5] and IOS [25] platform. Pa, Y.M.P et al. design a practical IoT honeypot and sandbox, and catch at least 4 distinct IoT malware families that target at Telnet-enabled IoT devices [23]. Chun-Jung Wu et al. capture logs of 3 million telnet sessions of IoT malware and design a method based on text mining algorithm for IoT malware behavior analysis [24]. Since a number of various IoT malware that spread by exploiting vulnerabilities of PE file format have been catched. June Ho Yang et al. design a command-line tool for IoT malware detection [25]. Byungho Min et al. design various advanced attacks targeting at IoT aspect of smart home, and evaluate the impact via practical evaluations and propose offensive techniques [26]. Software-defined networking [27] (short for SDN) has been popular in the recent years, which is a novel approach that allow network administrators to manage network services easily. Vandana C.P. design a new security framework for IoT based on SDN-IoT architecture [28].

6   Conclusion

In this paper, we seek to analyze two major kinds of malware targeting IoT devices. In malware based on brute force attack, we choose Mirai as an example to analyze. Mirai has some unique advantages such as monopolizing devices, hiding process information, advanced scan technology which make it more powerful than former malware. We make a statistics about the vulnerabilities in IoT devices, and conclude that IoT malware will utilize vulnerabilities such as buffer overflow and command injection more and more. We take Darlloz and BASHLITE as an example to analyze. Darlloz uses the CVE-2012-1823 to exploit IoT devices, BASHLITE uses the ShellShock to do these things. There are many topics about IoT devices in security conferences around the world in recent years, including secure architecture design, vulnerabilities analysis. Designing secure architecture can protect the devices from the root level. At the end of paper, we present strategies for protect IoT devices.

Acknowledgement. The IIE authors were supported in part by NSFC U1536106, 61100226, Youth Innovation Promotion Association CAS, and strategic priority research program of CAS (XDA06010701). Yingjun Zhang was supported by National High Technology Research and Development Program of China (863 Program) (No. 2015AA016006) and NSFC 61303248.

References

1. Symantec blog. https://www.symantec.com/connect/blogs/iot-devices-being-increasingly-used-ddos-attacks
2. Jing, Q., Vasilakos, A.V., Wan, J., et al.: Security of the Internet of Things: perspectives and challenges. Wirel. Netw. **20**(8), 2481–2501 (2014)

3. Zhang, Z.K., Cho, M.C.Y., Wang, C.W., Hsu, C.W., Chen, C.K., Shieh, S.: IoT security: ongoing challenges and research opportunities. In: 2014 IEEE 7th International Conference on Service-Oriented Computing and Applications, pp. 230–234. IEEE (2014)
4. Inside the Internet of Things village at DefCon. http://www.businessinsider.com/iot-village-defcon-2016-8
5. Chen, K., Wang, P., Lee, Y., et al.: Finding unknown malice in 10 seconds: mass vetting for new threats at the Google-Play scale. In: USENIX Security, vol. 15 (2015)
6. Enjoy Safer Technology. https://www.eset.com/int/
7. Dyn blog. http://dyn.com/blog/dyn-statement-on-10212016-ddos-attack/
8. Hackers create more IoT botnets with Mirai source code. http://www.itworld.com/article/3132570/hackers-create-more-iot-botnets-with-mirai-source-code.html
9. The Qbot. https://sourceforge.net/p/theqbot/wiki/Home/
10. Linux.Darlloz. https://www.symantec.com/security_response/writeup.jsp?docid=2013-112710-1612-99
11. Remaiten. https://en.wikipedia.org/wiki/Remaiten
12. Mirai Source. https://github.com/jgamblin/Mirai-Source-Code
13. GeekPwn blog. https://blog.geekpwn.org/2016/05/19/security-geek-winners-awarded-one-million-yuan-prize/
14. Common Vulnerabilities and Exposures. https://cve.mitre.org
15. Mirai bots attack 1 m German routers. http://www.theregister.co.uk/2016/11/28/
16. Symantec blog. https://www.symantec.com/connect/blogs/linux-worm-targeting-hidden-devices
17. CVE-2012-1823. https://cve.mitre.org/cgi-bin/cvename.cgi?name=cve-2012-1823
18. ShellShock. https://cve.mitre.org/cgi-bin/cvename.cgi?name=CVE-2014-6271
19. Busybox. https://en.wikipedia.org/wiki/BusyBox
20. Chakrabarty, S., Engels, D.W.: A secure IoT architecture for Smart Cities. In: 2016 13th IEEE Annual Consumer Communications & Networking Conference (CCNC). IEEE (2016)
21. Jerald, A.V., Rabara, S.A., Bai, D.P.: Secure IoT architecture for integrated smart services environment. In: 2016 3rd International Conference on Computing for Sustainable Global Development (INDIACom), pp. 800–805. IEEE, October 2016
22. Sun, H., Wang, X., Buyya, R., et al.: CloudEyes: cloud-based malware detection with reversible sketch for resource-constrained Internet of Things (IoT) devices. Pract. Exp., Software (2016)
23. Ham, H.S., Kim, H.H., Kim, M.S., et al.: Linear SVM-based android malware detection for reliable IoT services. J. Appl. Math. (2014)
24. Chen, K., Liu, P., Zhang, Y.: Achieving accuracy and scalability simultaneously in detecting application clones on android markets. In: Proceedings of the 36th International Conference on Software Engineering, pp. 175–186. ACM (2014)
25. Chen, K., Wang, X., Chen, Y., et al.: Following devil's footprints: cross-platform analysis of potentially harmful libraries on android and iOS. In: 2016 IEEE Symposium on Security and Privacy (SP), pp. 357–376. IEEE (2016)
26. Pa, Y.M.P., Suzuki, S., Yoshioka, K., et al.: IoTPOT: analysing the rise of IoT compromises. EMU 9, 1 (2015)
27. Wu, C.-J., et al.: IoT malware behavior analysis and classification using text mining algorithm (2016)
28. Yang, J.H., Ryu, Y.: Design and development of a command-line tool for portable executable file analysis and malware detection in IoT devices. Int. J. Secur. Appl. 9(8), 127–136 (2015)

29. Min, B., Varadharajan, V.: Design and evaluation of feature distributed malware attacks against the Internet of Things (IoT). In: 2015 20th International Conference on Engineering of Complex Computer Systems (ICECCS). IEEE (2015)
30. SDN. https://en.wikipedia.org/wiki/Software-defined_networking
31. Vandana, C.P.: Security improvement in IoT based on Software Defined Networking (SDN)

Design of OPC/DDP-Based Remote Monitoring System for Environmental Protection of the IoT

Hongzhi Pan[✉], Ting Zu, Rong Liu, Bo Liu, Qun Fang, and Xin He

Department of Computer Science and Technology, Anhui Normal University,
189 Jiuhua South Road, Wuhu 241002, Anhui, People's Republic of China
asdphz2015@163.com

Abstract. With the acceleration of industrialization and the increasingly serious environmental problems, environmental protection of internet of things (EPIoT) has been recognized as an efficient way for developing green industries. By analyzing the OPC protocol for the data acquisition and the DDP communication protocol for the data transmission, this paper designs and implements an OPC/DDP-based monitoring system, including automatic monitoring on environmental data, efficient data acquisition, remote scheduling of devices, remote and real-time data visualization. Furthermore, the system uses a reverse proxy technique in data processing to achieve cross domain management and keep the session. The system effectively solves the problem of collecting data and visually displaying data under severe environment. In addition, the design process is optimized by the remote control. Finally, the system provides a reliable support on the decision for environmental management.

Keywords: Environmental protection of Internet of Things · OPC · DTU · Data collection · Data transmission · Visualization

1 Introduction

Behind the tendency of rapid economic development, the environment problems, such as sewage from factories and ecological deterioration, become very tough. In the field of environmental protection, the construction and application of the Internet of Things (IoT) has become an important way to promote the upgrading of environmental management. The IoT-based application can further foster and develop a new strategic environmental protection industry, and has great impact on promoting the development of environmental protection in China.

In the environmental monitoring, the application of the IoT has become the trend technique for deployments [1]. Most of the traditional systems of environmental protection only involve a single data collection mode, and hence, the reliable data acquisition and transmission is not achieved. Moreover, the collected data can not be efficiently and visually displayed in those traditional systems. In order to solve these drawbacks, we propose an automatic monitoring system based on open platform communication (OPC)/ DTU & DSC communication protocol (DDP) for environment of things. Based on the reliable data collection and transmission of OPC/DDP, the system involves smart collection, transmission storage and visualization of data generated by various automatic

© ICST Institute for Computer Sciences, Social Informatics and Telecommunications Engineering 2017
F. Chen and Y. Luo (Eds.): Industrial IoT 2017, LNICST 202, pp. 187–195, 2017.
DOI: 10.1007/978-3-319-60753-5_20

environmental detection equipment. It divides into four stages, including environment sensing, data transmission, data center and payment. In addition, the system can support reliable decisions based on the data analysis.

In this paper, the OPC/DDP-based monitoring system is designed to allow various types of environmental perception elements and highly reliable data transmission using multi-protocol and multi-target. The system uses B/S platform to remotely coordinate various equipment with the aim of completing the effective control of environmental parameters, and visually display of the monitoring data.

The rest of the paper is organized as follows. Section 2 reviews the related work of environment protection of the IoT. The implementation of the proposed system is detailed in Sect. 3. Section 4 concludes this paper.

2 Related Work

Environmental protection of Internet of things refers to the traditional environmental protection industry to introduce automation and information technology to achieve scientific management of environmental protection system network, to build all-round, multi-level, full coverage of the ecological environment monitoring network [1]. To promote the efficient and accurate transmission of environmental information resources, through the construction of massive data resource center and unified service support platform to promote the ecological civilization construction and environmental protection scientific development goals [2].

At present, the Internet of Things at home and abroad has played a great role in environmental protection such as pollution prevention, ecological protection and so on. As of the first half of 2015 the country has 32 provinces, autonomous regions and 9,567 key sources of pollution to implement automatic monitoring. Jiangsu Province has completed the construction of heavy metal monitoring in Suzhou, Taihu Lake cyanobacteria, ammonia nitrogen, total nitrogen monitoring [3]; Wuxi focus on pollution sources and all key radioactive sources automatic monitoring system; Shanxi Province in more than seven hundred key enterprises set up intelligent monitoring Inner Mongolia Autonomous Region has also built a concept of environmental protection based on the concept of environmental monitoring platform to achieve a mobile device based on the environmental emergency and law enforcement applications [5]; Jiashan County, Zhejiang Province, the implementation of environmental monitoring, monitoring, monitoring, Also has completed the "environmental decision-making integrated information system", "intelligent pollutant total control system" and other sets of environmental protection system of things [6].

3 System Design and Implementation

3.1 Remote Monitoring System Components

Environmental protection equipment Remote monitoring system is a combination of hardware and software systems. It is necessary to have the functions of collecting, real-time online communication, alarm management, remote control, data storage, device data query, system log, setting and so on for monitoring data and running parameters generated by automatic monitoring equipment. At the same time also need to have strong anti-jamming capability, fault fast processing, data transfer and other functions.

The system consists of equipment layer, network layer, application layer composed of three levels. Environmental protection equipment remote monitoring system framework shown in Fig. 1.

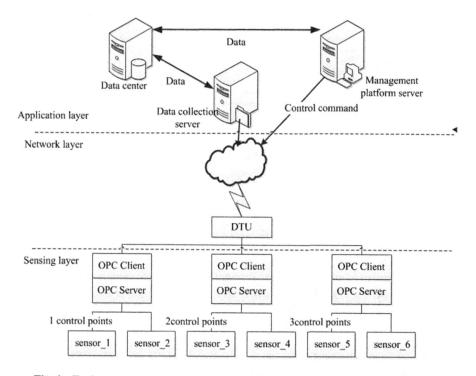

Fig. 1. Environmental protection equipment remote monitoring system frame diagram

3.2   Data Acquisition Based on OPC Client Function Design

Data acquisition based on OPC client development, the structure is shown in Fig. 2.

Data collection the client is mainly composed of three parts. Responsible for data acquisition of OPC client, the data real-time processing of data management module, and RS232 agent for sending data.

The realization of the detailed below two parts:

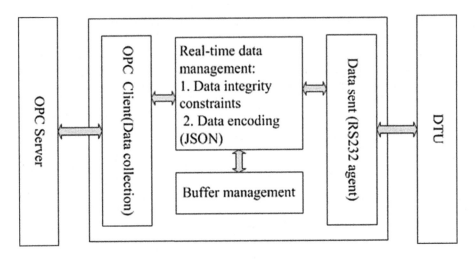

Fig. 2. Data acquisition client structure

The OPC Client. Data acquisition client using C# programming, the realization of OPC client process generally includes the object's statement, the server connection, add group and a data item and read data. Client implementation steps:

1. The OPC client initialization.
2. The OPC object statement with the server connection, the object of declaration is the required data items are defined. To connect to a remote server, you must have the remote server's IP address (opcServerIp) and remote server name (opcServer-Name), and then connect to the OPC server via opcServer.Connect (config.opcServerName, config.opcServerIp).
3. Create a group and add data item. First create the group with the code opcGroups = opcServer. OPCGroups; opcGroup = opcGroups. Add (OPCGROUP-NAME); then set the group properties, including group activity status, group update time, and so on. Finally add data items, code opcItems = opcGroup.OPCItems.
4. The OPC data read. Mainly through the Group's KepGroupDataChange event trigger to achieve.

The Realization of the RS232 Agent. Data acquisition client data needs to be sent by the network layer DTU to the data center, data acquisition client via a serial port to send data to the DTU.

1. Initialize the port function.
   Parameter Description: rs232Config: portName: "COM3", baudRate: 57600, dataBits: 8, stopBits: 1, parity: 0.
2. Handshake signal control.
3. Send data. public MessageSender (OpcServerConfig config, RS232Proxy rs232) this.config = config; this.rs232 = rs232.

3.3   DDP Protocol Design

DDP (DTU & DSC Communication Protocol) Communication Protocol is DTU (Data Transfer Unit) and DSC (Data Service Center) between the Communication Protocol. DTU (Data Transfer Unit), it is specifically designed to convert serial Data to IP Data or converts IP Data to serial Data transmission through wireless communication network of wireless terminal equipment [7]. DTU are widely used in meteorology, hydrology and water conservancy, geology, environmental monitoring, etc. [8]. (1) Its core function is the internal integrated TCP/IP protocol stack. (2) To provide two-way serial data conversion function. (3) Support automatic heartbeat, permanent online. (4) Support parameter configuration, permanent preservation. (5) support user serial port parameters Settings, etc. [9]. DSC (Data Service Center) is used to manage the DTU and DTU Data sending and receiving service software, it needs to be done through the dynamic library development kit and DTU communication between. Dynamic library includes and DTU communications required for all API functions, including the start of the service, service

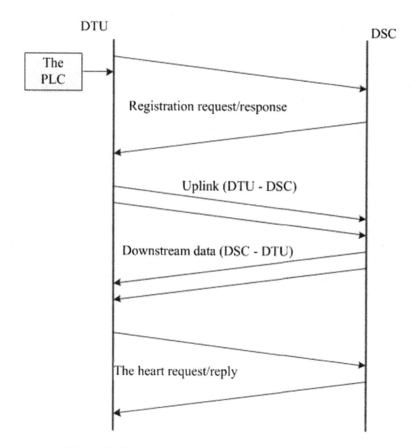

Fig. 3. DTU shake hands with DSC communication process

to stop sending, data receiving, data, parameter configuration, parameters in the query, etc. [10]. DTU with DSC communication process as shown in Fig. 3.

At this point DTU as a client, on-site PLC equipment to establish a connection with the DTU first, through the serial port to send data to the DTU, DTU and the data center to establish the connection through the registration package protocol to complete the connection process. After the connection, DTU and DSC data transmission between the transmission process, if there is disconnection and other circumstances, the heartbeat packet protocol to complete the disconnection automatically reconnect, automatic redial and other functions. To ensure the effective transmission of data.

3.4   Realization of the Function of the Cross-Domain and Keep the Session Based on the Reverse Proxy

Reverse Proxy (Reverse Proxy) is a proxy server to accept the connection request on the Internet, and then forward the request to the server on the internal network; and the results obtained from the server to return to the Internet request to connect the client, this When the proxy server on the performance of a server [11]. The usual proxy server, only for the proxy internal network connection request to the Internet, the client must specify the proxy server, and would have to be sent directly to the Web server http request sent to the proxy server. When a proxy server can proxy a host on an external network and access the internal network, this proxy service is called a reverse proxy service [12].

1. Cross-domain functions based on the reverse proxy.
   Cross domain is yes the script for the browser cannot perform other web sites, it was caused by the browser's same origin policy, is a browser security restrictions on javascript. In this paper, using NGINX reverse proxy cross-domain. Configure NGINX, multiple prefix in a server configuration for forwarding the HTTP/HTTPS requests to multiple real servers. All the URL on the server is the same domain name, protocol and port, for the browser, these urls are homologous, thus there is no limit to the cross-domain.
2. Session to maintain function based on reverse proxy.
   The client and the server often need to interact through many times of complete interaction at a time. Due to the interaction with the user's identity is closely related, therefore, related to the client application requests, often needs to be done forwarded to a server, and can't be load balancer forwarded to a different server for processing. So we need to keep on the load balancing configuration Session (Session Persistence) mechanism. The principle of Cookie session remains as shown in Fig. 4.

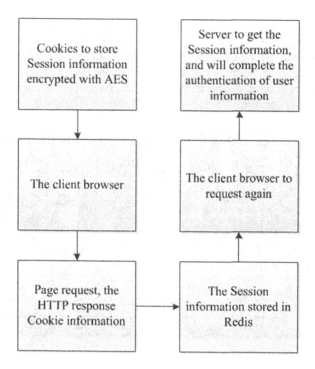

Fig. 4. The session workflow

3.5 The Implementation of Remote Monitoring System

Remote monitoring system to realize the function of remote monitoring of environmental data, it completed the real-time collection of field data, the security of the data transmission, data storage, data processing, data management, and other functions. In the process of data collection, using OPC architecture to complete real-time data acquisition; Communication protocol by DDP, terminal equipment and data center for the customer to build a wireless communication link, sends the data to the Kafka, ensure the safety of the data sent to the data center.

In the realization of the function of management, adopts B/S structure, using the bootstrap front-end framework for equipment, DTU, OPC client, data visualization, etc. Using a reverse proxy technology solves the problem keep the session, add the authentication. Server when the user login to set a cookie information encrypted with AES, at the same time will be the value stored in Redis, when a user request again, will bring back the cookie information parsing, if the server can parse correctly, remove the user information, the user authentication through, and then query the user's role, through the role of user menu list and interface permissions, validating the user interface of the current request permissions. Management platform management interface includes device management, protocol management, DTU management, project monitoring, system management. In the main interface shows the DTU status information, all the environmental monitoring points of the data statistics, abnormal circumstances such as real-time alarm information. Figure 5 is a real-time monitoring of the state of the enterprise production line, the figure shows the real-time data for each collection point, the abnormal situation of the alarm information, while silane can wash the various parts of the remote control system, the basic data analysis, To provide decision makers with accurate scheduling support.

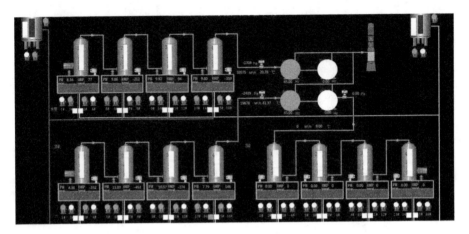

Fig. 5. An enterprise production line state of real-time monitoring

4   Conclusion

This paper designed and implemented a remote monitoring system based on OPC/DDP for environmental protection. The system not only has the "cross domain management, keeping the session, WEB publishing" properties, but also has a remote control, authority management, warning processing, visual display, etc. However, The completeness and security of data transmission is still an open question since the data transmission in DDP is transparent, which is left as a future study.

References

1. Xianfeng, W.: Based on the internet of things environment automatic monitoring data acquisition and transmission system architecture design and function implementation. J. Environ. Manage. China **4**, 53–57 (2013)
2. Silan, Z., Deming, X., XuDong, M., Hellmann, M.G.: Environmental iot in fuling shale gas development, the application of environmental monitoring research. J. Environ. Sci. Manage. **9**(3), 15–18 (2016)
3. Huang, J., Zhang, H., Jiang, L., et al.: The Taihu lake cyanobacteria blooms early warning monitoring the construction of a comprehensive system. J. Environ. Monitoring China **31**(1), 139–145 (2015)

4. Lee, J., Penryn, D.B., et al.: The pollution source in Shanxi Province the design and implementation of automatic monitoring and control system. J. Environ. Monitor. China **28**(3), 130–135 (2012)
5. Konka, P.-L.Y.: The general planning of the Inner Mongolia autonomous region environment informatization strategic vision research. J. Environ. Sci. Manage. **40**(6), 178–181 (2015)
6. Zou, X., Liu, L.: Jiashan county environmental monitoring system integration of environmental protection enterprises in zhejiang province "carefully crafted" - participate in emissions trading intention survey. J. Environ. Protect. **9**, 53–55 (2010)
7. Ball, F.W., Bing, H.: DTU passthrough mode study. J. Inf. Sci. Technol. **3**, 490–492 (2011)
8. Wang, Y., Wu, Y., Li, J.-C., et al.: The agricultural irrigation fertilization intelligent control system based on GPRS DTU application study. China's Rural Water Conservancy Hydropower **12**, 93–98 (2013)
9. Liu, Q., Lan, T., Circle, H., et al.: Intelligent GPRS DTU mixed embedded file system. Comput. Eng. **35**(12), 256–258 (2009)
10. Zhongbiao, Z.: An improved design of DTU communication protocols. Power Syst. Protect. Contr. **17**, 136–138 (2014)
11. Zheng, G., Yin, J., Zhu, X.: Use reverse proxy technology to protect the web server implementation. Comput. Secur. 30–32 (2010)
12. Pigeon, W.X., Dong, L.-L.: Single sign-on system based on the reverse proxy design. J. Comput. Appl. Softw. **28**(3), 156–158 (2011)

Smart Home Monitoring System Based on SOC

Haiquan Ma, Ping Wang$^{(\boxtimes)}$, Hong Fan, and Wujun Xu

Engineering Research Center of Digitized Textile and Fashion Technology,
College of Information Science and Technology, Ministry of Education,
Donghua University, Shanghai 201620, China
mahaiquan8@163.com, {PingWang,dhfanhong,WujunXu}@dhu.edu.cn

Abstract. Smart home technologies can provide financial savings, enhance convenience for consumers, contribute to more ecological and sustainable living, and reinforce the buyer's sense of safety and security. The Zynq-7000 AP SoC device is based on the Xilinx® All Programmable SoC architecture. These products integrate a dual core ARM® Cortex™-A9 MPCore™ based PS and PL in a single device. The PS is equipped with two Gigabit Ethernet Controllers. The goal of this paper is to present a smart home monitoring system, which utilizes face detection as identification. Combining with SOC technology, ZYNQ platform is used to accelerate the speed of video image processing and identification. The system consists of video image acquisition module, control recognition processing module and information display interactive module. With the intelligent analysis, early notice and warning on collected video information informs users via WeChat. The system meets the miniaturization, integration of the home environment at the same time to be more secure and fast real-time information feedback.

Keywords: Smart home · Zynq-7000 AP SoC · Face recognition · WeChat applications · Hardware acceleration

1 Introduction

With the continuous improvement of living standards, people expect home life can be more comfortable, safe and convenient. However, the traditional home applications cannot provide a satisfactory software and hardware conditions to meet these needs. In recent years, collaborative design of software and hardware has made smart home environment possible. Smart home needs provide not only WiFi solutions but also cloud storage and data analysis services. The companies have provided software and hardware solutions that traditional hardware products are now get connected to achieve data sharing for smart home. The Zynq®-7000 family is based on the Xilinx® All Programmable System on Chip (AP SoC) [1] architecture. Zynq-7000 is the first tightly integrated high-performance ARM Cortex-A9 hard core with programmable logic FPGA device. In the Zynq platform, the programmable logic can be regarded as the peripherals of the processor, and the programmable logic can be regarded as the

© ICST Institute for Computer Sciences, Social Informatics and Telecommunications Engineering 2017
F. Chen and Y. Luo (Eds.): Industrial IoT 2017, LNICST 202, pp. 196–204, 2017.
DOI: 10.1007/978-3-319-60753-5_21

main device of the processor. Through the perfect combination, it can not only play the advantages of running the operating system, but also show the advantage of FPGA to implement the parallel algorithm to accelerate and reconfigure dynamically.

Zynq-7000 series provides FPGA flexibility and scalability, while providing performance and power consumption and ease of use typically associated with ASIC and ASSP. Zynq-7000 SoC AP family of devices enables designers to use industry standard tools from a single platform for cost sensitive and high performance applications. Although each device in the Zynq-7000 series contains the same processing system (PS), programmable logic (PL) and I/O resources differ between devices [2]. Smart home monitoring system based on SOC in this paper also offers possibilities for energy and cost savings, greater home efficiency through automation, as well as improved home security. Smart homes have the potential to provide for consumers' growing expectations of convenience, sustainable living, safety, and security.

The rest of the paper is organized as follows. Section 2 introduces the architecture of ZYNQ 7000 series. Section 3 briefly illustrates face detection algorithm explored in this work. Section 4 shows the architecture of the proposed system on ZYNQ platform using Vivado HLS [3]. The achieved results are discussed in Sect. 5. Conclusions are offered in Sect. 6.

2   Architecture of ZYNQ 7000 Series

Zynq 7000 SoC from Xilinx is a series of chips that FPGA and CPU are built on the same chip, which can achieve rapid interaction in the accelerated program. Field Programmable Gate Array (FPGA) is becoming more and more popular in the field of computer vision. In view of its true parallel architecture, it can potentially speed up image processing to an order of magnitude. In addition to the FPGA design tools, Xilinx also sells a variety of different levels of FPGA and FPGA resources. They also sell a special type of FPGA chip with integrated CPU on the same chip, called Zynq. This type of chip is classified as SoC. Tight integration between PS and PL [4] is ideal for fast interaction between the accelerator and its controlling C program. With support for DDR3 speed memory interface, it allows the FPGA and CPU to share external memory that is usually much bigger than the available internal memory. All chips of the 7000 series use a Dual ARM Cortex-A9 as CPU. The chip used in this paper is called Zynq 7020 (XC7Z020) and is equivalent to the Artix-7 FPGA. Display and control for ARM part and IP core design for FPGA part are executed. Zynq 7020 possesses rich logic resources that are shown in Table 1. In this thesis the Zynq-7020 is used to test systems designed with the Vivado Design Suite, a toolchain of programs which Vivado HLS extends. The Zynq-7020 can be evaluated with the ZC702 Evaluation Kit that contains interfaces for expansion cards and HDMI [5] output among other features. The system uses camera with USB interface to obtain surveillance video for intelligent analysis (Fig. 1).

Table 1. Zynq 7020 chip resources.

Parameter	Description
Processor	Dual-core Cortex-A9 with NEON and FPU extensions
Maximum processor clock frequency	866 MHz
Programmable logic	Artix-7
Number of triggers	866 MHz
6 Enter the number of LUTs	53,200
32 Kb block RAM quantity	140
Number of DSP48 chips (18 × 25 bits)	220
Select IO input/output block number	HR:200 HP:0

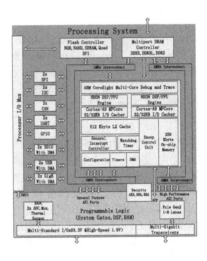

Fig. 1. Zynq-7000 AP SoC overview.

3 Face Detection Algorithm

3.1 AdaBoosting Face Detector

The AdaBoost Algorithm [6] is a kind of creative method for real-time target detection, and its training speed is very slow, but it is very fast. It is an integral image based on fast feature evaluation And the enhancement of feature selection, which is mainly used to quickly reject the attention cascade of non face to face windows.

Boosting is a classification scheme that works by combining weak learners into a more accurate ensemble classifier. A weak learner need only do better than chance.

Training consists of multiple boosting rounds. During each boosting round, we select a weak learner that does well on examples that were hard for the

Fig. 2. Image features.

previous weak learner, "Hardness" is captured by weights attached to training examples.

As shown in Fig. 2. The integral image computes a value at each pixel (x, y) that is the sum of the pixel values above and to the left of (x, y), inclusive. This can quickly be computed in one pass through the image.

Each Haar features correspond to a weak classifier, but not any Haar feature can better describe the face's gray distribution for a certain characteristics. How to choose from a large number of Haar features out optimal Haar features and make into classification that used for face detection is the key problem to AdaBoost algorithm training. The AdaBoost Algorithm is mainly implemented by calling the visual library of Open Source Computer Vision (OpenCV). OpenCV is the most popular computer vision library. It is a distributed under the BSD license (open source), cross-platform computer vision library, which can run on Linux, Windows, Mac OS and Android operating systems. It's lightweight and efficient - made up of a series of C function and a small amount of C++ class, at the same time provides the Python, Ruby, MATLAB language interface; realize the many general algorithm of image processing and computer vision. Xilinx provides a C++ library, which can accelerate the similar function of OpenCV. A library is a subset of OpenCV functions and data structures that can be synthesized by Xilinx rewriting.

3.2   KLT Face Recognition Algorithm

Face recognition is a supervised learning process. Intuitive distance was calculated directly, but there is a very big defect - too big amount of calculation. For an image size is 100 * 100, and there are 1000 training set, so the number of calculations required to identify an image is 1000 * 100 * 100. The recognition speed is very slow when the test set is large. A key way to solve the above problem is to dimension reduction of image using Karhunen-Loeve Transform (K LT) [7] by only retaining some key pixel that make recognition speed boost.

KLT transform performs the statistics of the variables in each variable rate of change (the difference between the average of multiple samples and one sample) to achieve dimension reduction, The rate of change is small (the eigenvalue of the covariance matrix is small) that doesn't make much contribution to the discrimination, so it can be discarded; And the variable with large change rate has a great influence on the discrimination, so it is necessary to keep the eigenvector with large eigenvalue to form a transformation matrix. Converting the newly acquired observations and the transposed conversion matrix can reduce the dimension of the original data. This process can be understood as a projection transformation that projects the original high-dimensional spatial coordinates into low-dimensional space. Since the transformation matrix (which is regarded as an orthogonal coordinate axis vector in a low-dimensional space) of the eigenvectors corresponding to several eigenvalues with the greatest contribution has been analyzed before, so this process can maximize the amount of data information is not missing.

The design uses the High-Level Synthesis Tools (HLSTs) which make the system design easier to modify and/or repair to design KLT IP core by Vivado [8]. The Vivado HLS [9] tool convert the C/C++ language to the RTL level HDL description. HLS presents a new design concept, which focus on FPGA design system modeling and improves the development efficiency. HLS Tools allow more software engineers have the opportunity to participate in FPGA design.

4   Architecture of Proposed System

Smart home monitoring system, including the terminal which placed in the user's home and WeChat subscription numbers that users can access through WeChat, two parts. The overall block diagram of the system is shown in Fig. 3.

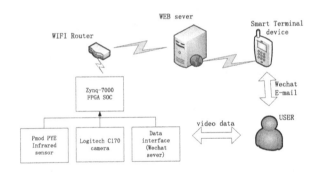

Fig. 3. Home monitoring system data flow.

The PS is equipped with two Gigabit Ethernet Controllers. Each controller can be configured independently. To access pins via MIO, each controller uses an RGMII interface (to save pins). Access to the PL is through the EMIO which provides the GMII interface.

The system uses C170 Logitech network camera to capture video and images, and stored in the wifi router. When a person or an animal to trigger the infrared sensor, the camera is triggered to start recording until the left trigger source monitoring area, the user can view the Home Furnishing by WeChat, and the transfer of view stored in the video server.

4.1   Camera Acquisition Module

C170 Logitech network camera is used to capture video and image, through universal serial bus (Serial Bus Universal, USB) will collect the video storage in SOC memory space. Linux system to carry out video capture, light loaded camera driver is not enough, also need to load V4L (referred to as V4L) module. V4L module supports the programming interface (API) can be applied to call, from the camera device to capture video streaming. The following is mainly about the acquisition of the video stream.

USB is a cable bus that supports data exchange between the host device and a large number of simultaneous access peripherals. Through a host scheduling, token based protocol, the connected devices share the USB bandwidth. When the main device is operating with other peripherals, the USB bus allows you to add, configure, use, and remove peripherals. ZYNQ has two USB controllers, in accordance with the On-The-Go 2 C OTG USB) standard. OTG added to the USB specification, to achieve point to point communication. Using OTG USB technology, consumer electronics, peripherals and portable devices can be connected to each other.

Based on OTG USB, both can be fully compatible with the development of USB peripherals, and can act as a host of USB. Based on the connector signal, the OTG state machine can determine the role of the device. And then, based on the connection mode, the device (host or peripheral) is initialized with the appropriate operation mode. When the device is connected, based on the implementation of the business, the device can use the OTG protocol to confirm its role.

4.2   The PYE Pmod Infrared Sensor Module

According to the requirements of this design, when some people or animals through the surveillance area will trigger the camera video, which requires the appropriate passive pyroelectric infrared sensor module. Combined with the design of the ZYBO development board, the company chose the digilent company's new products are still in the testing phase of the product PYE Pmod infrared human body induction module.

The design of the PYE Pmod infrared sensor module for the German company is still in the test phase of the external expansion.

Exhibition board. It uses a high sensitivity, strong reliability of the original import LHI778 probe, with the BISS0001. The sensor processing integrated circuit is a passive pyroelectric infrared switch. Because of its support in low voltage mode, it is widely used in all kinds of automatic induction and control system. The system uses infrared sensors to a large extent, reduce the power consumption of the system (Fig. 4).

4.3   Smart monitoring system

As shown in Fig. 5, Design system connection diagram including (1) WIFI Router: router network forwarding function; (2) Logitech C170 camera: the camera video

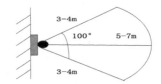

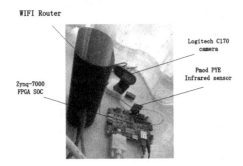

Fig. 4. Pmod PYE infrared sensor.

Fig. 5. Design system connection diagram.

data acquisition module; (3) Zynq-7000 FPGA SoC: infrared human body induction module system sleep and video trigger, reduce power consumption; (4) Pmod PYE Infrared sensor: ZYNQ development board as the core control board, including FPGA and ARM two components, data processing and operation display.

The system is open, the main program will enter the state of automatic detection, once someone or animal departure infrared sensor, the main program will be in accordance with the scheduled process or in accordance with the user's configuration to complete all the operations. At this point the user will receive a display home in the case of WeChat subscription number push, and can see the home video online.

WeChat, the leading Chinese mobile messaging app, has released an API for connected hardware that enables users to remote control smart devices through WeChat public accounts. WeChat can be used to send voice, images, and video to a TV, to interact with friends (such as to send reminders and TV "barrages.") WeChat is an information hub that can use its user base and social network relationships to link hardware products, manufacturers, and users, to encourage users to engage with and use hardware products, and to promote sales.

5   Experiments and Results

By using the advantages of the FPGA+ARM architecture of ZYNQ, software algorithm is mapped to hardware implementation. The experimental performance evaluation show that the algorithm can shorten the processing time significantly. Performance comparison between CPUs and SOC for face detection IP core is shown in Table 2.

Table 2. Performance comparison between CPUs and SOC for face detection IP core.

Experiment	Running time of PC	Running time of SOC
The first experiment	420.556 ms	301.416 ms
The second experiment	403.87 ms	297.045 ms
The third experiment	408.914 ms	306.995 ms

It can be found that the average running time is about 300 ms to deal with a face recognition for the hardware algorithm IP. This processing speed relative to the PC on the pure software algorithm reduces the processing time reduces nearly 100 ms, and the hardware implementation of the algorithm achieve a acceleration (Fig. 6).

Diagram of smart home monitoring system is shown in Fig. 7. Infrared camera sensor start the system when someone appear in the monitoring area. The system can accurately analyze the video image, the results are displayed on the platform, including the number of video statistics, matching the face recognition, processing time and receiving message via WeChat, as shown in Fig. 7. The user

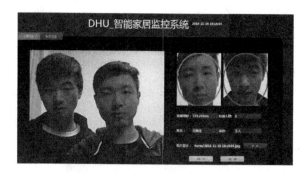

Fig. 6. Diagram of smart home monitoring system.

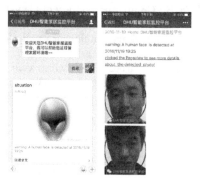

Fig. 7. Receive message screenshots via WeChat.

can view the face image data, also can click the URL to enter the WEB server to view video recording files.

6 Conclusions

In this paper, we show how face detection realizes based on the Zynq-7000 AP SoC device and receive message via WeChat. The system meets the miniaturization, integration of the home environment at the same time to be more secure and fast real-time information feedback. The implementation of face detection and tracking processing using C-based HLS is presented. The results show that hardware accelerators enhance the complex computation of the processing functions. The hardware accelerators on FPGA enhance the computational performance. There are many computer visions application which can take advantage of hardware accelerators to enhance performance of real-time highly computational applications. When targeting HLS design flow, the implementation of C/C++ code is rapidly developed for hardware accelerator.

References

1. Freund, Y., Schapire, R.E.: A decision-theoretic generalization of on-line learning and an application to boosting. J. Comput. Syst. Sci. **55**, 119–139 (1997)
2. Yao, M., Aoki, K., Nagahashi, H.: Segmentation-based illumination normalization for face detection. In: Computational Intelligence & Applications (IWCIA), pp. 95–100 (2013)
3. Li, C., Liu, J., Wang, A., Li, K.: Matrix reduction based on generalized method in face recognition. In: Digital Home (ICDH), pp. 35–38 (2014)
4. Xilinx. LogiCORE IP Video Direct Memory Access (axi vdma) (v3.1) Data Sheet.pdf
5. Xilinx. LogiCORE IP AXI Video Direct Memory Access (axi_vdma) v6.0 product Guide.pdf
6. Freund, Y., Schapire, R.: A short introduction to boosting. J. Jpn. Soc. Artif. Intell. **14**(5), 771–780 (1999)
7. Chatterjee, D., Chandran, S.: Comparative study of Camshift and KLT algorithms for real time face detection and tracking applications. In: IEEE International Conference on Research in Computational Intelligence and Communication Networks (2016)
8. Xilinx. ug902-vivado-high-level-synthesis. www.xilinx.com
9. Xilinx. ug871-vivado-high-level-synthesis-tutorial. www.xilinx.com

Improved One-Round Phrase Search Schemes Over Symmetrically Encrypted Data in Storage Outsourcing System

Ling Shen[1,2(✉)] and Jie Wang[3]

[1] Department of Computer Science,
Wuhan Donghu University, Wuhan 430212, China
aleenapple@163.com
[2] Wuhan University, Wuhan 430072, China
[3] Department of Computer Science,
University of Massachusetts Lowell, Lowell, MA 01854, USA

Abstract. Phrase search schemes over encrypted data are efficient methods for protecting users' data privacy in storage outsourcing systems. We analyze and improve two one-round phrase search schemes over encrypted data. One drawback of F. Kong's phrase search scheme is that it cannot support single-keyword search. We propose a modification and the improved scheme supports both single-keyword and phrase search. In M. Li's phrase search scheme, a simple unkeyed hash function is used instead of a keyed pseudo-random function. We present a security analysis and show that the usage of a keyed pseudo-random function can resist the leakage of some useful information. These phrase search schemes can be applied in cloud storage.

Keywords: Cloud storage · Information security · Searchable symmetric encryption · Phrase search

1 Introduction

The Internet of Things (IoT) and mobile technology are integrating various access devices such as radio-frequency identification (RFID) tags, sensors, smart phones, tablets, and wearable devices into a global network infrastructure [1–3]. The sharp increase of IoT, mobile devices, and social-networking services produces large amounts of data in either structured or unstructured format. While cloud computing and storage services [4] provides powerful, reliable, and on-demand computing and storage resources, users can outsource complex computation and their data to the public or private cloud services. For example, Microsoft's Azure storage service and Amazon's Simple Storage Service (S3) Storage services are public cloud storage services.

However, despite its benefits and popularity, cloud services face many security and privacy threats [5–9]. When users store their data into the remote cloud, they suspect that the cloud service providers may obtain their data. To protect their data privacy, users encrypt the data using secret cryptographic keys and send the cipher-text data to the cloud. The fundamental problem is how users can retrieve only files containing certain

© ICST Institute for Computer Sciences, Social Informatics and Telecommunications Engineering 2017
F. Chen and Y. Luo (Eds.): Industrial IoT 2017, LNICST 202, pp. 205–213, 2017.
DOI: 10.1007/978-3-319-60753-5_22

keywords from the remote cloud. As the data has been encrypted by users, the cloud is required to perform search operations over encrypted data. The Fully-Homomorphic Encryption Schemes (FHE) [10, 11], which can support any computation on encrypted data, maybe one of the most amazing solutions. However, the inefficiency of FHE schemes makes them hard to use in practice.

Searchable Symmetric Encryption (SSE) proposed by D. Song, D. Wagner, and A. Perrig [12] is a very efficient scheme for secure storage outsourcing. In SSE scheme, the remote untrusted server can perform searches on encrypted data and no plain-text data is leaked. In [13], R. Curtmola, J. Garay, S. Kamara, and R. Ostrovsky gave two formal security definitions for Searchable Symmetric Encryption (SSE) schemes, called non-adaptive indistinguishability security and adaptive indistinguishability security.

Multi-keyword search over encrypted data [14, 15] is a natural expansion to single-keyword search. In multi-keyword search scheme, also called conjunctive keyword search, the documents containing all of the query keywords are returned. The difference between phrase search and multi-keyword search is that phrase search requires the query keywords occur consecutively in the document. In 2012, S. Zittrower and C.C. Zou [16] introduced a phrase search scheme on encrypted data by storing keyword-location value for each keyword. Y. Tang, D. Gu, N. Ding, and H. Lu [17] proposed a two-phase phrase search scheme, which was provably secure in the non-adaptive setting. Z.A. Kissel and J. Wang [18, 19] presented an efficient verifiable phrase search scheme and a single-round phrase search scheme. In [20], F. Kong and J. Wang gave an analysis and improvement to Z. A. Kissel's scheme. M. Li et al. [21] proposed the LPSSE phrase search scheme by combing R. Curtmola's secure linked list structure and keywords' relative position information. H.T. Poon and A. Miri [22, 23] adopted Bloom filters to reduce the storage amount in their phrase search schemes.

In this paper, we propose further improvements of two one-round phrase search schemes, known as F. Kong's scheme and M. Li's scheme. In F. Kong's phrase search scheme, users cannot perform single-keyword search. We propose an improvement to support both single-keyword and phrase search by combing R. Curtmola's method. In M. Li's phrase search scheme, a simple unkeyed hash function $h()$ is used instead of a keyed pseudo-random function $h_s()$ in Y. Tang's scheme. We give a security analysis and show that some information may be leaked when unkeyed hash function $h()$ is adopted. Thus it is better to use the keyed pseudo-random function $h_s()$.

The rest of the paper is organized as follows. In Sect. 2, we review searchable symmetric encryption schemes. In Sect. 3, we analyze F. Kong's phrase search scheme and propose an improvement to support single-keyword search. In Sect. 4, we give the security analysis of M. Li's phrase search scheme and present the improvement method. Finally, we give the conclusion and future research work in Sect. 5.

2   Searchable Symmetric Encryption Schemes

Storage-as-a-Service (STaaS) is known as a kind of cloud service providing users with storage outsourcing. When users want to retrieve some encrypted documents from the cloud, they should send the query to the cloud, who can perform searches on encrypted data and return the result to the users. Searchable symmetric encryption schemes [12–23] are practical solutions for secure storage outsourcing.

2.1   Searchable Encryption Schemes and Security Definitions

D. Song, D. Wagner, and A. Perrig [12] presented practical methods for searches on encrypted data by scanning the cipher-text documents.

R. Curtmola, J. Garay, S. Kamara, and R. Ostrovsky [13] constructed two index-based Searchable Symmetric Encryption (SSE) schemes by using linked lists and look-up tables. They also gave two kinds of security definitions of searchable symmetric encryption schemes, known as non-adaptive indistinguishability and adaptive indistinguishability.

R. Curtmola et al. gave the conception of *History*, *Access Pattern*, and *Search Pattern* [13]. The trace of a history H_q denotes the information leaked about the history. The trace consists of the access and search patterns.

It was noted [13] that the accurate security definition for SSE is that nothing is leaked except the access pattern and the search pattern. The detailed descriptions of non-adaptive indistinguishability and adaptive indistinguishability are seen in [13].

2.2   Phrase Search Schemes Over Encrypted Data

In conjunctive keyword or multi-keyword search schemes on encrypted data [14, 15], the cloud tries to retrieve those documents containing all the keywords according to the query sent by users. In phrase search schemes on encrypted data [16–23], it is required that the keywords occur consecutively in the documents. Thus, we should preserve the location information of each keyword in the documents to judge whether the keywords occur as a phrase.

There are two kinds of methods of recording the location information of each keyword in the documents. One method [16] is to record the sequence number of each word in the documents. Another method [17] is to construct a relative position table of all the words in the documents.

S. Zittrower and C.C. Zou's phrase search scheme on encrypted data [16] stores the encrypted keyword-location information for each keyword in the documents. To resist statistical cryptanalysis, they truncated the encrypted words to a predefined number of bits.

In 2012, Y. Tang, D. Gu, N. Ding, and H. Lu [17] proposed a two-round phrase search protocol on encrypted data by using a binary matrix and a look-up table. In the first round, it is required to get a set of candidate documents containing each word in the phrase. In the second round, the cloud will find the documents containing the phrase by testing whether the keywords occur as a phrase.

In [19], Z.A. Kissel proposed a single-round phrase search scheme by using the encrypted next-word lists, which is an improved inverted index structure. In Z.A. Kissel's scheme, there are a set of postings list containing the document identifiers, number of occurrences, and the locations of each pair of words.

The idea of F. Kong's improved scheme [20] is to construct the encrypted next-word index for each pair of words (w_s, w_t) directly instead of using the next-word list N. The data structure of F. Kong's scheme is (A, P), where A is the encrypted list of all pairs of words (w_s, w_t) and P is the postings list of the corresponding locations of each pair of words in the documents.

M. Li et al.'s LPSSE phrase search scheme [21] is constructed based on R. Curtmola's scheme by adding the relative location information of words to the inverted index.

3   Improved F. Kong's Phrase Search Scheme Over Encrypted Data

In this section, we modify F. Kong's phrase search scheme to support one-keyword search over encrypted data.

3.1   The Idea of Our Modification

In R. Curtmola's non-adaptively secure SSE scheme [13], the encrypted index consists of an array of words and a look-up table. Each word w_i has a linked list which contains all the identifiers of the documents in $D(w_i)$. When the user wants to get the documents containing keyword w_i, he/she sends the query to the remote server. The server will find the linked list L_i of keyword w_i, and obtain all the document identifiers in the list L_i.

In [19], Z.A. Kissel's one-round phrase search scheme constructs the encrypted next-word lists to preserve the locations of each pair of words. In a next-word index, each word w_i is followed by a list of succeeding words $w_{i,1} \ldots w_{i,j} \ldots$ and the locations where a pair of adjacent words $(w_i, w_{i,j})$ occur. To perform one keyword search, the server must scan all the nodes in the next-word list of keyword w_i and form a set of all the document identifiers.

In F. Kong's phrase search scheme [20], the next-word list is built for each pair of encrypted words (w_i, w_j) instead of each word. For example, the server cannot know whether a pair of encrypted words (w_i, w_j) contain a keyword w_i or w_j. Therefore, the server cannot find the documents where a keyword w_i occurs.

The idea of our modification is adding the next-word list of each word to the index of pairs of words. Thus no matter one-keyword search or phrase search, the server can find the corresponding documents. We note that only document identifiers are recorded in the next-word list of each word and no one-word location information is leaked.

3.2   Our Improved Phrase Search Scheme

We use the similar notations and definitions in [19, 20]. Let $Pair_i$ denote a pair of words (w_s, w_t). Similar to F. Kong's scheme [20], our improved scheme also constructs an encrypted index (A, P), which consists of two arrays A and P. The difference is that the information of each word is added to the arrays A and P in our scheme.

Let $D = \{D_1, D_2, ..., D_n\}$ be the document collection and $\Delta = \{w_1, w_2, ..., w_d\}$ be the set of d words. Let $D(w_i)$ be the set of documents identifiers that contain keyword w_i. Let $p = (w_1, w_2, ..., w_n)$ be a phrase consisting of n words and $D(p_i)$ be the set of all the documents containing the phrase p_i. Let (G, E, D) denote a secure symmetric encryption algorithm. Three cryptographic pseudo-random functions φ, f, and ζ are described as follows:

$$\varphi: \{0, 1\}^k \times \{0, 1\}^{\lg(m|\Delta|)} \rightarrow \{0, 1\}^{\lg(m|\Delta|)},$$
$$f: \{0, 1\}^k \times \{0, 1\}^p \rightarrow \{0, 1\}^{k+\log(m|\Delta|)},$$
$$\zeta: \{0, 1\}^k \times \{0, 1\}^p \rightarrow \{0, 1\}^{\lg(|\Delta|)}.$$

The improved one-round phrase search scheme on encrypted data consists of four probabilistic polynomial-time algorithms, similar as the schemes in [19, 20]:

Step 1 – Key generation: The client generates three random cryptographic keys x, y, and ω from the space $\{0, 1\}^k$.

Step 2 – Building the Index: The client builds the encrypted next-word index (A, P) as follows. Then the client sends the (A, P) and all the encrypted documents to the remote cloud.

(i) The head list A:

We create the element nodes in the array A for each pair of words and single word respectively.

For a pair of words $Pair_i$, the element in $A[\zeta_x(Pair_i)]$ is $(k_{i,0}\|\varphi_\omega(s_i)) \oplus f_y(Pair_i)$. It is noted that $\varphi_\omega(s_i)$ is the address of the head node of the pair of words $Pair_i$ and $k_{i,0}$ is the cryptographic key for encrypting the corresponding posting list P.

Similarly, for each word w_i, the element in $A[\zeta_x(w_i)]$ is $(k_{i,0}\|\varphi_\omega(s_i)) \oplus f_y(w_i)$, where $\varphi_\omega(s_i)$ is the address of the head node of the word w_i and $k_{i,0}$ is the key for encrypting the corresponding posting list P.

(ii) The posting list P:

For a single word w_i, we store only the document identifiers containing w_i in the array P. For a pair of words $Pair_i$, we store not only the document identifiers containing w_i but also the location information in the array P.

The element in $P[\varphi_\omega(c)]$ is $E(n_{i,j})$ encrypted with the cryptographic key $k_{i,j-1}$. For a pair of words, we have

$n_{i,j} = \text{id}(d)\| l \| k_{i,j}\|\varphi_\omega(c + 1)$.
For a word w_i, we have
$n_{i,j} = \text{id}(d)\| k_{i,j} \|\varphi_\omega(c + 1)$.

The counter c is initialized to 1. The identifier $\text{id}(d)$ is the identifier for the document $d \in D(Pair_i)$ or $D(w_i)$. For a phrase, l is the location of the two-word phrase $Pair_i$ in the document d. The cryptographic key $k_{i,j}$ is the key for encrypting the next node of the posting list.

Step 3 – Generating the Trapdoor: The client computes the search trapdoor T_p for the phrase $p = (w_1, w_2, ..., w_n)$ and sends the trapdoor T_p to the remote cloud:

$$T_p = \{(\zeta_x(Pair_1), f_y(Pair_1)), (\zeta_x(Pair_2), f_y(Pair_2)), ..., (\zeta_x(Pair_{n-1}), f_y(Pair_{n-1}))\},$$

where $Pair_i$ is the pair of words (w_i, w_{i+1}) with $1 \leq i < n$.

For a single keyword w_i, the client computes the search trapdoor T_p for the keyword w_i and sends the trapdoor $T_{wi} = \{(\zeta_x(w_i), f_y(w_i))\}$ to the remote cloud.

Step 4 – Performing the Search: Once the cloud receives the trapdoor T_{wi} or T_p, it performs the query and returns all the documents containing the phrase $p = (w_1, w_2, ..., w_n)$ or the keyword w_i to the client.

Now we explain that the improved scheme supports the one-word search. For one-word search, upon receiving the query $T_{wi} = \{(\zeta_x(w_i), f_y(w_i))\}$, the cloud can find the element $(k_{i,0} \| \varphi_\omega(s_i)) \oplus f_y(w_i)$ in $A[\zeta_x(w_i)]$. Then it computes $A[\zeta_x(w_i)] \oplus f_y(w_i)$ and obtains $k_{i,0} \| \varphi_\omega(s_i)$. It is noted that $P(\varphi_\omega(s_i))$ is the head node of the posting list of the word w_i and $k_{i,0}$ is the encryption key. By decrypting using the cryptographic key $k_{i,0}$, the cloud recovers $id(d) \| k_{i,j} \| \varphi_\omega(c + 1)$, in which $id(d)$ is the identifier for the document $d \in D(w_i)$ containing the keyword w_i. Then the cloud scans all the nodes in the posting list by using a similar method. Therefore, the cloud obtains all the document identifiers containing the keyword w_i and return them to the client.

For phrase search, the cloud receives the $T_p = \{(\zeta_x(Pair_1), f_y(Pair_1)), (\zeta_x(Pair_2), f_y(Pair_2)), ..., (\zeta_x(Pair_{n-1}), f_y(Pair_{n-1}))\}$ and can obtains the document identifiers containing the phrase $p = (w_1, w_2, ..., w_n)$. This procedure is no difference with the schemes in [19, 20]. Thus the improved scheme supports one-keyword and phrase search and it is a remedy for F. Kong's scheme.

In fact, in Z.A. Kissel's phrase search scheme [19], we can perform one-keyword search besides phrase search. It is required to scan all the posting lists of the keyword w_i, which is followed by many words of all the existing pairs. It is a little more complicated than our scheme.

For security, our modification cannot bring new security risks. The symmetric encryption algorithm for encrypting keyword w_i or a pair of words $Pair_i$ must be a semantically secure symmetric algorithm [24, 25]. Thus the ciphertexts of (w_i, w_s), (w_i, w_t), or the keyword w_i are indistinguishable. So the cloud or the attacker cannot get useful information to learn whether an encrypted pair $Pair_i$ includes an encrypted keyword w_i. Therefore, our improved phrase search scheme has as good security as these schemes [13, 19, 20].

4   Analysis and Improvement of LPSSE Scheme

M. Li et al.'s LPSSE phrase search scheme [21] is proposed based on R. Curtmola's non-adaptive searchable symmetric encryption scheme by adding the relative location information of words to the inverted index.

Y. Tang et al. [17] proposed a two-round phrase protocol, in which the first round is to get all the document candidates containing all the words in the phrase and the second is to find the documents containing the phrase. M. Li et al.'s scheme can be finished in one round of communication at the expense of more search time.

M. Li et al.'s scheme [21] uses a similar construction of relative location information as Y. Tang et al.'s scheme [17]. However, they use a simple unkeyed hash function $h()$ instead of a keyed pseudo-random function $h_s()$.

Now we give a security analysis and show that some information may be leaked when unkeyed hash function $h()$ is adopted. For simplicity, we adopt the notations of Y. Tang et al.'s scheme.

The look-up table A for each document D [17] is built for recording the location of each word in document D. To avoid leaking the location information, they assign a unique random number r_i to represent the location of the ith word in D. The first column is $\Psi_z(w[i]\|id(D))$ and the remaining elements are $h_s(r_{i-1})\| r_i$. The cryptographic secret key s is computed by $f_{2t}(w[i-1]\|w[i]\|id(D))$. To check whether two words are located adjacently, we can compute $h_s(r_{i-1})$ of the first word and test whether it is equal to the right v bits the element of the second word in the table.

We note that no one can compute $h_s(r_{i-1})$ without the secret key s, which is given by $f_{2t}(w[i-1]\|w[i]\|id(D))$ in the client's query. However, in M. Li et al.'s scheme [21], they use a unkeyed hash function $h()$, which can be computed without a secret key. Thus some information may be leaked. For example, the client sends the query of the phrase $(w[1]\|w[2])$ to the remote cloud. In Y. Tang et al.'s scheme, the cloud can only judge whether the phrase $(w[1]\|w[2])$ is contained in a document D. However, in M. Li et al.'s scheme, the cloud can test the phrase $(w[1]\|w[2])$ and $(w[2]\|w[1])$ because both $h(r_{i-1})$ and $h(r_i)$ can be calculated. Thus we suggest that the keyed pseudo-random function $h_s()$ should be applied to improve the security of M. Li et al.'s scheme.

5 Conclusions

Searchable symmetric encryption techniques maybe one of the most efficient methods for secure cloud storage before full Homomorphic encryption schemes overcome their efficiency problem. We have given improvements of two one-round phrase search schemes, known as F. Kong's scheme and M. Li's scheme.

R. Curtmola et al. had propose an adaptively secure one-keyword search scheme. Unfortunately, these phrase search schemes are still non-adaptively secure. Therefore, it is an amazing work to construct adaptively secure phrase search schemes over encrypted data.

References

1. Xu, L.D., He, W., Li, S.: Internet of Things in industries: a survey. IEEE Tran. Ind. Inform. **10**(4), 2233–2243 (2014)
2. Dabbagh, M., Ammar, R.: Internet of Things Security and Privacy. In: Rayes, A., Salam, S. (eds.) Internet of Things From Hype to Reality, pp. 195–223. Springer, Cham (2017)

3. Sadeghi, A.-R., Wachsmann, C., Waidner, M.: Security and privacy challenges in industrial Internet of Things. In: Proceedings of the 52nd Annual Design Automation Conference, vol. 54. ACM, New York (2015)

4. Hashem, I.A.T., Yaqoob, I., Anuar, N.B., Mokhtar, S., Gani, A., Khan, S.U.: The rise of "big data" on cloud computing: review and open research issues. Inf. Syst. **47**, 98–115 (2015)

5. Chhabra, S., Dixit, V.S.: Cloud computing: state of the art and security issues. ACM SIGSOFT Softw. Eng. Notes (SIGSOFT) **40**(2), 1–11 (2015)

6. Tari, Z., Yi, X., Premarathne, U.S., Bertók, P., Khalil, I.: Security and privacy in cloud computing: vision, trends, and challenges. IEEE Cloud Comput. (CLOUDCOMP) **2**(2), 30–38 (2015)

7. Padilha, R., Pedone, F.: Confidentiality in the cloud. IEEE Secur. Priv. (IEEE SP) **13**(1), 57–60 (2015)

8. Ali, M., Khan, S.U., Vasilakos, A.V.: Security in cloud computing: opportunities and challenges. Inf. Sci. **305**, 357–383 (2015)

9. Cloud Security Alliance (CSA): Security guidance for critical areas of focus in cloud computing v3.0. White Paper. https://cloudsecurityalliance.org/guidance/csaguide.v3.0.pdf

10. Gentry, C.: Fully homomorphic encryption using ideal lattices. In: Proceedings of the 41st Annual ACM Symposium on Theory of Computing (STOC 2009), pp. 169–178. ACM, New York (2009)

11. Gentry, C., Groth, J., Ishai, Y., Peikert, C., Sahai, A., Smith, A.D.: Using fully homomorphic hybrid encryption to minimize non-interactive zero-knowledge proofs. J. Cryptol. (JOC) **28**(4), 820–843 (2015)

12. Song, D., Wagner, D., Perrig, A.: Practical techniques for searches on encrypted data. In: Proceedings of IEEE Symposium on Security and Privacy, pp. 44–55. IEEE (2000)

13. Curtmola, R., Garay, J., Kamara, S., Ostrovsky, R.: Searchable symmetric encryption: improved definitions and efficient constructions. In: ACM Conference on Computer and Communications Security (CCS 2006), pp. 79–88. ACM (2006)

14. Golle, P., Staddon, J., Waters, B.: Secure conjunctive keyword search over encrypted data. In: Jakobsson, M., Yung, M., Zhou, J. (eds.) ACNS 2004. LNCS, vol. 3089, pp. 31–45. Springer, Heidelberg (2004). doi:10.1007/978-3-540-24852-1_3

15. Cao, N., Wang, C., Li, M., et al.: Privacy-preserving multi-keyword ranked search over encrypted cloud data. IEEE Trans. Parallel Distrib. Syst. **25**(1), 222–233 (2014)

16. Zittrower, S., Zou, C.C.: Encrypted phrase searching in the cloud. In: Global Communications Conference (GLOBECOM), pp. 764–770. IEEE (2012)

17. Tang, Y., Gu, D., Ding, N., Lu, H.: Phrase search over encrypted data with symmetric encryption scheme. In: 32nd International Conference on Distributed Computing Systems Workshops, pp. 471–480. IEEE (2012)

18. Kissel, Z.A., Wang, J.: Verifiable phrase search over encrypted data secure against a semi-honest-but-curious adversary. In: IEEE International Conference on Distributed Computing Systems, pp. 126–131. IEEE (2013)

19. Kissel, Z.A.: Verifiable symmetric searchable encryption. Ph.D. Dissertation, University of Massachusetts Lowell, August 2013

20. Kong, F., Wang, J., Yu, J., Wang, X.: Analysis and improvement of a verifiable phrase search over encrypted data in a single phrase. In: 2015 10th International Conference on P2P, Parallel, Grid, Cloud and Internet Computing (3PGCIC), pp. 840–843. IEEE (2015)

21. Li, M., Jia, W., Guo, C., Sun, W., Tan, X.: LPSSE: lightweight phrase search with symmetric searchable encryption in cloud storage. In: 2015 12th International Conference on Information Technology-New Generations (ITNG), pp. 174–178. IEEE (2015)

22. Poon, H.T., Miri, A.: An efficient conjunctive keyword and phase search scheme for encrypted cloud storage systems. In: 2015 IEEE 8th International Conference on Cloud Computing, pp. 508–515. IEEE (2015)
23. Poon, H.T., Miri, A.: A low storage phase search scheme based on bloom filters for encrypted cloud services. In: 2015 IEEE 2nd International Conference on Cyber Security and Cloud Computing (CSCloud), pp. 253–259. IEEE (2015)
24. Katz, J., Lindell, Y.: Introduction to Modern Cryptography. In: Chapman & Hall/CRC Cryptography and Network Security Series. Chapman & Hall/CRC, Boca Raton (2007)
25. Stinson, D.R.: Cryptography: Theory and Practice. CRC Press, Boca Raton (2005)

A 0.6–2.4 GHz Broadband GaN HEMT Power Amplifier with 79.8% Maximum Drain Efficiency

Chun Ni[1,2(✉)], Zhongxiang Zhang[1,2], Meng Kong[1,2], Mingsheng Chen[1],
Hui Wang[1], and Xianliang Wu[1]

[1] School of Electronic and Information Engineering,
Hefei Normal University, Hefei 230601, China
aiheping.student@sina.com

[2] Anhui Engineering Research Center for Microwave and Communication,
Hefei 230601, China

Abstract. A highly efficient and broadband 10 W GaN HEMT power amplifier (PA) is presented, which employs the hybrid PA mode, transferring between continuous Class-F, continuous Class-B/J and continuous inverse Class-F. A GaN PA is designed and realized based on this mode-transferring operation using low-pass filter output matching network. The maximum theoretical efficiency of this hybrid continuous modes PA is more than 78.5%. Specifically, the operating bandwidth is determined by the low pass filter output matching network and the theoretical bandwidth can achieved multi-octave. The proposed design strategy is experimentally verified by a 0.6–2.4 GHz PA design with 79.8% maximum drain efficiency and 10 W output power. The footprint of the fabricated PA is 75 mm × 40 mm.

Keywords: Power amplifier · Continuous Class-F · Hybrid continuous modes · Low-pass filter

1 Introduction

The advantages of highly efficient power amplifiers (PAs) have been introduced in the literatures and a class-F PA is more attractive to reach this target. As is explained in [1], the square voltage waveform of the ideal Class-F PA operation is produced by odd harmonics and the half-sinusoidal current waveform is the result of fundamental and even harmonics. Given the condition with symmetrical drain current and voltage waveforms, drain efficiency of the ideal Class-F operation can be able to reach 100%. However, the Class-F PA has a main problem of narrow bandwidth. Since the Class-F PA has the intrinsic sensitivity to the load, it has been very difficult to design the Class-F PA with wide bandwidth in principle. A broadband Class-F PA achieving power added efficiency above 64% from 575–915 MHz is proposed in [2].

The harmonic load-pull technique was used to design the PA, where the output matching network was designed primarily to achieve quasi-optimal loads

© ICST Institute for Computer Sciences, Social Informatics and Telecommunications Engineering 2017
F. Chen and Y. Luo (Eds.): Industrial IoT 2017, LNICST 202, pp. 214–222, 2017.
DOI: 10.1007/978-3-319-60753-5_23

at the fundamental and second harmonics. The continuous Class-F working mode and its extension modes have been presented to broaden the design range of Class-F, which is proposed in [3] proving that the PA bandwidth can be widened. With the help of output capacitance C_{DS} of the nonlinear transistor model and simplified real frequency method, PA design can be attributed to the research of broadband fundamental matching [4].

2 PA Design Methodology

The bandwidth of the broadband PAs proposed in the literature can reach more than 50%. However, achieving efficiency more than 60% at RF frequency depends largely on the precise control of the first three harmonics in output stage, which will lead to low efficiency performance when the bandwidth is over more than an-octave. In our work a novel technique of designing PA with octave bandwidth and high efficiency is proposed. A hybrid PA mode which comprised of continuous Class-B/J, continuous Class-F and continuous inverse Class-F is utilized to design and implement a 0.6 GHz–2.4 GHz PA, and a low-pass filter topology is adopted to design the output matching network.

The normalized drain currents of continuous Class-B/J PAs are defined by Eq. (1), the same as Class-B power amplifier. The normalized drain voltages of Class-B/J PAs are shown in Eq. (2).

$$i_{CBJ}(\theta) = \frac{1}{\pi} + \frac{1}{2}cos(\theta) + \frac{2}{3\pi}cos(2\theta) + ... \tag{1}$$

$$v_{CBJ}(\theta) = (1 - cos\theta)(1 - \gamma sin\theta), -1 \leq \gamma \leq 1 \tag{2}$$

The normalized drain currents of continuous Class-F PAs are also defined by Eq. (1). The normalized drain voltages of Class-F PAs are shown in Eq. (3).

$$v_{CF}(\theta) = (1 - \frac{2}{\sqrt{3}}cos\theta + \frac{1}{3\sqrt{3}}cos3\theta)(1 - \gamma sin\theta), -1 \leq \gamma \leq 1 \tag{3}$$

The normalized drain currents of continuous inverse Class-F are defined by Eq. (4). The normalized drain voltages of inverse Class-F are shown in Eq. (5).

$$i_{CIF}(\theta) = [0.37 - 0.43cos\theta + 0.06cos(3\theta)](1 - \gamma sin\theta), -1 \leq \gamma \leq 1 \tag{4}$$

$$v_{CIF}(\theta) = 1 + \sqrt{2}cos\theta + \frac{1}{2}cos(2\theta) \tag{5}$$

The normalized voltages and currents of continuous Class-B/J and continuous Class-F based on equations are shown in Fig. 1. The blue curves show continuous Class-F voltage waveforms, the red curves show continuous Class-B/J voltage waveforms, and the black curve represents current waveform. The normalized currents and voltages of continuous inverse Class-F based on equations are shown in Fig. 2. The blue curves represent voltage waveforms, and the black curve represents current waveform.

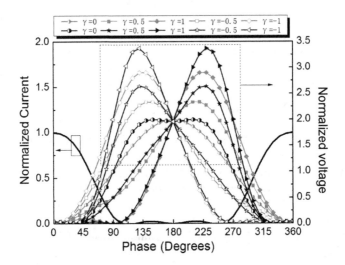

Fig. 1. Theoretical voltage and current waveforms of continuous Class-B/J and continuous Class-F (Color figure online)

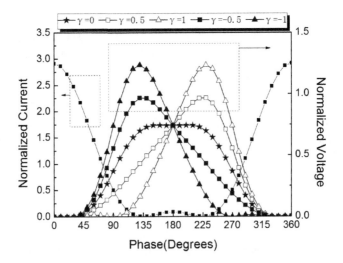

Fig. 2. Theoretical voltage and current waveforms of continuous inverse Class-F (Color figure online)

The continuous Class-B/J maintains the same DC voltage and fundamental voltage components as Class-B, therefore continuous Class-B/J can achieve equal power and efficiency of class-B. The ideal efficiency of continuous Class-B/J is 78.5% [4]. The above Eqs. (1) and (3) are used to prove that the theoretical drain efficiency of this continuous Class-F is able to achieve 90.7% [5]. The above Eqs. (4) and (5) are used to prove that the theoretical drain efficiency of this continuous inverse Class-F is able to achieve 81.85% [6].

Provided different γ values, different fundamental impedances can be presented with a larger range. Consequently, an ideal bandwidth is achieved by the combination kit of continuous PA modes, continuous Class-B/J, continuous Class-F and continuous inverse Class-F. The fundamental impedances can be calculated by Eq. (6).

$$Z_{CBJ} = R_L + jR_L\gamma$$
$$Z_{CF} = \frac{2}{\sqrt{3}} + jR_L\gamma$$
$$Z_{CIF} = \frac{1}{0.43\sqrt{2} + j0.37\sqrt{2}\gamma}R_L \tag{6}$$

Figure 3 illustrates the fundamental impedances spaces of continuous Class-B/J, continuous Class-F and continuous inverse Class-F. The fundamental impedances spaces of this hybrid PA mode are further enlarged compared to conventional continuous PA modes.

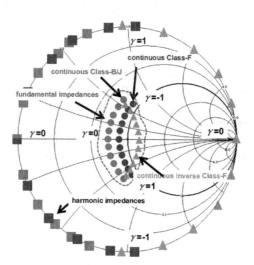

Fig. 3. The first three calculated harmonic impedances of continuous Class-B/J, continuous Class-F and continuous inverse Class-F in the smith chart

3   Matching Network Design

To realize broadband PAs needs a proper matching network. Literature [7,8] present the low-pass filter topology based on transmission line to achieve broadband and highly efficient PA. As is shown in Fig. 4, the output matching circuit and frequency response of the PA are given. Frequency response curve shows that the PA is working in continuous Class-B/J state at frequency point f_1, inverted Class-F state at frequency point f_2 and Class-F state at frequency point f_3.

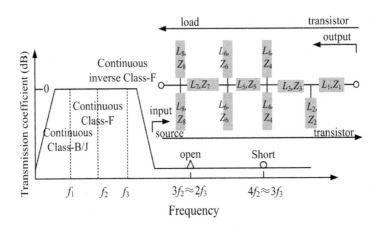

Fig. 4. Low-pass filter matching network for broadband PA using stepped transmission line transformer and the frequency response of the hybrid continuous PA mode

A bold improvement method is proposed that the second harmonic open circuit termination of continuous inverse Class-F PA and the third harmonic open circuit termination of continuous Class-F PA are both achieved by the output matching network. Thus, $3f_2$ is approximately equal to $2f_3$. Simultaneously, the third harmonic short circuit termination of continuous inverse Class-F PA and the fourth harmonic short circuit termination of continuous Class-F PA are also both achieved by the output matching network. It is obvious from the frequency response that $4f_2 \approx 3f_3$. The conversion of this working mode is able to broaden the bandwidth of PAs to a great extent. It is shown in the output matching circuit that high impedance transmission line can be utilized to be equivalent to inductance and low impedance open short wires is equivalent to capacitance, thus forming a third order low-pass filter matching circuit.

The input and output matching networks adopt stepped transmission line transformer and harmonic matching topology. In this design method, the input stepped transmission line transformer is applied to matching input impedance of the transistor to $50\,\Omega$ at fundamental frequency. The complete schematic of the PA, including input and output matching networks, is shown in Fig. 5. In order to obtain the impedance trajectories of the output matching network at I-gen plane in the smith chart, the approximated equivalent network of device output

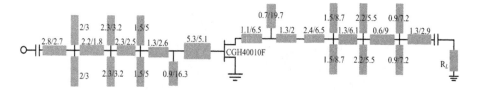

Fig. 5. Complete schematic with the dimensions of input and output matching network of the designed PA

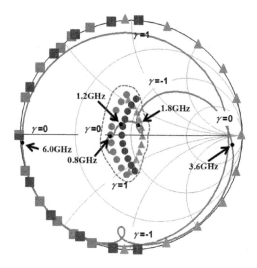

Fig. 6. Harmonic impedance trajectories of output matching network on I-gen planes in the smith chart

parasitic for CGH40010F is simulated by ADS. The fundamental impedance trajectories of the range from 0.6 GHz to 2.4 GHz are shown in Fig. 6.

From Fig. 6, the second and third harmonic terminals of continuous inverse Class-F are both at the optimal places, while the third and fourth harmonic terminals of continuous Class-F deviate from to the optimal places. However, great fundamental impedance matching status is obtained.

4   PA Design and Fabrication

The proposed PA is simulated with a constant drain supply voltage $V_{DD} = 28$ V and the gate bias voltage $V_{gg} = -2.5$ V which represents a bias condition of a conventional Class B amplifier. The optimum performance of continuous Class-B/J, continuous Class-F and continuous inverse Class-F have been achieved at frequency points of 0.9 GHz, 1.4 GHz and 2.1 GHz respectively. The substrate of the designed PA is RO4003C. American Technical Ceramics (ATC)

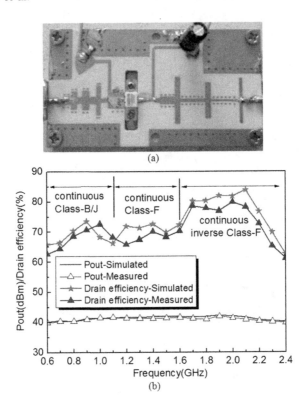

Fig. 7. Circuit and results. (a) the Fabricated PA circuit. (b) the simulated and measured drain efficiencies and output power of designed PA with respect to frequency

100A is used for DC-block, while ATC 100B and Panasonic electrolytic capacitors are used for bias line resonant capacitors. The footprint of the fabricated PA is 75 mm × 40 mm. Figure 7(a) shows the fabricated circuit of the design.

The PA is measured under the excitation of a single-tone continuous wave sweeping from 0.6 GHz to 2.4 GHz with the step size of 100 MHz. The simulated and measured drain efficiency in the whole frequency range are shown in Fig. 7(b). The measured drain efficiency range is from 61.1% to 79.8%, whose average value is about 70%. The output power are also taken into account and tested, as is shown with the power curves shown in Fig. 7(b). The output power is about 39.7 dBm to 41.6 dBm within the whole sweeping frequency band. An average gain of around 10 dB is measured.

The comparison between our work and some other recent contemporary broadband PA results is shown in Table 1, including bandwidth, output power, drain efficiency and PA mode. It can be seen from Table 1 that our work shows a great bandwidth performance due to the high operating frequency band of the designed PA. We attribute this excellent performance to the combined utilization of continuous Class-B/J, continuous Class-F and continuous inverse

Table 1. Broadband PA comparison with other researches

Ref	Bandwidth (GHz, %)	Power (W)	Drain Efficiency (%)	PA mode
2009 [4]	1.4–2.6, 60	9–11.5	60–70	Class-J
2012 [7]	1.45–2.45, 51	11–16.8	70–81	Continuous Class-F
2013 [9]	0.53–1.33, 87	8–13.8	70–87	Continuous Class-F
2014 [10]	1.6.4–2.7, 51	10.2–17.8	70.3–81.9	SCM
2016 [11]	2.4–3.9, 47.6	9.2–13.8	62.2–74.7	SICM
This work	0.6–2.4, 120	9.3–14.4	61.1–79.8	Hybrid PA mode

Class-F modes, and to the fact that the novel stepped transmission-line transformer is employed to optimize fundamental impedance and control the harmonic impedance directly.

5   Conclusion

A high efficiency broadband hybrid PA mode based on modified harmonic controlled network is presented. Both the multistage transmission line transformer and harmonic tuning circuits are used at the output matching network to increase the drain efficiency and broaden the bandwidth of the PA. The optimum performance of continuous Class-B/J, continuous Class-F and continuous inverse Class-F have been achieved at frequency points of 0.9 GHz, 1.4 GHz and 2.1 GHz respectively. The PA has achieved wide bandwidth of 0.6–2.4 GHz, with 61.1%–79% drain efficiency, 10 dB gain, and 10 W output power within the bandwidth.

Acknowledgments. This work was supported by the Key projects of natural science of Anhui Provincial Education Department (grant. KJ2015A292, KJ2015A202), the Science and Technology Project of Anhui Province, China (grant. 1708085QF150, 1501021041) and National Natural Science Foundation of China (grant. 61601166, 51477039), Scientific Research Starting Foundation for New Teachers of Hefei Normal University (No. 2015rcjj05).

References

1. Krauss, H.L., Bostian, C.W., Raab, F.H.: Solid State Radio Engineering. Wiley, New York (1980)
2. Butterworth, P., Gao, S., Ooi, S.F., Sambell, A.: High efficiency Class F power amplifier with broadband performance. Microw. Opt. Technol. Lett. **44**(3), 243–247 (2005)
3. Carrubba, V., Clarke, A.L., Akmal, M., et al.: On the extension of the continuous Class-F mode power amplifier. IEEE Trans. Microw. Theor. Tech. **59**(5), 1294–1303 (2011)
4. Wright, P., Lees, J., Benedikt, J., Tasker, P.J., Cripps, S.C.: A methodology for realizing high efficiency Class-J in a linear and broadband PA. IEEE Trans. Microw. Theor. Tech. **57**(12), 3196–3204 (2009)

5. Carrubba, V., Clarke, A.L., Akmal, M.J., et al.: The continuous Class-F mode power amplifier. In: 40th European Microwave Conference, pp. 1675–1677. IEEE Press, Paris (2010)
6. Carrubba, V., Clarke, A.L., Akmal, M., Lees, J., Benedikt, J., Cripps, S.C., Tasker, P.J.: Exploring the design space for broadband pas using the novel continuous inverse Class-F mode. In: 41st European Microwave Conference, pp. 333–336. IEEE Press, Manchester (2011)
7. Tuffy, N., Guan, L., Zhu, A., Brazil, T.J.: A simplified broadband design methodology for linearized high-efficiency continuous Class-F power amplifiers. IEEE Trans. Microw. Theor. Tech. 60(6), 1952–1963 (2012)
8. Chen, K., Peroulis, D.: Design of highly efficient broadband Class-E power amplifier using synthesized low-pass matching networks. IEEE Trans. Microw. Theor. Tech. 59(12), 3162–3173 (2011)
9. Lu, Z., Chen, W.: Resistive second-harmonic impedance continuous Class-F power amplifier with over one octave bandwidth for cognitive radios. IEEE J. Emerg. Sel. Topics Circuits Syst. 3(4), 489–497 (2013)
10. Chen, J., He, S., You, F., Tong, R., Peng, R.: Design of broadband high-efficiency power amplifiers based on a series of continuous modes. IEEE Microw. Wirel. Compon. Lett. 24(9), 631–633 (2014)
11. Shi, W., He, S., Li, Q.: A series of inverse continuous modes for designing broadband power amplifiers. IEEE Microw. Wirel. Compon. Lett. 26(7), 525–527 (2016)

Dynamic Research on 2-Stage Reluctance Electromagnetic Launcher

Baomi Jing[1], Tongqing Liao[1(✉)], Sheng Wu[2], and Li Yang[1]

[1] School of Electronic and Information Engineering, Anhui University, 111 Kowloon Road,
Hefei 230039, Anhui Province, People's Republic of China
tongqing7577@sina.com
[2] Department of Computer, Hefei Normal University, 327 Jinzhai Road, Hefei 230061,
Anhui Province, People's Republic of China

Abstract. During the process of electromagnetic launching, the electromagnetic force applied to the projectile correlate with the structure, trigger position and initial velocity. So, it's very important to choose appropriate trigger position with different initial velocity in multi-stage reluctance launcher system. Two dimension finite element models of reluctance electromagnetic launcher are established based on the simulation environment of Ansoft Maxwell 2D. The effect of trigger position, initial velocity and their rational combination on multi-stage reluctance launcher are simulated and discussed. It can be seen from the results of simulation that different initial velocities have their optimum trigger positions in multi-stage reluctance launcher system. And then, their rational combination can improve their performance effectively.

Keywords: Reluctance electromagnetic launcher · Trigger position · Initial velocity

1 Introduction

Electromagnetic emission technology can convert electrical energy into electromagnetic energy, which has many advantages, such as high efficiency, excellent performance and good controllability. So, it has a tremendous practical value in the military and civilian areas.

The theory and control scheme were carried out by Electromechanical Research Center on the University of Texas at Austin campus, in the 20th Century [1]. Poland's B. Tomczuk and M. Sobol have analyzed reluctance launcher's magnetic field [2]; Malaysia's M. Rezal has done some excellent work on single-stage reluctance launcher by simulation and experimental [3]. In recent years, China has also carried out researches on reluctance launcher. Meng Xueping and Zhi Binan conducted some experiments, such as research on energy conversion efficiency of the single-stage reluctance coil launcher [4–6].

The above research mainly focuses on single-stage reluctance launcher. In this article, it mainly focuses on dynamic research on multi-Stage reluctance Launcher.

© ICST Institute for Computer Sciences, Social Informatics and Telecommunications Engineering 2017
F. Chen and Y. Luo (Eds.): Industrial IoT 2017, LNICST 202, pp. 223–229, 2017.
DOI: 10.1007/978-3-319-60753-5_24

2   Theoretical Analysis

Reluctance launcher consists of solenoid-driven coils and ferromagnetic material Projectiles. Figure 1(a) is the 2-stage reluctance launcher schematic. When the switch is closed, Pulsed magnetic field is produced by capacitors discharge through switch to 1-stage driving coil. The projectile is sped up by changing reluctance in reluctance coil launcher. When the projectile moves to the center of the driving coil, the magnetic flux is easy to pass because of the smaller air gap of the magnetic circuit, the smaller reluctance of the magnetic circuit leads to the less force that acting on the projectile. When the projectile passes through the center of the driving coil, the attraction turns to tension. So some measures must be taken to prevent the projectile from pulling back. When the projectile just achieved the 2-stage driving coil, the photoelectric switch is turned on, so that the 2-stage pulse storage capacitor begins to discharge.

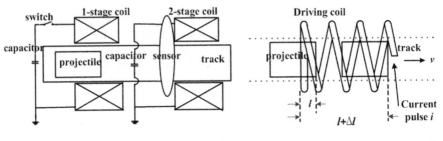

(a) 2-stage reluctance launcher schematic   (b) Force analysis of projectile

Fig. 1. Reluctance launcher schematic and force analysis of projectile

Then, the force applied to the projectile in solenoid can be obtained by using the principle of virtual displacement [7]. As shown in Fig. 1(b), defining the distance from the top of the projectile to the bottom of the driving coil is l, the displacement is Δl. The calculation of force applied to the projectile does not need to calculate the magnetic field energy of the entire system according to the principle of virtual displacements, only need to calculate magnetic field energy's difference between the two positions of the projectile in Fig. 1(b).

Magnetic energy difference is:

$$\Delta W_m = \frac{1}{2} \int_{A \cdot \Delta l} (\mu - \mu_0) H^2 dV \tag{1}$$

Then the force applied to the projectile can be obtained:

$$F_p = \frac{\Delta W_m}{\Delta l} \approx \frac{1}{2}(u - u_0)H^2 A = \frac{1}{2}(u - u_0)(\frac{Ni}{l_x})^2 A \tag{2}$$

Where u_0 is the permeability of the vacuum, H is the magnetic field intensity of solenoid. A is the cross-sectional area of the driving coil, u is the constant permeability, there is a current i through solenoid which the length is l_x, N is the number of solenoid turns.

It can be seen from Eq. (2) that the force applied to the projectile is mainly related to the parameters of external circuit, solenoid and projectile. When solenoid and projectile's physical parameters are determined, i is the key factor to determine the acceleration force.

Equation (1) can only be a rough analysis of the force applied to the projectile. Then, we will analyze the relevant parameters of the force accurately by finite element analyzing software Ansoft Maxwell.

3   Simulation Study

3.1   Simulation Architecture, Parameters and External Circuit

In Ansoft Maxwell, inductance can be computed which is very different by analytic calculation [8]. So, this paper simulated 2-stage reluctance launcher system based on the 2D transient field solver of Ansoft Maxwell.

Figure 2(a) shows the simulation model of the 2-stage reluctance launcher, including the motion region, the solution region, the driving coil and projectile. The projectile is a solid cylinder with diameter of 20 mm and height of 50 mm, whose material and mass are iron and 124 g respectively; The two driving coils have exactly the same structure with inner radius of 12 mm, outer radius of 28 mm, height of 50 mm, a total of 200 turns, and the material is copper. And the driving coil resistance is about 0.133Ω. The material properties of the Motion and Solution fields are air. The mesh is taken by system default.

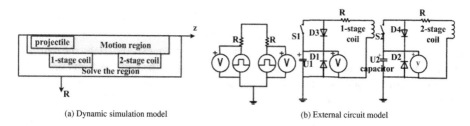

(a) Dynamic simulation model   (b) External circuit model

Fig. 2. Dynamic simulation model and the external circuit model

In Fig. 2(b), the external circuit model is made by Maxwell Circuit Editor software. And the parameter of capacitor is 600 v, 1000 uf. U_1 is the power of the 1-stage reluctance launcher and U_2 is the power of the 2-stage reluctance launcher; S_1 and S_2 are controllable switches which the discharge circuit is automatically altered by; D_1 and D_2 are free wheeling diodes that act as protection capacitors to prevent reverse voltage reversal. The roles of D_3 and D_4 protect the switch.

3.2   Effect of Trigger Position on Reluctance Launcher

In the process of simulation, the external circuit which shown in Fig. 2(b) provides excitation power for the launcher. It can be seen from Fig. 1(b) that l is 0 when the top of the projectile just enters the coil, l is 50 mm when the projectile just completely enters the coil and l is 100 mm when the projectile completely leaves the coil.

Due to the complexity of the dynamic process, the projectile is affected by both the accelerating force of the magnetizing current and the deceleration force generated by the eddy current magnetic field during the simulated process. According to Fig. 3(a), the launcher provided with an optional power, when the projectile is close to the center of the driving coil, the reverse force begins to appear. Therefore, when the projectile moves to the center of the driving coil, the switch should be turned off immediately.

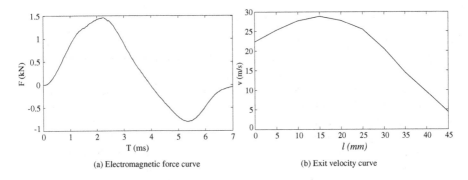

(a) Electromagnetic force curve   (b) Exit velocity curve

Fig. 3. Dynamic simulation curve

According to the dynamic simulation analysis of the force, trigger position can be selected in the range of 0-50 mm, and the step length is 5 mm. As shown in Fig. 1(b), the trigger position is l. Change l and keep other model parameters invariant, the dynamic simulation results are shown in Fig. 3(b). It can be seen that the outlet velocity gradually increases with the increase of displacement, and then decreases.

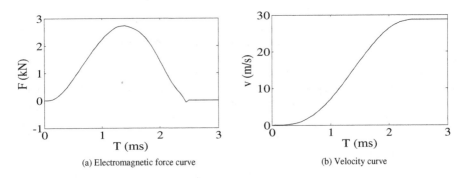

(a) Electromagnetic force curve   (b) Velocity curve

Fig. 4. Dynamic simulation results

Figure 4 is the electromagnetic force and velocity curves when l (*trigger position*) = 15 mm. The above analysis shows that a series of best discharge positions which can make the projectile get the maximal velocity exist in a given reluctance launcher.

3.3   Initial Velocity of the Projectile

In fact, the projectile can posses arbitrary initial velocity. But, initial velocity of the projectile will have an impact on the performance of launcher. At the same time, trigger position will be greatly changed with different initial velocities. The initial velocity is chosen as the exit velocity $v_0 = 28.86$ m/s which is shown in Fig. 4(b), the simulation results are shown in Fig. 5.

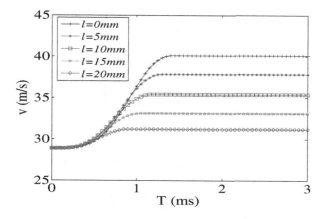

Fig. 5. Simulation results of exit velocity at $v_0 = 28.86$ m/s

When the initial velocity is 28.86 m/s, the best trigger position is $l = 0$ mm. And so on, when other parameters remain unchanged, we can get the initial speed of the best trigger position (as shown in Table 1). It can be seen from Table 1 that with the increase of projectile initial velocity, the best trigger position changes a little. When $v_0 \geq 15$ m/s, the best trigger position is almost always fixed at $l = 0$. This is because the time of operation is too short to complete, the rising edge of the current is not yet fully act on. So, force does not reach the peak but the projectile has separated itself from the effective magnetic field. It can be seen that the initial velocity of the projectile has a great influence on the performance of the reluctance launcher.

Table 1. Simulation results vary with the initial velocity

v_0(m/s)	Δv(m/s)	l (mm)	v_0(m/s)	Δv(m/s)	l (mm)
0	28.55	15	25	13.2	0
5	25.2	10	30	11	0
10	12.55	3	40	6.6	0
15	19.8	0	50	3.35	0
20	16.7	0	100	0.45	0

The spacing between 2-stage coil and 1-stage coil which we named relative space is s. The flight time and relative space have a proportional relationship when projectile flies in the primary and secondary coils. Relative space s can't be too small, otherwise the primary and secondary coils will work together on the projectile (s $\geq$ 50 mm). But, the flight time will be too long if relative spacing is too large, and the overall efficiency will be reduced. So the best spacing can be set as s = 50 mm. The above simulation can be summarized as two points. (1) Multi-stage reluctance launchers have a optimal trigger position and an initial velocity which is numerically equal to the exit speed of the previous stage. (2) The stage number of multi-stage reluctance launcher need to be choose carefully. Although the exit velocity of projectile will increases with the raise of the stage number. But, the speed increments will be smaller and gradually approach zero when the speed exceeds a critical value.

3.4   Combination Triggering Position with Initial Velocity

It can be seen that different initial velocities of projectile should choose corresponding trigger positions which has great influence on the performance of reluctance launcher. Without loss of generality, 2-stage reluctance launcher will be analyzed in this article. All parameters are the same except for trigger position. Therefore, we discuss in two cases: (1) The first and second launchers discharge at the optimal trigger position, namely $l_1 = 15$ mm, $l_2 = 0$ mm; (2) The two discharge position are set to $l_1 = 15$ mm, $l_2 = 15$ mm.

Simulation results are shown in Fig. 6. Figure 6 (a) is the diagram force-time. Obviously, in the first case, the drive current of the second launcher is larger, leading to force applied to the projectile is larger. Figure 6(b) is the diagram speed-time. In the first case, when t $\approx$ 5.65 ms, the projectile reaches the outlet of the second stage driving coil, at which time the exit velocity is 41 m/s. In the second case, when t $\approx$ 5.90 ms, the projectile reaches the outlet of the second driving coil, at which time the exit velocity is 39 m/s. Thus, it can be seen that the performance in the first case is better than in the second case.

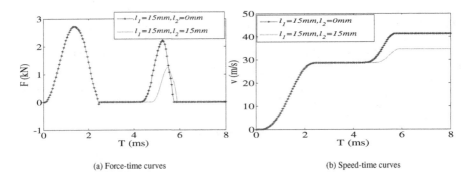

(a) Force-time curves   (b) Speed-time curves

Fig. 6.   Simulation results

4   Conclusion

The trigger position and initial velocity of projectile have great influence on the perform-ance, and their rational combination can improve the efficiency in the 2-stage reluctance launcher. Some methods on how to improve the exit speed of the two-stage reluctance launcher can be get. (1) Make sure that the projectile injection speeds (equivalent to a single stage of the initial velocity) at all levels have corresponding optimal trigger posi-tions, and the driving coil begins to discharge in this position; (2) The relative space need to be selected reasonably. (3) The stage number of multi-stage reluctance launcher must be selected carefully.

References

1. Ingram, S.K., Pratap, S.B.: A control algorithm for reluctance accelerators. IEEE Trans. Magn. **27**(1), 156–159 (1991)
2. Tomczuk, B., Sobol, M.: Field analysis of the magnetic systems for tubular linear reluctance motors. IEEE Trans. Plasma Sci. **41**(4), 1300–1305 (2005)
3. Rezal, M., Iqbal, S.J., Hon, K.W.: Development of magnetic pulsed launcher system using capacitor banks. In: The 5th Student Conference on Research and Development (2007)
4. Xueping, M., Bin, L., et al.: Research on energy conversion efficiency of the single-stage reluctance coil launcher. J. Armored Force Eng. Coll. **27**(3), 59–62 (2013)
5. Xueping, M., Bin, L., Zhiyuan, L., et al.: Influence analysis of the initial velocity of the projectile on the launcher properties of the reluctance coil launcher. J. Ordnance Eng. Coll. **25**(6), 39–43 (2013)
6. Binan, Z., Bin, L., et al.: Effect of trigger position on the reluctance launcher. Electron. Measur. Technol. **33**(4), 45–48 (2010)
7. Peng, C.: Research on new electromagnetic emission technology. National defense science and Technology University (2005)
8. Bo, Z., Hongliang, Z., et al.: Application of Ansoft 12 in Engineering Electromagnetic Field. China Water Power Press, Beijing (2010)

Characteristic, Architecture, Technology, and Design Methodology of Cyber-Physical Systems

Chao Liu, Fulong Chen$^{(\boxtimes)}$, Junru Zhu, Ziyang Zhang, Cheng Zhang, Chuanxin Zhao, and Taochun Wang

Department of Computer Science & Technology, Anhui Normal University, Wuhu, 241002, Anhui, China
{lcahnu,long005,jrzhu_study,zzy000,zhangcheng, zhaocx,wangtc}@ahnu.edu.cn

Abstract. Cyber-physical systems (CPS) involve in a variety of computing model integration and collaborative work. There are some problems such as un-unified design methods, worse elasticity, high complexity, difficult to implement cyber-physical co-design and co-verification, etc. Aiming at the co-design of embedded components, sensing components, controlling components, communication components and physical components in heterogeneous environments, this paper proposes the characteristics, architectures, technologies, and design methodologies of CPSs. It's necessary to design CPSs in the model-driven design process to establish CPSs and confirm its correctness, support cyber-physical co-design and correctness by construction so as to avoid modifying repeatedly the design when problems are found in the system realization process, and provide the necessary theoretical and practical technical supports to establish CPSs.

Keywords: Cyber-Physical systems · Co-modeling · Component · Co-verification

1 Introduction

Cyber-Physical System (CPS) [1] is a new generation of multi-dimensional intelligent system integrated computing, communication and control, widely used in aviation, automotive [2, 3], chemical, pharmaceutical, infrastructure, energy [4, 5], health, manufacturing, traffic control [6], home [7], entertainment, robotics [8] and consumer electronics and other fields.

CPS is a multidimensional and complex system which combines computing, network and physical environment. As shown in Fig. 1, the real time sensing, dynamic control and information service of the large-scale engineering system are realized through the organic integration and deep collaboration of 3C technology (Computation, Communication and Control). CPS implements the integration of computing, communication and physical systems. It can make the system more reliable and efficient with real-time collaboration, and has important and wide application prospects. With ubiquitous environmental sensing, embedded computing, network communication and network control systems engineering, CPS has the function of computing, communication, precise control, remote cooperation and autonomy. It pays attention to the close combination

© ICST Institute for Computer Sciences, Social Informatics and Telecommunications Engineering 2017
F. Chen and Y. Luo (Eds.): Industrial IoT 2017, LNICST 202, pp. 230–246, 2017.
DOI: 10.1007/978-3-319-60753-5_25

and coordination of computational resources and physical resources, mainly used for some intelligent systems, such as robots, intelligent navigation, etc. In recent years, CPS has not only become an important direction of research and development of academic and scientific community, but also it is expected to become the industry field of the priority development of the business community. The development of CPS research and application is of great significance to accelerate the integration of industrialization and information technology.

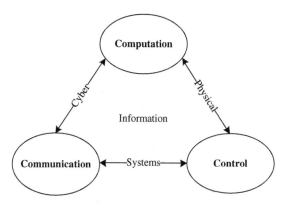

Fig. 1. 3C view of CPS.

In order to meet the CPS's idea of the integration of computing, communication, control and physical equipment, and make the engineering system more efficient, more efficient, more functional and superior performance, it needs to evolve the existing physical and information systems involved in the evolution of science and technology, and establish a scientific and technological infrastructure to meet the needs of CPSs.

In the process of CPS building, we have to face some challenges, such as re-arrangement of the abstract layer in the design flow, the development of new heterogeneous model combination based on the semantic foundation and the description of the different physical and logical modeling language based on the semantic foundation, research on the science and technology foundation of a system combination and integration which is model-based, accurate and predictable, development of new CPS open architecture which will allow us to build the national and global level CPSs, new flexible CPS design automation infrastructure, etc. CPS will change the way that people interact with the physical world, and its application is very wide, including smart grid systems, intelligent transportation systems, aerospace and electronic systems, intelligent medical systems, information appliances systems, environmental monitoring, intelligent building, industrial control, defense systems, weapons systems, etc. It will become an important driving force for the new technological revolution. CPS combines a variety of technologies, such as sensing, decision-making, execution, computing, networking, and physical processes. It is the key field of science and technology and economic development in the new century.

2   Characteristics

CPS is developed on the basis of embedded system, sensor technology and network technology. According to the actual needs, a complete CPS should have the following characteristics.

- **Reliability**. The physical reality of the world is always changing.CPS is working in such an environment. Therefore, CPS must have the ability to cope with the unexpected situation and subsystem failure. Reliability, as an important index of the system, has been widely recognized by people. Especially the requirement of CPS is more prominent. Only high reliability as a guarantee, CPSs involving people's lives and safety can safely be used by people.
- **Concurrency**. Concurrency is the basic feature of the event in the physical environment. At present, the computing mode is in order. And people seem to have been fully adapted to this mode. But CPS is a system that combines computing and physical processes. New concurrent computing software systems must be developed to meet the needs of CPS.
- **Real-time**. The real-time nature of the information world is that the same time that the event occurred in the physical world is also reflected in the information world. CPS has a constant interaction between computational process and physical process. It is needed to perceive the physical process and to intervene in the process of physics in real time. This puts forward the very high requirement to the system's real-time performance.
- **Massive information processing**. CPS is a multidimensional and complex system which combines computing, network and physical environment. The type and quantity of information that the system needs to receive and process is very large, e.g., smart grid CPS needs to receive the voltage, current, temperature and other information of each node. The number of these nodes is extremely large. Therefore massive computing is a common feature of CPS.
- **Distribution**. In CPS, there are a lot of embedded systems. They form a distributed computing network. However the capacity of each node is limited. Therefore CPS is a typical distributed computing system.
- **Autonomy**. The autonomy of the system is one of the most representative features of CPS. The system can respond to the changes of the external environment and make the appropriate response in time so as to ensure the normal operation of the system. And this kind of reaction can be carried out by human intervention.
- **Security**. For any valuable system, security is an indispensable prerequisite. Especially for the CPS which can affect the physical environment, it needs to enjoy a higher security.
- **Dynamic reorganization**. CPS faces a huge physical environment. In this physical environment, all kinds of resources are changing at a time. If we cannot make the system adjust itself according to the actual situation, i.e. effective dynamic reconfiguration, it is possible to make the system unstable or unsafe because of the depletion of some resources.

– **Heterogeneity**. In CPS there are a variety of devices, including sensors, processors, memory, etc. These devices may come from different manufacturers. They may use different instructions, and depend on different operating systems. How to ensure that these devices can achieve interoperability between the CPS is a problem must be solved. This also determines the CPS must have the characteristics of heterogeneity.

3 Related Terms

CPS is very easy to be confused with of Internet of Things (IoT), Machine-To-Machine (M2M), Sensor Network Wireless (WSN) and so on.

– **M2M**. From a narrow sense, M2M represents the communication between the machine and the machine. In a broad sense, it can also indicate the communication between people and machines. At present, most of the M2M refers to the communication between non information technology (IT) machine and other equipment or IT system.
– **WSN**. WSN refers to a large number of sensor devices through wireless communication way to connect and form a sensor network.
– **IoT**. IoT refers that through the Internet and other means of communication, computing systems, sensors, controllers and objects (or environment) are connected to form a network connecting human with things and things with things for informatization, remote management and intelligent control.
– **CPS**. CPS is a complex system which combines the computation, the network and the physical environment, and realizes real time sensing and dynamic control of physical devices or environments by computing, communication and control.

In summary, M2M emphasizes the communication between the machine and the machine, WSN focuses on the multi hop transmission of sensing information, CPS emphasizes the process of feedback and control, and IoT emphasizes the information perception and transmission of all things.

4 Architecture

Based on the environment perception, CPS is a controlled, reliable and extensible network physical equipment system with the capability of computing, communication and control. By the feedback loop of the interactive computational processes and physical processes, it realizes the deep integration and real-time interaction, adds or extends new functions, and detects or controls physical entities in a safe, reliable, efficient, and real-time manner. Physical devices in CPS refer to objects in nature. Therefore they not only refer to the cold equipment, but also include living organisms, such as people.

4.1 Composition Structure

Tan et al. [9] proposed a representative CPS composition structure. The composition structure is divided according to the different space. At the same time, it gives the detailed process of sensing event flow and control event flow. Through this structure, we can clearly understand the interaction between the physical world, the cyber space and the human space. The physical world is the basis of CPS. The information source of the whole system and the final feedback of the information all exist in the physical world. In the physical world, there are various devices which can interact directly with the physical environment. We can call the terminal device at the front end of the system Mote. These Mote constitute the front end of CPS in the physical world. The physical world front end of CPS consists of two parts: the perception part and the execution part.

CPS is full of all kinds of physical nodes in the physical environment. These heterogeneous nodes may be very close or thousands of kilometers apart. How to make these nodes communicate with each other and to support the interoperability between each other is the problem that CPS network needs to solve. Network for CPS, is the basis for the realization of information sharing. Compared to the common network layer of the computer network, CPS network construction is more difficult. CPS network not only needs to provide the basis for the application of resource sharing network, but also to shield the heterogeneity of a very large physical nodes and realize the seamless connection of the system. At the same time, it also provides users with the plug and play services. As a result, the CPS network has a higher demand for technology. In addition to the access control technology, routing technology, network transmission technology in the common computer network, CPS also needs some new technologies as the support, e.g., the description and semantic analysis technology of heterogeneous data generated by heterogeneous nodes, node localization technology caused by node mobility, new storage technologies for solving the massive data, network congestion technologies for solving massive data transmission, etc.

The third part of the structure of CPS is the CPS control unit. The event driven control unit receives the event and physical world information perceived by the sensing unit through the CPS network, and according to certain rules, deals with them and generates the processing information. These processing information will be transmitted through the CPS network to the implementation unit and the sensing unit, and complete the interactive process of the whole system.

4.2 Hierarchical Structure

In addition to the above described CPS composition structure, the CPS can be divided into a hierarchical structure model. According to the function of CPS equipment, the whole CPS is generally divided into physical layer, network layer and application layer.

- **Physical layer**. The physical layer mentioned here refers to the hierarchy of the system nodes in which the computing function is embedded into the physical process. In brief, physical devices that interact with the environment are collectively referred to as the physical layer. This layer includes sensing devices for environmental sensing, execution devices for reacting to environmental state, energy units for supplying energy to other devices, etc.
- **Network layer**. There are some differences between the network layer and the network in the composition structure. In the latter, it also includes database servers.

The main function of the network layer in the hierarchical structure is to carry out the network transmission. Network layer is to shield the heterogeneity of the physical layer units and provide support for CPS cell interconnect. In order to achieve better network transmission and solve the load problem caused by the large amount of data on the network, Krishna et al. [54] proposed the concept of CPI (Cyber-Physical Internet) to establish a network of computing physics similar to the Internet, so as to support the interconnection and interoperability of all devices in CPS.

– **Application layer**. It is the top layer. It is user oriented, responsible for the entire CPS presented to users. This layer encapsulates details of the physical layer and the network layer, and generates different application modules, such as monitoring module, data acquisition module, data display module, etc., so that users do not need to care about the details of the physical layer and the network layer, and directly focus on the business processing. The application layer is mainly to collect the task requirements and decompose the task reasonably, and then according to these sub tasks, query and configure resources, position and schedule resources to complete specific tasks.

5 Integrated Technologies

CPS requires a lot of technologies as the basis and support, such as computer system technology, embedded system technology, wireless sensor network technology, IoT technology, network control technology and hybrid system technology, etc. Although, based on the above technologies, but because of its inherent characteristics, and there are some differences between the above technologies and CPS. Therefore, in order to achieve a better CPS abstraction and modeling, to build a suitable CPS validation system, it is necessary to understand the existing technology in depth, and on this basis to improve and optimize.

5.1 Computer System Technology

The computer system mainly consists of two parts: hardware and software. CPS must also have the software and hardware components as well as the functions, such as CPU, memory and external device, operating system, language processing system, data processing system, etc. However, CPS has many differences from the common computer system in the specific design and implementation of the components. The design of the existing computer system is based on the goal of efficient data storage, conversion and processing. Differently, the ultimate goal of CPS is to realize the real-time and effective interaction between the computing process and the physical process. Therefore, the focus of CPS is on the system's real-time, security, reliability, confidentiality, adaptive and other characteristics. The common computer systems have not paid special attention to these characteristics. However, the existing grid technology, parallel computing technology in the computer system, to a certain extent, satisfies the requirements of distributed control and efficient computation of CPS, and provides a great technical support for the development of CPS.

5.2 Embedded System Technology

An embedded system is a system used to control or monitor machines, devices, factories, and other large scale equipment, i.e., it is a special computer system which is application-centered, based on computer technologies, software and hardware modifiable, strictly required on function, reliability, cost, volume and power consumption. It can be seen that the embedded system is mainly developed and designed according to software and hardware collaboration. The combination of computing unit and physical object in CPS can also be considered as a kind of generalized hardware and software collaboration, but different from the traditional collaboration of embedded systems. CPS requires hardware must contain information components. For traditional hardware and software collaboration, in order to get a stable integration environment, the function of embedded systems is enhanced by embedding a certain computing device and the corresponding software in the physical device. The integration of information and physics in CPS is to make the system better adapt to the uncertain and dynamic environment, and more attention is paid to the deep coupling of computing resources and physical resources, and how to effectively utilize existing resources and so on. Although there are some differences between embedded technology and CPS, CPS still need embedded technology as a support.

5.3 Wireless Sensor Network Technology

Wireless sensor networks consist of a large number of inexpensive micro sensor nodes deployed in the monitoring area, which form a multi hop ad hoc network system by wireless communication. The purpose is to sense, collect and process the information of objects in the network coverage area, and send it to the observer. Sensors, sensing objects and observers constitute the three elements of the wireless sensor network. The development of wireless sensor network technology promotes the development of CPS. The existing wireless network technology provides a good platform for the development of CPS. Unfortunately, wireless sensor network technology has limitations, e.g., when the node is put into the monitoring site, they are basically static in space, i.e., the monitoring position is fixed, and cannot make the corresponding adjustment according to the changes of the environment. At the same time, in addition to sensor nodes, CPS also contains actuator nodes, compared to the wireless sensor network, more complex. Because of the autonomy of the node (especially the actuator node), the topological structure of the structure must be dynamically configured in space and time, there should be a clear coordination and communication protocol between the nodes, and the universal solutions in different environments are necessary. In addition, CPS also needs to be improved through the network control strategy and battery equipment to extend the service life of the sensor nodes.

5.4 IoT Technology

Through radio frequency identification, infrared sensor, global positioning system, laser scanner and other information sensing equipment, according to the agreement, IoT connects the things to the Internet for information exchange and communication, so as to achieve a "thing-thing connected" or "object-object connected" network with intelligent identification, positioning, tracking, monitoring and management. There are some differences between IoT and CPS. First, CPS is aimed at the remote communication and control of physical components (including human), and IoT is aimed at the perception of the object state. Human use sensors to sense the state of objects, but they can't control the state of the object. Second, in IoT, communication occurs mainly between objects and people or between objects and processors, and in addition to the above two kinds of communication, CPS has a communication between objects and objects, so as to achieve the goal of self-interaction between components. Although there is a difference between CPS and IoT, the development of the IoT technology has greatly promoted the realization of CPS. IoT can not only provide a "thing-thing connected" network communication environment for the realization of CPS, the involved radio frequency identification technology, wireless sensor technology, embedded system technology and nanotechnology can provide help for the realization of CPS.

5.5   Network Control Technology

Networked Control Systems (NCS) is a fully distributed, networked real-time feedback control system. It refers to a set of field sensors, controllers and actuators, and communication networks, used to provide data transmission between devices and enable users of different locations in the region to achieve resource sharing and coordination. Similar to CPS, NCS aims at interaction between objects. However, in CPS, in order to improve the real-time performance and accuracy, using decentralized control, on the basis of self-sensing control of each node, it realizes the system's operation and decision based on the control mode of the central linkage adjustable feedback control, and by improving the performance of node autonomy, it achieves the system's self-regulatory capacity and efficiency improvement.

5.6   Hybrid System Technology

Hybrid system is a kind of dynamic system composed of continuous subsystem and discrete subsystem. CPS is a hybrid system, and many models of hybrid systems can be applied to the research of CPS, such as discrete event model, computational intelligence model, game theory and so on.

6   Challenges and Problems in Design

As shown in Fig. 2, CPS specially emphasizes the process of sensing, transmission, processing, and control of user space, cyber space, information space and physical space. The real time, dynamic information control and information service of physical entities are highlighted. The basic feature is a perceptual feedback loop which can interact with the physical world. It influences the feedback loop through the computing process and physical process, achieves close interaction with the physical process, and thereby adds or expands new capabilities to the physical system. CPS is composed of complex and varied functions [10], and needs to be coordinated with communication, sensing, control and physical components. It makes it difficult to grasp the development of the system, and it is an urgent need and urgent task to discuss its efficient cooperative design method.

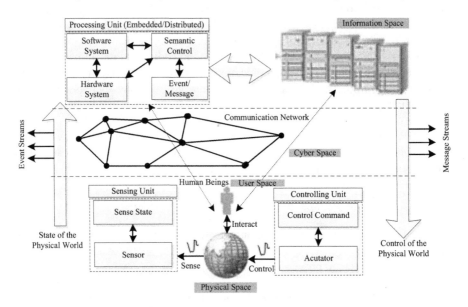

Fig. 2. Application system architecture of the CPSs.

The traditional embedded system is enclosed. It particularly emphasizes computational processing power. In addition to the I/O ports that are used to connect the basic external modules, there is no external extension interface. It cannot meet the design requirements of controllability, trustworthiness, extensibility of physical devices. A complete CPS is designed to be an interactive network composed of physical devices. It involves tn The collaborative work of heterogeneous units, such as humans, machines, things and so on, not just a single device. The combination of computing and physical entity units will be more compact. The physical component is different from the software component and hardware component. The safety and reliability of the system is higher than that of the general computing system [11]. CPS needs to be improved in terms of adaptability, automation, efficiency, functionality, reliability, security, availability, and so on [12].

The heterogeneity of CPS components is mainly reflected in three aspects:

- First, software components and hardware components are included in the embedded system. Their analysis, design, coding, testing methods are significantly different.
- Second, for the CPS components, such as embedded software components, embedded hardware components, sensing components, control components, communication components, and physical components, there is not consistent in terms of function,

computing model (continuous and discrete), description (text and graphics) and validation (formal verification, simulation and test), difficult to co-design.

- Third, the types, models and connection forms of these components used in different application environments are different. There is a large difference in scale. In design, the system needs to be more flexible (elastic). When the system is complex to a certain degree, if the direct programming is used for design, the system will increase the possibility of fault or even failure.

In view of the complex work of the collaborative design of CPS components, in order to meet the requirements of good performance, low cost and high reliability, and improve the quality and efficiency of the system development, the design needs to be carried out under the description that the design cycle can completed. Therefore, the first step in collaborative design of all kinds of components should be to establish a system model, which is an abstract description of the system. Its content mainly includes three points: the requirement analysis is transformed into a system implementation that is remodelable, verifiable, and visualized so that it is easy to verify whether the designed system is in conformity with the requirement analysis, and also easy to understand and modify the design; it can represent the structure and behavior of the system; it can represent the non-functional constraints of the system.

CPS collaborative design, including collaborative design between designers and among different models of sub components, is becoming an urgent problem to be solved. One of the most effective methods to solve this kind of complex problem is the theory of hierarchical and collaborative modeling [13], i.e., closely combined with the external physical environment factors of CPS, the complex problem is divided into several sub problems so as to solve one by one. Hierarchical cooperative modeling is to divide the complex system with multi computing models into some layers, link up the system structure and system behavior to be designed, and visually control the architecture so as to discover more details of needs and better solve the problem. In addition, the system design also follows a law that the sooner the verification, the sooner found the problem, the price paid is smaller. Effective system model and specification are conducive to the division of design and professional production, and is conducive to collaborative verification and correctness-by-construction, and thereby is conducive to saving design and production costs.

Based on the above analysis, CPS design is facing some problems and challenges.

- There is no uniform standard for analysis and design, e.g., their methods are not unified. From analysis and design to production and programming, there is not a consistent engineering method. This makes the impact of human factors in every process of product form is very serious.
- The results of analysis and design cannot be reused [14] when developing similar projects or products. The configuration in the process of design and after the completion of design cannot achieve flexible regulation from the general framework to the specific application, i.e., not remodelable [15].
- CPS design is a collaborative design process [16], e.g., collaborative design for a variety of heterogeneous computing models [17–22], including continuous systems, discrete systems, etc., and collaborative design of heterogeneous components,

including software, hardware, sensors, controllers, communication units, physical systems, etc. Single model or modeling method is difficult to meet the needs of the design of heterogeneous components in CPS [23, 24].

7 Design Methodology

7.1 Overview

In accordance with whether the formalization is supported, traditional embedded system modeling methods can be divided into formal and non-formal methods. The formal methods are described in terms of symbolic and mathematical language, including algebraic language such as OBJ, Clear, ASL, One/Two ACT, etc., process algebra language such as CSP, CCS, π calculus etc., temporal logic language such as PLTL, CTL, XYZ/E, UNITY, TLA, etc., and network language such as Petri Nets [25–28], UML, FSM, FNN [29], etc. The limitation of Petri Nets is that the complexity of the system will rapidly lead to the non-understanding of the system. Due to the lack of explicit support for concurrency and hierarchy, for complex systems, FSM may have "state explosion" and "migration expansion" phenomenon. The non-formal methods, such as structured method and object-oriented method, can basically describe the functional properties of the system, and simulation can be used to verify the correctness of the system. But the description ability of the non-functional attributes is limited, and it is not conducive to rigorous verification through mathematical methods.

According to the composition elements of the modeling objects, the modeling methods can be divided into process based, task based, and component based approaches. Component-based approaches [30–33] also include object-oriented (such as real-time UML), middleware (such as COBRA, EJB, SOM, DCOM and other business standards), actor-oriented [34], field-oriented, resource-oriented technologies.

According to the system description, the modeling methods can be divided into state-oriented (such as FSM and Petri Nets), activity-oriented (such as data flow diagram and control flow graph) [35], structure-oriented (such as component connection diagram), data-oriented (such as the entity relationship diagram and Jackson diagram) and heterogeneous model (such as the control/data flow graph).

According to the development methods, there are two kinds of methods including Top-Down (such as Simulink, SDL, StateCharts, etc.) and Bottom-Up (such as HDL, UML, IDL, ADL, Modelica, etc.). The former is suitable for system requirement analysis, high level architecture description and system evaluation. The latter is suitable for the description, design and verification of the low layer architecture.

These methods have played an important role in the traditional system design. However, in the collaborative design of CPS, they face new problems and insurmountable difficulties.

7.2 Key Methods

CPS is different from the usual pure software or hardware system, but integrated with software, hardware, sensing, control, communication, and physical systems [36–38]. Some functions can be achieved by software, can also be achieved through hardware, but also can be completed by the physical device. The challenge of CPS design is not only related to the computer software and hardware, and also involves a number of non-computer engineering problems, such as mechanical dimensions, power consumption and manufacturing cost, etc. Even for the problem of computer engineering, most systems also have special requirements for real-time, reliability, and multi rate problems. With the increasing application demand, CPS function is becoming more and more powerful, the system architecture is becoming more and more complex, and the requirements are also naturally improved like boats going up with the level of the water.

In order to support the design of CPS in the heterogeneous environment, OMG proposes a Model Driven Architecture (MDA) method, which is an open frame based on UML, MOF, XMI, CWM and so on, supports software design and model visualization, XML data storage and exchange, separates the commercial application logic from the supporting platform technology, and establishes the abstract model of the embedded software system. In the promotion of MDA, a variety of modeling and verification methods to support the collaborative design of embedded systems have emerged.

Model Integrated Computing (MIC) [30], proposed by Vanderbilt University, based on the use of UML/OCL meta model language, extends the use and scope in the system development, provides a flexible framework for the development of CPS, and can meet the requirements of the rapid development and application of engineering personnel in specific areas, e.g., military, aviation, chemical engineering, etc., without needing too many software development foundation. At present, the team also realized that the support of the heterogeneous model is the next research direction.

Sifakis et al. proposed the BIP (Behavior/Interaction/Priority) [31] CPS abstract modeling method based-on components. This method supports for the glue operation of heterogeneous components. The modeling results can be compiled into the specified platform C++ code. And the model checking theory is proposed for model verification. However, there is still a lack of modeling and verification platform support, also need to provide a further extension of the physical component modeling and verification.

After studying the characteristics and challenges of CPS in depth, Lee who is a leading figure in the CPS study, believes that the CPS can also be called a deep embedded system. And by summarizing the existing simulation control modeling method, he puts forward the concept of "cyber systems need to be physical" and "physical systems need to be cyber" to solve the modeling of physical entities and cyber entities and the interaction between them. In his method, the physical subsystem is packaged abstractly in a software system, so that the physical subsystem has the characteristics of interaction with the information layer. At the same time, he abstracts software components and network components, so that they have the time characteristics of the physical world in real time. Lee et al. [34] also proposes a system level, hierarchical and heterogeneous actor-oriented modeling language based on Ptolemy, using XML as the basic behavior and structure description language, realizing the modeling environment towards parallel, real time embedded applications. This method is mainly used to verify the model of embedded systems and CPSs. It does not have the comprehensive and compile function for the target system, and does not support the implantation of the new behavior model. Liu [39] further expands the CPS as the Cyber Physical Social System (CPSS), introduces cognitive and social domains into CPS, and realizes collaborative modeling of cyber, physics, cognition and social space. In theory, the modeling space of CPS is greatly expanded.

The researchers have come to realize the importance of CPS collaborative modeling and verification. DEVS [40] is a kind of discrete event system simulation theory which is built by Zeigler based on the study of general systems theory. It has simple operation semantics, and there is a simple corresponding relationship with the real system. However, DEVS is a kind of poor semantic system description method. Its advantage lies in the support of the system's structure, communication mechanism and time concept. The disadvantage is the lack of a description of the system behavior. The openness of model structure is low. And its abstract mathematical description from the specific modeling of the system is still a long distance. Liu [41] embeds StateCharts to DEVS, using these characteristics that StateCharts is suitable to establish the behavior model of the system and describe the conversion rules of states, to realize the complementary advantages. In this improvement method, a simple, intuitive system model can be established. This method can effectively improve the design efficiency of CPS and complete the automatic mapping of high-level modeling to the bottom layer code.

In addition, in the rapid development at the same time, Modelica is highly concerned by the industrial sector. Many of the relevant industry's top companies have launched their support programs. Under the support of Modelica, Taha et al. [42] completes the Acumen project, and proposes a modeling and verification method for hybrid systems. In this method, continuous functions are used to model continuous systems and discrete simulation. Tan [9] describes the connections between the CPS components using events, which are divided into temporal and spatial events, and establishes the hierarchical event model. Then the event model of concept lattice is proposed, and the event type, the internal attribute and the external attribute are defined. Compared with the time driven model [43, 44], the event driven model [45] can better reflect the interaction between components in CPS.

In the field of specific application, Parolini [46] proposes a control oriented model in which the computational network and the thermal network are used to construct the system model, so that the effective control of energy efficiency of data center is realized. Saber [47] divides the cyber physical energy system into stochastic model, intelligent dynamic load balance model and smart grid model, including energy, grid - based vehicles and heat units, maximizing the reuse and utilization of energy. Saeedloei [48] emphasizes the importance of the programming model, in which the methods such as co-induction, limiting factor and co-winding communication are used for logic programming of CPS, so that the formal modeling and verification of the reactor temperature control system are realized. Lin [49] uses agent-based modeling method to model the CPS system by using agent to eliminate the difference and represent the properties of information layer and physical layer in CPS system. These applications [50–54] are highly targeted, and have low open support and different description methods for different models. The validation of the collaboration is limited by their model openness.

8   Conclusions and Future Works

The above problems restrict the development of CPS theory and technology, and become the main bottleneck for many years to limit CPS to large scale applications. This makes most of the organizations and groups, who are engaged in the development of CPS applications, basically adopt the operation mode of small group and even small workshop, so that the development of more complex or large-scale system becomes very difficult or even impossible to carry out, or because of the changing needs of the system or the flow of team members, the project falls in failure. Therefore, an open modeling approach is needed to support the collaborative design of embedded, sensing, control, communication, physical and other components for modeling CPS, and an extensible consistent description method is provided to specify these heterogeneous components, and then to carry out the collaborative verification.

Acknowledgement. The authors would like to thank our colleagues and students in Engineering Technology Research Center of Network and Information Security at Anhui Normal University. We thank National Natural Science Foundation of China under Grant No. 61572036, University Natural Science Research Project of Anhui Province under Grant No. KJ2014A084, Anhui Province University Outstanding Youth Talent Support Program under Grant No. gxyqZD2016026 and Anhui Provincial Natural Science Foundation under Grant No. 1708085MF156.

References

1. Marwedel, P.: Embedded Systems Design - Embedded Systems Foundations of Cyber-Physical Systems. Springer, Heidelberg (2011)
2. Wang, Y., He, L.: The application of CAN bus microcontroller MC9S08DZ60 in automotive electronic control unit. In: Proceedings of the International Conference Science and Engineering, pp. 2608–2611 (2013)
3. Lee, I., Hatcliff, J., King, A., Roederer, A.: Challenges and research directions in medical cyber-physical systems. Proc. IEEE **100**(1), 75–90 (2012)
4. Sridhar, S., Govindarasu, M.: Cyber-physical system security for the electric power grid. Proc. IEEE **100**(1), 210–224 (2012)
5. Ili'c, M., Xie, L., Khan, U., Moura, J.: Modeling of future cyber-physical energy systems for distributed sensing and control. IEEE Trans. Syst. Man Cybernet. Part A Syst. Hum. **40**(4), 825–838 (2012)
6. Derler, P., Lee, E., Sangiovanni-Vincentelli, A.: Modeling cyber-physical systems. Proc. IEEE **100**(1), 13–28 (2012)
7. Lai, C., Ma, Y., Chang, S., Chao, H., Huang, Y.: OSGi-based services architecture for cyber-physical home control systems. Comput. Commun. **34**(2), 184–191 (2011)
8. Fink, J., Kumar, V.: Robust control for mobility and wireless communication in cyber-physical systems with application to robot teams. Proc. IEEE **100**(1), 164–178 (2012)
9. Tan, Y., Vuran, M., et al.: A concept lattice-based event model for cyber-physical systems. In: Proceedings of the International Conference on Cyber-Physical Systems, pp. 50–60 (2010)

10. Sha, L., Meseguer, J.: Design of complex cyber physical systems with formalized architectural patterns. In: Wirsing, M., Banâtre, J.-P., Hölzl, M., Rauschmayer, A. (eds.) Software-Intensive Systems and New Computing Paradigms. LNCS, vol. 5380, pp. 92–100. Springer, Heidelberg (2008). doi:10.1007/978-3-540-89437-7_5

11. Wang, B., Zhou, T., Liu, J.: Recommendation Systems, Information Filtering and Internet-Based Information-Physics. Complex Syst. Complex. Sci. 7(2), 46–49 (2010)

12. Chen, H., Cui, L., Xie, K.: A comparative study on architectures and implementation methodologies of internet of things. Chin. J. Comput. 36(1), 168–188 (2013)

13. Yu, Z., Jin, H., Goswami, N., Li, T., John, L.: Hierarchically characterizing CUDA program behavior. In: Proceedings of the IEEE International Symposium on Workload Characterization, vol. 76 (2011)

14. Wang, C., Li, X., Zhou, X., Ha, Y.: Parallel dataflow execution for sequential programs on reconfigurable hybrid MPSoCs. In: Proceedings of the International Conference on Field-Programmable Technology, pp. 53–56 (2012)

15. Chen, Y., Chen, T., Guo, Q., Xu, Z., Zhang, L.: An elastic architecture adaptable to millions of application scenarios. In: Park, J.J., Zomaya, A., Yeo, S.-S., Sahni, S. (eds.) NPC 2012. LNCS, vol. 7513, pp. 188–195. Springer, Heidelberg (2012). doi:10.1007/978-3-642-35606-3_22

16. Tokuno, K., Yamada, S.: Codesign-oriented performability modeling for hardware- software systems. IEEE Trans. Reliab. 60(1), 171–179 (2011)

17. Song, T., Kim, J., Pak, J., Kim, J.: Chip-package co-modeling & verification of noise coupling & generation in CMOS DC/DC buck converter. In: Proceedings of the International Zurich Symposium on Electromagnetic Compatibility, pp. 285–288 (2009)

18. Fan, G., Yu, H., Chen, L., Liu, D.: Strategy driven modeling and analysis of reliable embedded systems. J. Softw. 22(6), 1123–1139 (2011)

19. Wan, J., Zhang, D., Zhao, S., et al.: Context-aware vehicular cyber-physical systems with cloud support: architecture, challenges, and solutions. Commun. Mag. IEEE 52(8), 106–113 (2014)

20. Zhang, Z., Porter, J., Eyisi, E., et al.: Co-simulation framework for design of time-triggered cyber physical systems. In: Proceedings of the ACM/IEEE International Conference on Cyber-Physical Systems, pp. 119–128 (2013)

21. Molina, J., Damm, M., Haase, J., Holleis, E., Grimm, C.: Model based design of distributed embedded cyber physical systems. In: Haase, J. (ed.) Models, Methods, and Tools for Complex Chip Design. LNEE, vol. 265, pp. 127–143. Springer, Cham (2014). doi: 10.1007/978-3-319-01418-0_8

22. Shin, D., He, S., Zhang, J.: Robust, secure, and cost-effective design for cyber-physical systems. IEEE Intell. Syst. 29(1), 66–69 (2014)

23. Rajhans, A., Bhave, A., Ruchkin, I., et al.: Supporting heterogeneity in cyber-physical systems architectures. IEEE Trans. Autom. Control's Spec. Issue Control Cyber-Phys. Syst. 59(12), 3178–3193 (2014)

24. Li, H., Dimitrovski, A., Song, J., Han, Z.: Communication infrastructure design in cyber physical systems with applications in smart grids: a hybrid system framework. IEEE Commun. Surv. Tutorials 16(3), 1689–1708 (2014)

25. Xia, Y., Dai, G., Tang, F., Zhu, Q.: A stochastic-petri-net-based model for ontology-based service compositions. In: Proceedings of the International Symposium on Theoretical Aspects of Software Engineering, pp. 187–190 (2011)

26. Ding, Z., Jiang, C., Zhou, M., Zhang, Y.: Preserving languages and properties in stepwise refinement-based synthesis of petri nets. IEEE Trans. Syst. Man Cybern. Part A Syst. Hum. 38(4), 791–801 (2008)

27. Liu, S., Mu, C.: Petri net EPRES for embedded system modeling. J. Tsinghua Univ. (Science and Technology) **49**(4), 490–493 (2009)

28. Hao, K., Guo, X., Li, X.: The Pi+ Calculus-An extension of the pi calculus for expressing petri nets. Chin. J. Comput. **34**(2), 193–203 (2011)

29. Xu, Y., Gao, P., Liu, Z., Xu, P.: Armed forces knowledge management risk evaluation based on FNN. In: Proceedings of the International Conference on Industrial Engineering and Engineering Management, pp. 1833–1837(2011)

30. Roy, N., Dubey, A., Gokhale, A., Dowdy, L.: A capacity planning process for performance assurance of component-based distributed systems. In: Proceedings of the International Conference on Performance Engineering - A Joint Meeting of WOSP/SIPEW, pp. 259–270 (2011)

31. Bliudze, S., Sifakis, J.: Synthesizing glue operators from glue constraints for the construction of component-based systems. In: Proceedings of the International Conference on Software Composition, pp. 51–67 (2011)

32. Dang, T., Jeannet, B., Testylier, R.: Verification of embedded control program. In: Proceedings of the European Control Conference (ECC 2013), pp. 4252–4256 (2013)

33. Yan, Y., Wang, W., Wu, H.: Research and implementation of embedded PLC Domain-oriented Component-based model. Comput. Appl. Softw. **29**(2), 125–128 (2012)

34. Lee, E.: The past, present and future of cyber-physical systems: a focus on models. Sensors **15**(3), 4837–4869 (2015)

35. Guo, B., Zeng, S., et al.: Hierarchical control and data flow graph modeling method in energy-aware hardware/software partitioning. Sichuan Daxue Xuebao **43**(4), 83–88 (2011)

36. Sztipanovits, J., Bapty, T., Neema, S., Howard, L., Jackson, E.: OpenMETA: a model- and component-based design tool chain for cyber-physical systems. In: Bensalem, S., Lakhneck, Y., Legay, A. (eds.) ETAPS 2014. LNCS, vol. 8415, pp. 235–248. Springer, Heidelberg (2014). doi:10.1007/978-3-642-54848-2_16

37. Poovendran, R.: Cyber-physical systems: close encounters between two parallel worlds. Proc. IEEE **98**(8), 1363–1366 (2010)

38. Wan, K., Hughes, D., Man, K., et al.: investigation on composition mechanisms for cyber physical systems. Int. J. Des. Anal. Tools Circuits Syst. **2**(1), 30–40 (2011)

39. Liu, Z., Yang, D., Wen, D., Zhang, W., Mao, W.: Cyber-physical-social systems for command and control. IEEE Intell. Syst. **26**(4), 492–496 (2011)

40. Zeigler, B.: Requirements for standards based dynamic interoperation of critical infrastructure models. In: Proceedings of the Workshop on Grand Challengers in Modeling, Simulation, and Analysis for Homeland Security, pp. 1–5 (2010)

41. Liu, C., Wang, W., Zhu, Y.: Research on a composable modeling approach of embedding the state machine into DEVS. J. Nat. Univ. Defense Technol. **27**(5), 56–61 (2005)

42. Taha, W., Brauner, P., Zeng, Y., et al.: A core language for executable models of cyber-physical systems. In: Proceedings of the International Conference on Distributed Computing Systems Workshops (ICDCSW 2012), pp. 303–308 (2012)

43. Eidson, J., Lee, E., Matic, S., Seshia, S., Zou, J.: A time-centric model for cyber-physical applications. In: Proceedings of the International Workshop on Model Based Architecting and Construction of Embedded System, pp. 21–35 (2010)

44. Zhang, Z., Eyisi, E., Koutsoukos, X., et al.: A co-simulation framework for design of time-triggered automotive cyber physical systems. Simul. Model. Pract. Theory **43**(4), 16–33 (2014)

45. Talcott, C.: Cyber-physical systems and events. In: Wirsing, M., Banâtre, J.-P., Hölzl, M., Rauschmayer, A. (eds.) Software-Intensive Systems and New Computing Paradigms. LNCS, vol. 5380, pp. 101–115. Springer, Heidelberg (2008). doi:10.1007/978-3-540-89437-7_6

46. Parolini, L., Sinopoli, B., Krogh, B., Wang, Z.: A cyber-physical systems approach to data center modeling and control for energy efficiency. Proc. IEEE **100**(1), 254–268 (2012)

47. Saber, A., Venayagamoorthy, G.: Efficient utilization of renewable energy sources by gridable vehicles in cyber-physical energy systems. IEEE Syst. J. **4**(3), 285–294 (2010)

48. Saeedloei, N., Gupta, G.: A logic-based modeling and verification of CPS. In: Proceedings of the ACM SIGBED Review - Work-in-Progress (WiP) Session of the 2nd International Conference on Cyber Physical Systems, vol. 8(2), pp. 31–34(2011)

49. Lin, J., Sedigh, S., Hurson, R.: An agent-based approach to reconciling data heterogeneity in cyber-physical systems. In: IEEE International Symposium on Parallel and Distributed Processing Workshops and Phd Forum, pp. 93–103 (2011)

50. Xie, K., Chen, H., Li, C.: PMDA: a physical model driven software architecture for internet of things. J. Comput. Res. Dev. **50**(6), 1185–1197 (2013)

51. Pan, G., Li, S., Chen, Y.: ScudContext: large-scale environmental context services infrastructure towards cyber-physical space integration. J. Zhejiang Univ. (Eng. Sci.) **45**(6), 990–991 (2011)

52. Zhao, J., Wen, F., Xue, Y., Dong, Z.: Modeling analysis and control research framework of cyber physical power systems. Autom. Electr. Power Syst. **35**(16), 1–8 (2011)

53. Ma, H., Song, Y., Yu, S., Ma, H., Song, Y., Yu, S., et al.: The research of IoT architecture model and internetworking mechanism. Sci. Sinica **43**(10), 1183–1197 (2013)

54. Krishna, V., Saritha, V., Sultana, P.: Cyber physical internet. challenges, opportunities, and dimensions of cyber-physical systems. pp. 76–97 (2015)

Author Index

Printed in the United States
By Bookmasters